Praise for *Empire of Deception*

"[A] thrilling, too-wild-for-fiction tale. Reading *Empire of Deception* was like getting on the storied Cyclone roller coaster at Coney Island . . . holding your breath throughout its peaks and valleys, then getting out of the car, flushed and shaken, only wanting to ride it all over again."
                                                                    —*The Globe and Mail*

"Intoxicating and impressively researched, Jobb's immorality tale provides a sobering post-Madoff reminder that those who think everything is theirs for the taking are destined to be taken."
                                                    —*The New York Times Book Review*

"This is a fast-paced, fact-laden narrative populated by red-blooded personalities."   —*Winnipeg Free Press*

"Comprehensively researched and enthralling. . . . High-stakes hijinks give the story a rollicking feel, but Jobb manages great poignancy, too. . . . This lively and sweeping account seems to have already given a master con artist his due, putting him in the 'pantheon of pyramid-building swindlers.'"   —*The Washington Post*

"Not since Erik Larson's *The Devil in the White City* has an author so eloquently captured the shadowy character of the city."   —*BookPage*

"For fans of true crime. . . . A fine saga of charmed lives, selfish desire, smooth salesmanship, head-shaking trust, plain deceitfulness and a family's shame."   —*The Chronicle Herald* (Halifax)

"Dean Jobb skillfully dusts off this century-old tale with a fast-paced narrative, a keen eye for detail and a cast of characters in which the free-for-all city of Chicago plays a prominent role. . . . [A] masterfully told story."   —*Star Tribune* (Minneapolis)

"Lively, entertaining, and depressingly relevant history. . . . Reads like a novel and will be enjoyed by fans of popular history as well as true crime." —*Library Journal* (starred review)

"A brilliantly researched tale of greed, ambition, and our desperate need to believe in magic, it's history that captures America as it really was—and always will be." —Douglas Perry, author of *Eliot Ness: The Rise and Fall of an American Hero*

"A story that seems to be as American as it can get, and it's told well. . . . Lively and captivating." —*The Christian Science Monitor*

"The parallels between Koretz and Madoff are fascinating: Both men 'dropped hints' and 'played hard to get,' only selling shares to those who persistently begged for them. And both confined their sales, at least at first, to an inner circle of those who knew and trusted them, making their betrayals all the more brutal." —*The Columbus Dispatch*

"A dramatic read and a useful lesson!" —Michael Korda, author of *Charmed Lives*

"Jobb expertly mixes newspaper research with witness interviews to weave a rollicking narrative. . . . The result is a memorable, fast-moving work of history." —*Atlanta Jewish Times*

"A guilty-pleasure reminder that the most audacious bad guys have always been the most entertaining. . . . [It] reads like a Gatsby-Ponzi mashup." —Neal Thompson, author of *A Curious Man*

"Begin with a Bernie Madoff–wolf-in-sheep's-clothing con man pursued by a power-hungry public prosecutor; add the great hog-trough feeding frenzy of 1920s Chicago; stir with great writing and enterprising research; and there you have it: a wonderfully entertaining read!" —Michael Lesy, author of *Wisconsin Death Trip*

EMPIRE OF DECEPTION

Leo Koretz.

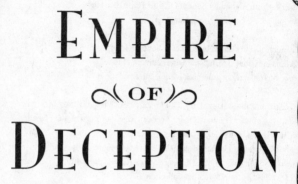

EMPIRE

⸎ OF ⸎

DECEPTION

From Chicago to Nova Scotia—
The Incredible Story of a
Master Swindler Who Seduced
a City and Captivated
the Nation

DEAN JOBB

HARPER ● PERENNIAL

Empire of Deception
Copyright © 2015 by Dean Jobb.
All rights reserved.

Published by Harper Perennial, an imprint of HarperCollins Publishers Ltd,
by arrangement with Algonquin Books of Chapel Hill, a division of
Workman Publishing Company, Inc., New York.

Originally published in Canada by Harper Avenue, an imprint of
HarperCollins Publishers Ltd, in a hardcover edition: 2015
This Harper Perennial trade paperback edition: 2016

Photo credits: frontispiece, pages 1, 65, 85, 136, 227, 239: Chicago History Museum;
page 7: *Chicago Tribune* (Tribune Content Agency); page 17: Courtesy Mary Goodman;
page 146: Thomas Raddall Fonds, Dalhousie University Archives; page 175: *Halifax
Evening Mail*, November 25, 1924; page 192: Library of Congress, Prints and
Photographs Division; pages 199, 204: Nova Scotia Archives; pages 40,
50, 100, 131, 170, 214, 250, 254: author collection.

HarperCollins books may be purchased for educational, business, or
sales promotional use through our Special Markets Department.

HarperCollins Publishers Ltd
2 Bloor Street East, 20th Floor
Toronto, Ontario, Canada
M4W 1A8

www.harpercollins.ca

Library and Archives Canada Cataloguing in Publication
information is available upon request.

ISBN 978-1-44344-109-4

Design by The Book Designers.
Map, page 35, by Michael Newhouse / Newhouse Design.

Printed and bound in the United States of America.
RRD 10 9 8 7 6 5 4 3 2

For Kerry

CONTENTS

The Players xiii

ACT 1

1 Our Ponzi 3

2 Ambitions 14

3 The Law 26

4 The Gamble 30

5 The Dupe 37

6 The Big Idea 42

7 The Syndicate 47

8 The Hanging Judge 62

9 The Sting 70

10 The Confidence Man 78

11 The Crime Fighter 83

12 The Bubble 89

13 The Flight 99

14 The Smash 111

ACT 2

15 The Sensation 119

16 The Double Life 127

17 The Victims 137

18 The Manhunt 147

19 The Alias 153

20 The Guide 160

21 The Hideaway 166

22 The Prince of Entertainers 174

23 The Crime of the Century 179

24 The Pariah 186

25 The Womanizer 191

ACT 3

26 The Trap 201

27 The Gang War 209

28 The Prisoner 213

29 The Return 218

30 The Confession 228

31 The Reckoning 238

32 The Final Swindle 245

Epilogue 255

Acknowledgments 267

A Note on Sources 271

Notes 275

Index 327

THE PLAYERS

The Swindler

Leo Koretz, a millionaire Chicago lawyer and stock promoter, developer of Arkansas rice farms, and member of the Bayano Syndicate; Also known as **Lou Keyte,** a wealthy New York writer and literary critic, and **Al Bronson,** a Chicago salesman

The Koretz Family

Mae Isabel, Leo's wife, a former teacher

Mentor Henry, later known as **Red Kearns,** their son, and **Mari Bertha,** their daughter

Henry, an insurance agent, and **Marie,** Leo's parents

Leo's brothers **Adolph** and **Ludwig,** owners of paint and wallpaper stores; **Julius,** a salesman; **Ferdinand,** a buyer for a department store; and **Emil,** a partner in a real estate firm

The Investors

Francis Matthews, an attorney with the Chicago law firm Moran, Mayer, and Meyer

Henry A. Klein, a wealthy financier and former distillery operator

Charles Cohn, a partner in a Chicago insurance firm

Samuel Richman and Samuel Cohen, Chicago lawyers

Milton Mandel, Leo's doctor, and his sister Sarah, a retired teacher

Felix A. Levy, Leo's rabbi and the leader of Emanuel Congregation

Salo Auerbach, a Chicago theater owner, and his wife, Anna

Josephine Schroeder, the secretary at Leo's law firm

Victor Polachek, an executive of the Hearst newspaper chain

Isaac Wilbraham, a retired railroad dining car steward

Alfred Lundborg, a Chicago tailor

The Investigators

Robert Crowe, Cook County state's attorney, a former judge,
and a powerful Republican politician in Chicago

John Sbarbaro, an assistant state's attorney and part-time undertaker

Stanley Klarkowski and William McSwiggin,
assistant state's attorneys

Edwin Olson, U.S. district attorney,
and assistant district attorney Harry Hamlin, Chicago

Lou Keyte's Nova Scotia Circle

Laurie Mitchell, the overseer of Pinehurst Lodge, a sports fisherman,
hunting guide, and close friend of the author Zane Grey

Thomas Raddall, a Liverpool bookkeeper, later one of Canada's leading
authors of historical fiction

George Banks, editor of the *Gold Hunter and Farmers' Journal*
in Caledonia; his daughter, Mabelle Gene Banks, was rumored to be
Lou Keyte's fiancée

Walter and Maurice Scott, employees of Pinehurst Lodge

Joseph Connolly, a Halifax lawyer

Francis Hiltz, a Halifax tailor

Act 1

The corner of State and Madison streets in Chicago's Loop, 1924.

OUR PONZI

THEY WERE DESCENDING on Chicago's newest hotel to honor a financial wizard. The Oil King, some called him, with a mixture of reverence and gratitude. Others dubbed him the New Rockefeller, a nickname as grand and audacious as he was, one that celebrated his greatest financial triumph to date. Leo Koretz, the man of the hour, had thumbed his nose at John D. Rockefeller and his mighty Standard Oil Corporation and was making this select group of Chicagoans very, very rich.

The evening was billed, tongue in cheek, as "a testimonial banquet tendered to Mr. Leo Koretz by the friends and relatives whom he has dragged from the gutter." It was June 22, 1922. The setting was the Drake Hotel, fourteen stories of limestone-clad Italianate grandeur on the northern edge of downtown Chicago, with its broad back to Lake Michigan and a view from the front rooms of Michigan Avenue, the city's skyscraper-studded main drag. The "most spacious hotel in the United States," proclaimed the embossed, leather-bound city guide found in each of its eight hundred rooms, whose "reputation for elegance and quality may never be surpassed in this generation."

Seventeen tuxedo-clad former gutter dwellers filed through the Drake's brass revolving doors and ascended a flight of wide stairs. They crossed the lobby's marble-tiled floor, passed an oasis of potted palms, and entered a private dining room. Inside, the table was overflowing with fresh-cut flowers. One glance at the centerpiece confirmed that this was the place. In the midst of the flowers was a plaster model of a seaway carved through a wilderness of mountains and jungle—a replica of the Panama Canal Zone. "O, we spread it on thick," recalled Charles Cohn, a partner in an insurance firm and a charter member of the Leo Koretz fan club. "Expense was absolutely disregarded in getting up that dinner."

The sky was clear, and a stiff wind off the lake kept the air cooler than the guests were accustomed to on the second evening of summer. There was plenty of news to loosen tongues as they found their seats. Prohibition agents had raided a dozen illegal saloons on Chicago's South Side the night before, making Cohn and his companions wary of returning to their favorite speakeasy. The president of the University of Illinois was assuring parents his school was doing its part to rein in the rebellious youth of postwar America. And everyone had read the reports from the Illinois coal-mining town of Herrin, where a bloody clash between strikers and scabs had left twenty-three men dead. Shocking, the diners nodded in solemn agreement. Senseless. Perhaps it was best that King Coal's days were numbered. Oil was the fuel of the future, and it was oil that had brought them together this evening.

Cohn and his companions could only marvel at their good fortune. Their friend Leo had let them in on the ground floor of Chicago's best-kept investment secret—the Bayano Syndicate, a moneymaking machine that controlled five million acres of timberland in the Republic of Panama. For more than a decade, investors had been earning fat profits from the sale of mahogany and other exotic woods. But the discovery of oil on the property in 1921 had transformed Bayano into a petroleum heavyweight that produced tens of thousands of barrels of crude every day. It was little wonder that Standard Oil had offered $25 million—more than $300 million in today's dollars—for a small stake in Bayano. Leo had rejected the offer, assuring his dumbfounded investors that they could do much better if they held on to their stock and went head-to-head with the Old Rockefeller. He had been right, as usual. By 1922, Bayano stock was paying dividends of 5 percent *a month*—an astounding 60 percent annual return.

The Oil King strutted into the Drake that night as if he owned the place. Leo had a large suite on the sixth floor, so every doorman and porter knew him—and his reputation as a good tipper. He was meticulous about his appearance and flaunted his discriminating eye for tailored suits and silk shirts. Neckties were in fashion, but he usually sported a bow tie, ensuring he would stand out in a crowd. Even so, a stranger would have been surprised to learn that this middle-aged man was a financial genius and a multimillionaire. Take away the expensive clothes and he looked, well, *ordinary*.

Leo Koretz (his surname was pronounced "korits") was of average height, five foot nine, and a tad overweight at 170 pounds. His stroll through the lobby displayed the stoop of his shoulders and the slight paunch over his belt. His light brown hair was well groomed but thinning on top, exposing even more of his high forehead. Only his gray-blue eyes, framed by horn-rimmed glasses with lenses as round as his face, told a different story. A writer of detective stories—reading them was Leo's guilty pleasure—would have pulled out all the stops to describe the way those eyes turned a spotlight on the world. Penetrating, piercing, razor sharp. It was as if he could peer straight into a person's soul.

Leo was "the wealthiest Jew in Chicago," in the estimation of one Chicago newspaper. To another he embodied the American Dream, "an outstanding example of the Horatio Alger type of self-made young man." An immigrant from central Europe, he had started at the bottom, as an office boy at the law firm Moran, Mayer, and Meyer, and slogged through years of night classes to earn a law degree. He practiced law, but his real talent was making money. Soon he was advising members of his inner circle to invest in mortgages, Arkansas rice farms, and the Bayano enterprises that were making him—and his friends—unimaginably rich.

Bayano profits paid the lease on an Arts and Crafts mansion overlooking the lake in the posh suburb of Evanston and filled it with antiques and fine furnishings. They surrounded his wife, Mae, and their young daughter with live-in servants and sent their teenage son to private school. The mansion was "one of those kinds of places where a person knows without looking that there are Rolls-Royce automobiles in the garage," in the words of one newsman. There were two, in fact, and when Leo was not being chauffeured around town in a gleaming Rolls, he was traveling on Bayano business. He was a regular at the St. Regis Hotel in New York, where the cashier, Basil Curran, was convinced his net worth must have been in the $20 million range—a quarter of a billion dollars in today's terms. In Chicago, Leo schmoozed with the city's elite. He belonged to a long list of clubs and, in the *Chicago Daily Tribune*'s eyes, enjoyed "a rating of 100 per cent in both social and business circles." He was a lavish entertainer who hired musicians or acting troupes to stage private performances at downtown hotels for his friends and investors. When other wealthy Chicagoans hosted parties, his name was often on the guest list.

Everyone wanted to be around him, and not just because he knew the secret to making money. Bighearted Leo, Lovable Lou—his other nicknames said it all. He was charming, with a quick wit and an ingratiating way of cracking jokes at his own expense. He exuded "a personal magnetism that was well-nigh hypnotic," W. A. Swanberg, a Pulitzer Prize–winning author, would later note. "He had a handclasp and warm smile that made men—and women—feel that he loved them." Especially women. He was "a genius with the ladies," a writer for the *Chicago Evening American* declared with envy, and doted on the wives of his investors and business associates.

"His manners were wonderful," recalled Anna Auerbach, a Bayano investor. "Why, a woman was made a social success if she could but persuade Leo Koretz to come to one of her parties." Smart, classy, fluent in German, and able to toss in a few Czech phrases as well, he captivated listeners with his deep, suave voice. He was the kind of smooth talker who could sell refrigerators in Alaska.

The guest list that June night was a who's who of prominent businessmen, doctors, and lawyers. Most, like Leo, were drawn from

Leo Koretz's lakeside mansion on Sheridan Road in Evanston,
just north of Chicago—a stately home fit for an Oil King.

Chicago's large and influential German Jewish community. Charles
Cohn had known him since their school days and had been profiting
from his friend's stock schemes for a decade. He was one of the syndicate's bigger investors, holding $55,000 worth of Bayano's green-
bordered share certificates. Samuel Cohen, another major shareholder,
was a lawyer with the downtown firm Elmer and Cohen. If Leo had
been asked to name his best friend, the answer would most likely have
been Cohen. Another longtime friend, Henry Klein, had struck it rich
selling whiskey; when Prohibition forced him into early retirement, he
had entrusted his money to Leo. Seated across the table was another
old friend, Francis Matthews, a lawyer from the blue-chip firm where
Leo got his start as an office boy.

There were plenty of Koretzes on hand. Leo's five brothers were
not accustomed to rubbing shoulders with such an upscale crowd—
Adolph and Ludwig each operated a paint and wallpaper store, Julius
sold women's hats, Ferdinand was a buyer for a department store, and

Emil, a former postal clerk, managed rental properties—but all held sizable blocks of Bayano shares. Even their elderly mother was sitting on a $38,000 Bayano nest egg. "He has always been good to us," Emil would later say, speaking for the entire family. "We were proud of him—so proud!"

To the Chicago sportswriter Westbrook Pegler, the twenties were "the era of wonderful nonsense." It was a time of dance crazes and bathtub gin, of bob-haired flappers and ballyhoo. And the well-heeled businessmen assembling at the Drake were proof, as well, that the postwar economy was booming. "More people were comfortably well-off, well-to-do, or rich than ever before," the economist John Kenneth Galbraith would note a generation later. It was as if the United States Constitution guaranteed every American the right to life, liberty, and a pile of cash. F. Scott Fitzgerald captured the mood of the times in a best-selling novel of 1920, *This Side of Paradise*. "I want a great deal of money," declared the main character, the pampered, self-centered Princeton graduate Amory Blaine. "That's what every one wants nowadays, but they don't want to work for it."

If easy money was the goal, Chicago was the place to find it. The novelist Henry Blake Fuller called it "the only great city in the world to which all its citizens have come for the one common, avowed object of making money." The city, which accounted for much of the population of the surrounding jurisdiction of Cook County, was the nation's railroad hub, linking the industrial East to the western half of the continent. Thirty-four railroads served the city, and it was said there was more track in the Chicago area than in all of the United Kingdom and northern Europe. It was a city of superlatives. "No other place butchers as much meat, makes as much machinery, builds as many railcars, manufactures as much furniture, sells as much grain, or handles as much lumber," marveled one writer in 1919. The city's wealth and power made it a center of culture and learning, with fine museums and art galleries, well-tended parks, and thousands of acres of forest preserves within its boundaries.

There was another Chicago, with its own dubious superlatives. A dark, violent world of slums and crooks festered in the shadow of the city's soaring skyline. It had become known across America as the Wicked City, a modern-day Sodom and Gomorrah where corrupt cops and civic officials allowed brothels and gambling dens to operate in their midst. Crime was on the rise as Prohibition drove the liquor trade underground and trigger-happy gangsters battled for profits and turf. There was a murder almost every day, making Chicago a deadlier place to live than much-larger New York City. As Leo and his friends gathered at the Drake, a young hoodlum and bootlegger named Alphonse Capone was beginning his ruthless campaign for underworld supremacy.

As Capone's power grew, Cook County State's Attorney Robert Crowe was making headlines as a crusader against this surge of gangland crime. Crowe was bright and ambitious, a former judge who had become one of the most powerful Republicans in the city. By 1922 the mayor's office, and perhaps even the governorship, seemed to be within his grasp. But corruption pervaded politics and justice in Chicago, and Crowe was not immune to the disease. He enlisted crooks and thugs to intimidate his political opponents and win elections, and some of his prosecutors made little effort to hide their ties to the underworld. Crowe's rapid rise in this cutthroat world paralleled Leo's dizzying ascent in the financial realm. Crowe and Leo knew each other, had begun their legal careers together. Their worlds would collide barely a year and a half after the banquet at the Drake, in a way Leo had long feared and Crowe could never have suspected.

Everything about the Chicago of Leo Koretz and Robert Crowe was big and brash. It was the Windy City as well as a wicked one, but the moniker had nothing to do with the winds blowing in from the prairie or the lake; the New York newspaperman who first used the term was mocking the bravado that surrounded everything about the place. The population was approaching three million, and the skyscraper—devised and perfected by Chicago architects—was transforming the city into one of the most modern in the world. Chicagoans amassed fortunes as big as their buildings. George Mortimer Pullman made his producing the passenger railcars that bore his name. Samuel Insull controlled most of the city's utilities, from the electrical grid to streetcars and railroads. Marshall Field—famous for admonishing an employee to "Do as the lady wishes!"—had started out as a dry goods clerk and built the country's largest department store chain. Chicago was a place where an ambitious, self-made lawyer could be reborn as an investment guru.

LEO'S BAND OF PULLMAN, Insull, and Field wannabes took their places at the Drake's banquet table. The menu set a lighthearted tone for the evening. The entrée was Bayano duckling, with Panama salad-oil dressing for the greens. The meal would be washed down with beverages "sanctioned by the U.S. shipping board," a nod to the dry times. A booklet printed on fine vellum—"the last word in appropriateness," as one observer put it—accompanied each place setting. The cover featured a photograph of a boy above the caption "The Child of Yesterday." It was young Leo with a thick mop of hair and a scarf tied around his neck. Inside was a flattering shot of "The Man of Today," with much thinner hair and a confident smile. Below it, for the amusement of the diners, was a biographical sketch of "The Man of the Evening." "Leo Koretz was born near Prague, in Bohemia," it began—and that much, at least, was true. "From birth he refused nourishment unless fed with an 18 carat gold spoon," it claimed. "At 5 years he first showed signs of great financial genius, negotiating a deal for the world's supply of apple sauce." The sketch continued:

> Believing a legal training would help him keep what his
> financial genius enabled him to get, he became a lawyer. . . .
> With insatiable hunger for new worlds to conquer, our
> Ponzi next cast his eyes upon the rich timber forests of Cen-
> tral America and soon we find him dominant in the field.

"Our Ponzi"—the diners roared with laughter at that one. Charles Ponzi was a notorious swindler who had claimed he could generate enormous profits by buying and selling international postal-reply

coupons—vouchers redeemable in stamps—and profiting from exchange rates. He had set up shop in Boston in 1920, promising to
double investors' money in just ninety days. But there was no postal-
coupon bonanza. Every dollar in profit Ponzi paid out came from the
money invested by latecomers, creating a giant pyramid that collapsed
the moment the pool of suckers dried up.

Leo a Ponzi? Bayano's riches nothing more than an elaborate fraud
created years before Ponzi ever heard of postal-reply coupons? Preposterous. Leo's friends were kidding when they called him a Ponzi, and
they thought they were being clever when they went on to call him a
Wallingford—the con man Get-Rich-Quick Wallingford was the title
character of a silent film released at the end of 1921. Bayano's investors had seen with their own eyes the contracts to buy oil tankers and
build pipelines; they had huddled with Leo to pore over blueprints of
the impressive facilities in Panama.

Leo transacted his Bayano business upstairs, in suite 629 of the
Drake, away from his downtown law office. Each of the diners had
been granted the privilege of visiting this inner sanctum, with its fine
antiques and large windows overlooking Lake Michigan. There they
had toasted their good fortune with Hennessy Three Star cognac,
White Horse scotch, and Gordon's gin, liberated from the $5,000
liquor cache that Leo—a man who was always thinking ahead—had
prudently assembled before the Eighteenth Amendment cut off the
supply of booze.

This Ponzi, this Wallingford, had never *asked* any of them to hand
over a penny. The men gathered at the Drake had begged for the
chance to invest. Leo had been reluctant to let his friends and relatives buy Bayano shares. One businessman spoke for many when he
grumbled that he had tried to buy Bayano stock but "Koretz would
not take my money." Some well-heeled Chicagoans were astonished
when he returned their five-figure checks. "I tried to dissuade people,
objected at times," Leo later claimed, sounding as surprised as anyone
at the gold rush he had created. "It was awfully hard to keep them
from buying stock." His approach was low key, "a sort of negative

salesmanship which had very positive results," noted one admirer of his talents as a promoter. "It was what he *didn't* say. . . . He always had an air of secrecy, a knowing air of withholding valuable information." Leo dropped hints to create excitement about Bayano's prospects, then inflated demand by making the shares hard to get. Greed and the marketplace did the rest.

"I mentioned to a friend that oil had been discovered on the land," he once explained. "The news spread rapidly. They began to besiege me with money." Stock certificates with a face value of $1,000 resold for up to $5,000 each.

The sketch of Leo's ascent to the pinnacle of high finance was getting to the best part, the discovery of oil at Bayano. The diners read on:

While searching for legal precedents in a habeas corpus case the thought suddenly came to him that at the present rate of consumption the oil supply of the world would be exhausted in the year 2017.

Being desirous of perpetuating the oil supply, our wizard took his pick and shovel and flew to Panama. At a depth of 2,204 feet his pick struck a solid substance and a few more blows turned up a can of oil.

He promptly wired John D. Rockefeller and asked him what to do with the can, and John met him at the border and offered him 2,000,000 yen for his holdings, which we are happy to say he promptly declined.

Our intrepid explorer has now returned to Chicago to report to the minority shareholders, his friends, and relatives here gathered.

The lights dimmed for the highlight of the evening, a slide-show tribute. A stereopticon projector flashed cartoon images onto a screen, and bursts of laughter greeted the appearance of each new panel. One depicted Leo as a scowling pirate, complete with saber and skull-and-crossbones hat, beside the caption "In his former existence, he probably was a buccaneer on the Spanish main." In the panel labeled "He ropes his friends in," investors waved wads of bills as he doled out stock certificates. In the final slide, "Leo Koretz, Oil King," Leo sat on a throne of cash, looking a bit bored, a crown perched on his oversize head. A figure identified as Sam Cohen bowed before him, saying, "Yes, my lord, what is your pleasure?" The hapless Cohen was the target of jibes and elbows as the room filled with laughter.

Sam Cohen was the butt of the joke, but every Bayano investor was as grateful to the Oil King as he was—and just as subservient. "Everybody had confidence in him and just seemed to take his word, and never worried about the details," explained a lawyer who had known Leo for years. He was "the very soul of honor," chimed in another close friend. "His followers were devout; it was a religious devotion," insisted Charles Cohn. "I had every confidence in the world." It was as if money grew on the mahogany trees that had launched the Bayano Syndicate on the road to financial success.

Leo's shareholders, friends, and relatives laughed and talked into the night, eating their Bayano duckling and perhaps calculating in their heads how much their stock would be worth in five or ten years. None suspected that the man whose generosity and business acumen they were celebrating was also a man with many secrets.

Had one of them, by chance, shown the photograph of the Man of Today to the staff at the Shirley Apartments on the other side of town, the janitor would have instantly identified Leo as Al Bronson, a traveling salesman. Within a couple of years, a lot of people in Canada's seaside province of Nova Scotia, some twelve hundred miles east of Chicago, would have remarked on how much Leo resembled their new American friend, the writer and literary critic Lou Keyte. A thick reddish beard obscured Keyte's face, but he was about the same age, and like Leo, he was rich, charming, and generous, and a dapper dresser.

Strangely, it would have been impossible to find anyone in Panama who recognized the man in the photograph or had ever heard of Leo Koretz.

AMBITIONS

ROBERT CROWE WOULD have recognized the Man of Today from the photograph distributed at the Drake Hotel that night. Leo and the Cook County state's attorney had started their careers together, as rookie lawyers at the Moran, Mayer, and Meyer law firm. That was twenty years before Bayano investors gathered to honor their benefactor, and long before Crowe discovered the truth about the syndicate. Perhaps it was a lucky break, he later joked, that he had never spoken to Leo about his Panamanian oil fields. He might have been tempted to buy some shares for himself.

Leo and Crowe were almost the same age, born just six months apart, and had graduated from law school in the same month of the same year, June 1901. They had probably discovered, at some point during the two years they worked at Moran, Mayer, and Meyer, that they shared a passion for detective stories. And both were the golden boys of their families, ambitious young men destined for great things.

There were differences, of course. Leo was foreign born and Jewish, the son of an insurance agent. Crowe had been born in Illinois but was the son of Irish immigrants, and his father had the connections needed to land a secure job as a court official. Leo had struggled to earn his law degree, taking night courses while holding down a job. Crowe's family had enough money to send Robert to Yale Law School.

Leo had a thin face back then, with hooded eyes and a wide smile.

His hair was combed into a pompadour but was already beginning to recede at the temples; the broad starched collars of the time made his long neck look a bit longer. Easygoing and easy to be around, Leo was full of fun and one-liners. The office joker. Not Crowe—he was serious, almost humorless, sizing up the world with close-set, accusing eyes. He was short and stocky, but a sharp mind and forceful personality made him loom larger in person. He was combative, all business. His chin jutted from his crescent-shaped face, and he led with it. A hard man to like, but a hard one to resist. He was as aggressive as Leo was outgoing.

There was another difference between them, one that, many years later, put them on a collision course. It was not their methods—both would prove to be devious men who were willing to do what had to be done to get ahead. It was what drove their ambitions. Robert Crowe was determined to wield great power. Leo Koretz yearned for great wealth. And the excesses and corruption of the twenties, the era of wonderful nonsense, would help each man to get what he wanted.

LEO'S FIRST GLIMPSE OF America was from the liner SS *Werra* as it steamed into New York Harbor on a September day in 1887. The Statue of Liberty, newly dedicated and clad in a skin still fresh and coppery brown, glinted in the sunlight. Buildings rose in a saw-toothed line along the tip of Manhattan Island. A massive circle of brown sandstone squatted at the water's edge—Castle Garden, a former fortress pressed into service as the entry point for a steady stream of immigrants to America.

Leo and his family were among more than four hundred thousand newcomers processed that year at Castle Garden, the predecessor of Ellis Island. They waited patiently on rows of wooden benches inside the rotunda, enduring cold and filth and a stench only a good cigar could conquer. Leo's father did his best to outwit the ticket agents who overcharged for train fares, the money changers who cheated on exchange rates, the baggage handlers who forced immigrants to pay twice. It was, said one observer, "a system of wholesale robbery," and the lesson for eight-year-old Leo, perhaps, was how easily a shrewd operator could relieve people of their money. After the private sector took its cut, each new arrival paid a government levy of fifty cents a head before immigration officials sent them on their way.

Leopold Koretz had been born on July 30, 1879, in Bohemia, a western province of Austria-Hungary. His father, Heinrich, was a merchant in Rokycany, a metalworking town of a few thousand about forty miles southwest of Prague. Heinrich had married Marie Eisner in 1866, and Leo was the seventh of their nine children.

Bohemia was a region of rugged mountains and dense forests at the heart of Europe, its western border cutting a deep wedge into the underside of neighboring Germany. It was also a troubled land, rife with ethnic tension. Over the centuries, Germans had migrated eastward and become the dominant culture, overshadowing the native Czechs: Bohemia's official language was German, confirming the Czechs' second-class status. Caught in the middle was a small German-speaking Jewish minority, accounting for less than 2 percent of the population. Rokycany—the Koretzes and other Germans called it Rokitzan—was predominantly Czech and awash in Catholic churches and Christian monuments. There were fewer than fifty German residents in the 1880s, by one estimate, and the Koretzes may have been the only Jews in town.

As the nineteenth century waned, Czech nationalism was on the rise. An anti-German backlash and a wave of anti-Semitism made it a good time for Jews to leave, and America promised a fresh start. The oldest of the Koretz boys—Max, Ferdinand, and Adolph—left first, while still teenagers. The rest of the family—Leo, his parents, and the five remaining siblings—received permission to emigrate in July 1887. Even with eight tickets to buy, Heinrich could afford a second-class cabin on the Norddeutscher Lloyd steamer *Werra,* sparing the family the cramped quarters, poor food, and foul air usually found in steerage.

The Koretzes sailed from Bremen in late August. *Werra* was one of a new class of liners that were among the largest, fastest, and most

Leo, right, as a boy in Bohemia with his younger brother, Julius.

luxurious of their time, able to cross the Atlantic in little more than eight days. Mark Twain sailed on one of the vessels and declared it "the delightfulest ship I ever saw." There were smoking rooms and saloons for the men, drawing rooms for the women, and wide decks for everyone to stroll. On this trip, *Werra* also carried a consignment of gold and silver worth more than $700,000, a fitting cargo to accompany Leo Koretz to America.

After a rough crossing—*Werra* plowed through a pair of powerful hurricanes—the liner arrived on September 6. When the Koretzes emerged from Castle Garden, Heinrich piled his family onto a train. They were headed west, like so many others, to the city Leo's father had chosen as the place to make a fresh start. It was a name railroad ticket agents heard over and over, day after day, in German accents as heavy as Heinrich's.

Chicago.

A BAND OF HAZE hovering above the flat horizon announced Chicago's sprawling presence long before trains arrived from the east. Mills and factories and the chimneys of countless houses spewed clouds of coal smoke that "settle in a black mass," a visitor noted in 1889, creating a gloomy world where "one can scarcely see across the streets in a damp day." It was as if the smoke had never cleared from the Great Fire of 1871, which had killed hundreds, left tens of thousands homeless, and reduced much of the city to hollowed-out ruins. A new Chicago had risen from the ashes. By the time Leo arrived, just sixteen years after the disaster, it was a booming railroad and industrial center and the second most populous city in America.

"No city in the world grew faster in the 1880s or was more chaotically alive," remarked the historian Donald Miller. People made pilgrimages to Chicago "to see the shape of the future." Chicago boasted some of the highest office towers in the world by the 1880s, monuments to progress in brick and stone. Many stood ten stories or more, so tall that a new word, *skyscraper,* was coined to describe them.

The city's ambitions knew no bounds. "Sir," a railroad brakeman assured a visitor in 1881, "Chicago is the boss city of the universe." The poet Carl Sandburg extolled it in verse as the "Stormy, husky, brawling, / City of the Big Shoulders," an unstoppable economic force. The city's stockyards and slaughterhouses were both a wonder and a blight—so vast and efficient that they became a macabre must-see for visitors, so exploitive and horrific to work in that they became fodder for Upton Sinclair's muckraking novel, *The Jungle*. With the phenomenal growth that followed the fire came a host of problems: poor sanitation, crowded slums, rampant crime, labor unrest, official corruption. A year before Leo's arrival, a bomb thrown in Haymarket Square during a rally demanding an eight-hour workday killed seven policemen. Raw sewage dumped into Lake Michigan, the source of the city's drinking water, caused deadly outbreaks of typhoid fever; among the many victims was Leo's oldest brother, Max, who succumbed to the disease in 1889 at twenty-two.

A section of the city's waterfront, known as the Levee, was a cesspool of saloons, brothels, and gambling dens of such "unbelievable depravity," wrote Herbert Asbury, an early chronicler of America's underworld, that "the most disreputable superlative that could be imagined would fail to do it justice." The area was so dangerous that one judge suggested anyone who ventured there deserved to be robbed. Chicago became notorious as a place of wickedness and a hotbed of crime. The British writer Rudyard Kipling visited, shook his head in disgust, and vowed never to return to a city "inhabited by savages." The police were too overwhelmed to bring criminals to justice, or too crooked to care, and the biggest crooks were too well connected to politicians to worry about facing prosecution. Robert Crowe would immerse himself in this shadowy, corrupt world and claim to be a politician and a crime fighter; it was almost impossible, however, to be both.

And yet, for many, Chicago's extremes—the rapid and relentless growth, the chasm between rich and poor, the skyscraper temples standing like bulwarks against the sin of the Levee—conspired to create a place bursting with promise and excitement. To Mark Twain it was "astonishing Chicago—a city where they are always rubbing the lamp, and fetching up the genii, and contriving and achieving new impossibilities."

Leo and his family were newcomers in a city of newcomers. Chicago's population doubled to more than one million during the 1880s, and more than a third of the population was foreign born, injecting the city with a globe-spanning array of cultures and languages. The "first and only veritable Babel of the age," a visiting English journalist said of the city. "Not if I had a hundred tongues, every one shouting a different language in a different key, could I do justice to her splendid chaos." Almost a half-million people of German descent were adding their voices to the splendid chaos of Chicago by 1890, making them by far the city's largest ethnic group.

The Koretzes joined a Jewish community growing in number and influence; by the turn of the century, one of every twenty Chicagoans was Jewish. There were almost a half-million Jews in the United States by the late 1880s, and their presence, in the words of one observer, had become "an accepted part of American life." Most were German speaking, allowing them to find a place in established German communities, and most were adherents of Reform Judaism, which relaxed or eliminated the traditions and cultural trappings that made Orthodox Jews stand out. Prayers were read in a language the congregation understood, not Hebrew; men and women sat side by side in the synagogue and could stray from a kosher diet. Reformers even changed the observance of the Sabbath from Saturday to Sunday, to ensure that Jewish shopkeepers and their employees did not have to choose between their faith and losing business.

Heinrich Koretz changed his first name to Henry, landed a job as an insurance agent, and settled his family in a German enclave north of the city center. North Town, as it was known, was Leo's neighborhood until he was sixteen. The Great Fire had leveled most of its homes and churches, but it had been rebuilt into a thriving suburban community. The neighborhood's German heritage was proclaimed in street names—Goethe, Schiller, Wieland—and celebrated in taverns that offered oompah bands as well as steins of beer. Tall townhouses of brick and stone lined the streets, tastefully trimmed with Italianate and Queen Anne flourishes. The horse-drawn pump wagon of Engine Company No. 27 was stationed just up the street from Leo's home on North Wells Street, ready to battle the next conflagration.

North Town was a place where shrewd businessmen were building empires. In 1883, Oscar Mayer, a young butcher from Württemberg, opened the sausage shop that would make him a household name. Western Wheel Works, the world's largest bicycle maker, chose North Town as the site for a towering factory erected in 1891. The son of a German cobbler would soon rent space in the factory to make custom shoes to ease the pain of people with foot conditions; his name was Dr. William Scholl.

In astonishing Chicago, ambition knew no bounds. In 1893, in the midst of one of the worst depressions in American history, the city defied economic gravity and staged the World's Columbian Exposition to mark the four hundredth anniversary of the discovery of America. A palatial city of domes, arches, and spires sprang up on the lakeshore; at night everything was bathed in electric light, a showcase for the incandescent bulbs that were replacing the gaslight of the waning century. To one newspaperman, at a loss for meaning if not for words, the fair was "an immense epitome of what is prominently valuable in modern progress." The Koretzes undoubtedly joined the millions who strolled the grounds, explored pavilions brimming with the latest inventions and displays from exotic lands, and marveled at the midway and its showpiece ride, George Ferris's twenty-six-story wheel.

Back in North Town, Leo could see the skyscrapers of downtown Chicago poking their heads above the hazy horizon. His older brothers had left school and gone to work, and he would soon be old enough to find a job, perhaps earning a few dollars a week at the bicycle factory. He could make footwear for Dr. Scholl or sausages for Oscar Mayer. Or maybe, like them, he would find a way to build a business empire of his own.

Few of Chicago's young people stayed in school for long; only two-thirds were still in class at age twelve, complained one educator of the era, and barely one in a hundred completed high school. Leo was among the ambitious 1 percent. Education would be his ticket out of North Town.

LAKE VIEW HIGH SCHOOL on Chicago's North Side was housed in three stories of Victorian overkill, with a central bell tower looming over a redbrick facade topped with gables and balustrades. The school set high standards for its students: *Ad astra per aspera* was its motto—"Through hardships to the stars." Future graduates would include politicians, scientists, business leaders, and the movie icon Gloria Swanson. Leo entered ninth grade in the fall of 1894, a few weeks after his fifteenth birthday. Like other kids from neighboring suburbs, he had to score well on an entrance exam to win one of the fifty or so places in the first year of the four-year program.

Leo excelled in pursuits not found in the curriculum. One was separating people from their money. He was "the great money-raiser of the school," by one account. "When any good cause came up Koretz was the collector for the fund." He would be remembered as someone who "could get blood from a turnip." Years later, classmates asked to describe him offered the words "idealistic" and "scrupulous character." His other talent was persuasion. He joined the debating society and became Lake View's go-to guy in matches against other schools. In his graduating year he teamed up with another student to win a debate held downtown in the eight-hundred-seat Steinway Hall, a contest that attracted several column inches of press attention.

On a mild, damp June evening in 1898, Leo and ninety-four classmates collected their diplomas at a church auditorium trimmed in flowers and the class colors. Historians would come to regard that year as a pivotal one for the United States, marking its transformation from young nation to global superpower. The United States had been at war with Spain since April, to avenge the sinking of the battleship *Maine* in Havana Harbor and to support Cuban rebels fighting for independence. Underlying these lofty goals was a strategic motive: banishing the last European colonial power from the Western Hemisphere. After the valedictory address, Leo was one of four students invited to speak.

His address, "For Conquest or for Humanity," explored the double-edged rationale for war. Days later a fearless cavalry officer named Theodore Roosevelt led his Rough Riders through a hail of bullets in the famous charge up San Juan Hill.

As the twentieth century dawned, the *Chicago Daily Tribune* paused to remember the advances of the previous "century of usefulness"—the telegraph and the telephone, electric light, railroads, steamboats, even everyday items such as kitchen stoves and postage stamps—and predicted that an artistic and cultural renaissance lay ahead. "The purely material may claim less attention," its editorial writer opined, "and Mammon come to be less regarded."

But for Leo Koretz, a young man starting his career in lockstep with the new century, money and the purely material sounded just fine. All he needed was to find a profession that would make it easy to get his hands on both.

PATRICK CROWE, THE MAN in charge of lighting the gas lamps that cast a pale glow over the streets of Peoria, Illinois, was one of the British government's most implacable foes in America. In the early 1880s, a band of Irish extremists, popularly known as the Fenian Brotherhood, launched a campaign of terror to free Ireland from British rule. Bombings rocked London, Glasgow, and other British cities; assassins ambushed and killed the chief secretary for Ireland in a Dublin park. Irish Americans were behind many of the plots, and Crowe was a key figure in the Fenian movement. Described as "a man of small stature, with a dark, intellectual countenance," he advocated the use of force to win independence for his homeland. He even claimed to have put his words into action. In 1881 he made headlines by boasting he had built some of the bombs wreaking havoc on the other side of the Atlantic. Follow-up reports of Crowe's arrest for illegally exporting explosives proved unfounded, and some newspapers dismissed his statements as fearmongering and bravado. No true terrorist, one editor noted, would attract such attention to his nefarious work.

While his bomb-making claims may have been bogus, Robert Crowe's father had reason to hate the British. Patrick and his wife, Annie, had been born in County Galway in the 1840s, the hungriest years of the Great Famine. They joined the exodus to America—Patrick was granted citizenship in his early twenties—and lived in New York and Missouri before settling in Illinois. Peoria was a steamboat stop on a waterway linking Chicago, about 150 miles to the northeast, to the Mississippi River. Abraham Lincoln stood on the steps of Peoria's courthouse in 1854 and made his first speech demanding an end to slavery, setting America on the path to civil war. It was a city of distilleries and farm-machinery factories considered so typically American that it became a truism of the entertainment industry that if an act was a hit in Peoria, it would be a hit everywhere. Patrick Crowe was a jack-of-all-trades, identified in the city directory over the span of a few years as a grocer, a contractor, and a plumber as well as superintendent of streetlamps. The last of Patrick and Annie's eleven children, Robert Emmett, was born in Peoria on January 22, 1879.

By the time Robert was old enough to attend school, his family had moved to Chicago and settled at 365 West Congress Street, on the West Side. It was the heart of one of the city's poorest areas, the Nineteenth Ward, soon to be the site of Hull House, the civic reformer Jane Addams's pioneering community center. Being Irish gave the Crowe family a leg up, since the Irish were one of the larger ethnic groups in the city and punched above their weight in local politics. They dominated the police and fire departments and doled out coveted jobs on the public payroll. In the 1890s they controlled a third of the seats on the city council and elected John Patrick Hopkins, the son of immigrants from Ireland's County Mayo, as mayor.

By one account, Patrick Crowe had another leg up. A man who had managed "to momentarily terrorize and paralyze the great United Kingdom" was welcomed as a hero. And a man who had named his son after a freedom fighter—Chicago's Irish community gathered each March to mark the birthday of Robert Emmet, executed for treason in 1803—had his pick of government jobs. Cook County hired Patrick as a clerk, and he was promoted to court bailiff and deputy sheriff.

There was enough money to propel the family into the middle class; one of Robert's brothers trained as a lawyer, another studied to be a bookkeeper, and a sister became a teacher.

Robert Crowe inherited his father's distaste for Britain. "I never had any liking or respect for her laws as they applied to my ancestors," he once noted. As a child he became a fan of pulp-fiction novels, devouring everything from French police procedurals to the exploits of the thief-turned-detective Arthur J. Raffles. And he was among that 1 percent of young Chicagoans to finish high school, graduating from West Division High in 1898, the same year Leo addressed his own graduating class at Lake View.

Like Leo, Crowe was well spoken and persuasive; he was a "fluent talker," as one newsman later put it. And like Leo, he was eager to make his mark.

THE LAW

AMERICA, THOMAS MORAN assured seventy-six new additions to Chicago's legal fraternity, needed more lawyers. "As the country grows older and richer there always will be an increase in demand for attorneys," the dean of Chicago-Kent College of Law said, his voice filling Steinway Hall just as Leo's had during his high school debates. "The prospects of success in the profession," Moran predicted, "were never as bright as they are at present." Among the members of the class of 1901 assured a bright future in the lawyer-friendly twentieth century was Leo Koretz.

After graduating from Lake View, Leo had landed a job as an office boy at Moran's law firm. Adolph Kraus, a founding partner in Moran, Mayer, and Meyer, had been born in Rokycany, and that hometown connection may have helped Leo to land the clerking job. But once he was there, it was probably Moran who encouraged him to take advantage of evening lectures at Chicago-Kent, which was housed in a downtown building not far from the firm's offices. The school, created through a merger of Lake Forest's law school with the upstart Kent College of Law, prided itself on accepting students "without distinction as to sex or color." Three women earned degrees in 1899, and Ida Platt, who graduated with honors in 1894, was only the second black woman to practice law in the United States. The faculty and guest speakers included judges and former judges who hammered home a message that lawyers must conduct themselves with honesty and integrity. "In the practice of law," the former judge Simeon Shope reminded Leo's graduating class in June 1901, "it is stalwart manhood and rugged honesty that wins."

While Leo was working around the clock to earn his degree, Robert Crowe had the luxury of studying law as a full-time student at Yale. One of the oldest law schools in the country, Yale had yet to gain national prestige—one historian dismissed it as "a local school with pretensions"—but its distinguished alumni included congressmen, ambassadors, and justices of the United States Supreme Court. Enrollment stood at about two hundred when Crowe was admitted in the fall of 1898, after passing an entrance exam that gauged his knowledge of grammar, history, and the US Constitution.

Yale was on a mission to do more than merely train lawyers; professors sought to instill "the principles and rules of legal science." Crowe and his classmates gathered at long oak tables in the library to plow through thick textbooks, then gathered in the classroom to discuss leading cases. Arthur Corbin, a future Yale professor who was two years ahead of Crowe, remembered being surrounded by classmates "docile enough and lazy enough to desire to be 'told' the law," not to question the validity of those timeworn legal principles. Corbin found the workload light and so did Crowe. "I paid more attention to Raffles," Crowe admitted, "than I did to real property."

Despite Yale's narrow, black-and-white view of the law, Crowe was exposed to the wider world. A young British member of Parliament named Winston Churchill visited in 1900 and, the *New York Times* reported, "spoke feelingly of the bonds between England and America." Bourke Cockran, a former congressman, echoed the optimism of Chicago-Kent's Thomas Moran and told Yale students that their profession offered unlimited opportunities for "the capable man." President William McKinley's attorney general, John W. Griggs, agreed to deliver the keynote address to Crowe's graduating class.

The Republicans, the party of McKinley and Griggs, were a political force on campus, claiming the allegiance of most of the student body. Crowe was among hundreds of students who gathered in the fall of 1900 to form a Republican club. They "marched in company formation" to the meeting hall, a newspaper reported, with a regimental band and Yale's football and baseball stars leading the way. Crowe, now in his senior year, was elected treasurer. A band and drum corps was formed, and members donned uniforms to parade at Republican rallies in New Haven and neighboring cities. New York's popular governor, Theodore Roosevelt, who became McKinley's vice president that fall, was invited to address the club.

By the time Crowe heard Attorney General Griggs, one of his new heroes, speak at his graduation exercises, he had a law degree and a track record as a leader in Republican politics. He returned to Chicago to make good use of both.

THE FIRM OF MORAN, Mayer, and Meyer was founded in 1881 when two lawyers, Adolph Kraus and Levy Mayer, squared off over the sale of a horse. Their courtroom showdown forged a partnership that grew into one of the city's leading law firms, with a roster of big-business clients that included many national firms.

Kraus had left the firm by 1901, when Leo and Crowe began to work alongside some of the wealthiest and most powerful lawyers in Chicago. The firm's leader was Mayer, the son of German immigrants and a prodigy who had graduated from law school at eighteen and, like Crowe, was a Yale man. Mayer was "a martyr to his work" who "gave the very best that was in him to every case he worked on," noted one of his partners, Alfred Austrian. By the turn of the century, Mayer was one of the most prominent corporate lawyers in America and a specialist in mergers and acquisitions.

Mayer acted for the powerful trusts that were consolidating their grip on the country's major industries, from distilling and brewing to sugar refining, banking, and natural gas distribution. A vocal opponent of antitrust legislation, he defended corporate takeovers in the pages of the *New York Times* in 1902 and accused courts and lawmakers of stunting economic growth. "The so-called trust," he wrote, was a corporate version of that most American of ambitions—"the ambition of the individual to accumulate wealth." Fighting antitrust laws made Mayer enormously wealthy. He was reputed to have billed more than $1 million in a single year and, when he died in 1922, left an estate then valued at $8.5 million.

For two years, Leo and Crowe helped to solve the legal problems of Moran, Mayer, and Meyer's business clients. They learned the intricacies of corporate law. They were at the table when Levy Mayer and other legal heavyweights cut deals and outwitted opponents. Crowe saw how powerful men controlled people and events. Leo realized that a savvy lawyer could make a fortune. Both had left the firm by 1903 to set up their own law practices, but their paths would cross again.

THE GAMBLE

LEO'S FRIENDS LOVED to tell a story about one of his first legal clients, an elderly woman who directed that her entire estate be used to care for her dog after her death. She had bequeathed the beloved pet to Leo, who was to hold her money in trust and look after the dog for the rest of its life.

The tale, for the most part, was true. Wills became one of Leo's specialties after he struck out on his own, and when Mrs. Alwin Schaeffer died in 1908, Leo was named sole trustee for her $30,000 estate. Schaeffer left small amounts to brothers and nephews in her native Germany, but she directed that much of the money be used to hold picnics twice a year for Chicago's orphaned children of Bohemian and German descent. Leo's job was to organize the picnics and to ensure the epitaph "Here Lies Sleeping Beauty" was inscribed in German—in gold letters—on her gravestone. His final duty was to find a new home for her poodle, Lottie, with "one of the richest families in the city" and to draw a hundred dollars a year from the estate for the dog's maintenance.

But there was more to the story. "Leo took the dog home. But poor doggie died suddenly one night," one friend explained. "And then, of course, all the money went to Leo. That was Leo's first adventure with somebody else's money."

AFTER LEAVING MORAN, MAYER, and Meyer, Leo set up his own law practice downtown—in the Loop, as everyone called it, because the tracks of streetcar lines and elevated railroads encircled the city's core in a band of steel. For a time he worked in partnership with Daniel Belasco, who was building a lucrative practice suing railroad and tram companies on behalf of those killed and maimed trying to traverse level crossings or navigate Chicago's clogged streets. Leo, though, for all his charm and debating skills, had no interest in cross-examining witnesses or scoring points in the courtroom. He stayed in the background and pushed paper, preferring to handle divorces, draft wills, and settle the financial affairs of deceased clients.

A friend of Leo's from their school days who also became a lawyer, Maurice Berkson, never thought Leo was cut out for a legal career. "He always had ambitions to be a business success," recalled Berkson. Leo himself soon realized that practicing law was not the ticket to easy wealth he had expected. "I was a very poor, struggling young lawyer, hungry for anything in the way of a client," he would recall. "I needed money badly."

That was when it all began. He "took a chance," Leo admitted many years later, and made his first "dip into dishonesty." One day in 1905 a friend came to his law office with money to invest. "I took it and, well," he said, "I gave him a fake mortgage for it."

The client thought the money had been lent to someone who was buying property and the buyer would pay back the principal and interest over time, in the same way a bank would make a mortgage loan. But this mortgage was secured against a property that did not exist, and Leo forged a signature for the fictitious buyer. He used some of the proceeds to cover principal and interest payments on the mortgage as they fell due, but he pocketed the rest. When the money ran out, "I simply set to work and drew up another fake mortgage," he explained, "and sold it to somebody else." He drafted another, then another, then another—so many that when he was asked about them almost twenty years later, he could not even hazard a guess at the number.

Each new mortgage was tied to nonexistent land or buildings and provided the money he needed to meet the payments due on earlier ones. Once the wheels were set in motion, Leo felt powerless to stop them.

"Each fake called for some more fakes to cover the first ones up," he said. "I got deeper in the hole." Soon he was in too deep to even think about going back. He was churning out phony mortgages, as he put it, "like street car transfers."

By 1905, Leo had another reason to make as much money as he could as quickly as he could. She was a teacher with jet-black hair and the doe eyes of a matinee star. Mae Isabel Mayer had grown up in the fashionable Kenwood–Hyde Park area of Chicago's South Side, the sixth of seven children—she had five sisters—and she was as clever as she was beautiful. Regarded as a brilliant student at Hyde Park High School, she had a personality that, as one acquaintance put it, "radiated warmth." Her German Jewish parents (the family was not related to Leo's former boss, Levy Mayer) had moved to Chicago from Kentucky in the early 1880s, shortly before she was born. When she met a charming young lawyer named Leo Koretz, her future seemed assured.

Leo and Mae announced their engagement in the fall of 1905. Her parents, Henry and Bertha Mayer, held a reception to celebrate at their Champlain Avenue home, and Rabbi Joseph Stolz of Isaiah Temple, a South Side synagogue, solemnized the marriage on January 30, 1906. He was twenty-six; she was twenty-three.

The Jewish enclaves of the South Side had been established after the Great Fire, and their residents were among the most prosperous in the city. The area became known as the Golden Ghetto, a wordplay that set its Americanized residents apart from the poorer eastern European Jews who filled the squalid tenements of the Maxwell Street ghetto in downtown Chicago. For Leo, marrying into the Golden Ghetto was a step up the social ladder. The son of Henry Koretz, an insurance agent from the North Side, was now the son-in-law of Henry Mayer, a dental supplies salesman with a red sandstone townhouse in one of the better areas of the city and enough money to employ an

Irish maid. The newlyweds moved in with Mae's parents but would need a place of their own soon so that they could start a family.

About the time of his marriage, Leo's eyes began to bother him. His eyesight was bad enough—by now he saw the world through thick glasses—but something had flared up. Frequent headaches and eye trouble would torment him for the rest of his life. Doctors suspected Chicago's smoky air was the cause of the trouble, and he was advised to get out of the city and spend time outdoors. A friend steered him to what seemed like the perfect cure: a job selling farmland in the clean air of the Arkansas countryside.

The prairie on Arkansas's eastern border with Mississippi and Tennessee was regarded as "one of the last agricultural frontiers in America"—uncultivated, sparsely populated, the preserve of "the cattleman, the trapper and the outlaw." That changed in the early 1900s when a local farmer named William Fuller returned from a hunting trip to Louisiana, where rice was extensively grown, convinced that "we had a good rice country if we had the water."

Rice must be planted and harvested in dry soil but grown in waterlogged fields, and Fuller pioneered the systems of wells, pumping stations, and levees needed for controlled flooding. Rice also had an image problem in the United States—many Americans were "prejudiced against it as a food, and think of it as a cheap boarding-house dish to be used as a last resort," noted a 1911 agricultural report—but high yields and good prices convinced other farmers to follow Fuller's lead. Rice production in eastern Arkansas jumped from a mere 310 bushels in 1899 to more than 1.25 million in 1909.

Rice production created a land boom as speculators snapped up acreage. Land in Illinois and other midwestern states was expensive, and farmers were eager to move to where it was still cheap; "many tillers of the soil in this state," a Chicago paper noted, "sold their $130-an-acre property and went south to cultivate land which cost one-sixth that amount." One land company chartered a train twice a month to bring in prospective buyers, free of charge, to inspect its holdings.

Leo spent six months in the tiny Arkansas town of Wheatley,

halfway between Little Rock and Memphis, selling farmland. He was an odd choice for the job, a bespectacled city boy with a law degree who knew next to nothing about farming, hired to convince weathered "tillers of the soil" to pull up stakes and start over. He was out of his depth, but he found someone to give him a crash course in rice farming: Henry K. Smith, a farmer and president of a Wheatley bank, lauded as "one of the first to realize the unlimited possibilities of raising rice" in the region. Smith showed him around and, as Leo recalled it, "taught me farm values." The selling part—that was something he was good at. If he could sweet-talk investors into putting money into fictitious mortgages, if he could win over the clever folks who judged high school debating contests, he could sell farmland to farmers.

He and Smith hit it off, and when Leo returned to Wheatley for a second sales stint, he proposed that they sell shares in Smith's farm. They became partners and bought up surrounding land under the corporate name Little Prairie Farms. Leo bought and incorporated two more farms, Prairie Blossom in Wheatley and Letchworth in Des Arc, about twenty miles away. He was president of all three companies and estimated his holdings stood at about three thousand acres, making him a big player in an area with an estimated forty thousand acres in rice production by 1910. Land values were going through the roof. Farms worth $10 an acre in 1905 were fetching $100 an acre five years later, but that was a conservative figure; by another account, the per-acre price ballooned as much as 1,000 percent in the first few years of the rice boom.

Leo continued to visit Arkansas every few months but spent most of his time back in Chicago, running his law office and tending his stable of bogus mortgages. Soon he was selling shares in rice farms to his Chicago friends and convincing others to take mortgages—more fake ones—on the properties. The "majority" of the rice farm mortgages, he admitted, "did not exist." To make the documents look official, he kept two embossing seals in his office. One bore the inscription "Circuit Clerk Seal Prairie County, Ark"; the other stamped mortgages and

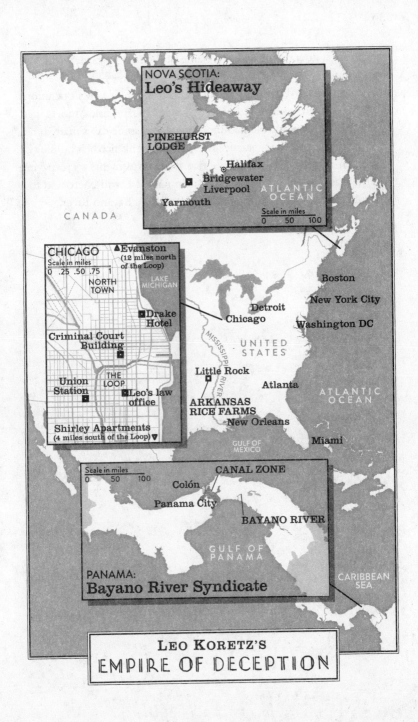

NOVA SCOTIA:
Leo's Hideaway

PINEHURST
LODGE

· Halifax
■ Bridgewater
Liverpool
Yarmouth

ATLANTIC
OCEAN

Scale in miles
0   50   100

CANADA

CHICAGO
Scale in miles
0 .25 .50 .75 1

▲ Evanston
(12 miles north
of the Loop)

NORTH
TOWN

LAKE
MICHIGAN

■ Drake
Hotel

Criminal Court
Building ■

Union
Station ■

THE
LOOP

■ Leo's law
office

Shirley Apartments
(4 miles south of the Loop) ▼

MISSISSIPPI RIVER

Detroit
Chicago

Boston
New York City
Washington DC

UNITED
STATES

Little Rock ◻

Atlanta

ATLANTIC
OCEAN

ARKANSAS
RICE FARMS

New Orleans

Miami

GULF OF
MEXICO

Scale in miles
0   50   100

CANAL ZONE

Colón ·
Panama City ·

BAYANO RIVER

GULF OF
PANAMA

CARIBBEAN
SEA

PANAMA:
Bayano River Syndicate

LEO KORETZ'S
EMPIRE OF DECEPTION

related legal documents with the name of Richard Hazard, a fictitious notary public.

Years later, investigators trying to make sense of Leo's operations in Arkansas were confronted with a "tangle" of land titles, mortgages, and other documents. He had mortgaged, "in some cases many times over," they discovered, "practically every foot of his rice belt holdings."

Then in 1907, just as Leo's rice farm investments were paying off, he was introduced to a businessman named David Nieto and to a scheme to develop the timberlands of Panama's Bayano River.

THE DUPE

THE BAYANO RIVER—now called the Chepo—traces a lazy arc for about 130 miles from its headwaters in the mountains that separate the Atlantic and Pacific Oceans. It empties into the Pacific at the narrowest point along the umbilical cord of isthmus that binds North and South America, making the valley an early contender as the route for the Panama Canal. But surveyors and engineers concluded that the terrain was too rugged and the cost and construction challenges would be too great. When the canal opened in 1914, its Pacific terminus was about thirty miles west of the point where the Bayano's slow-moving, muddy waters meet the ocean.

In the early twentieth century, eastern Panama was "one of the wildest, least-known corners of the entire world," the historian David McCullough noted in his account of the herculean effort to build the canal. While the American-controlled Canal Zone drew a thin line of civilization across the isthmus, few outsiders had braved the oppressive heat to venture into the jungles and mountains, an untamed kingdom ruled by alligators, poisonous snakes, and disease-carrying mosquitoes. More was known about the surface of the moon than about the resources that might lie beneath Panama's lush, green exterior. A feature article in the February 1922 issue of *National Geographic* described the country as a "far-away, mysterious place" that "most people think of as so remote that they can never hope to go there." The Bayano region—named for King Bayano, an African slave who led a sixteenth-century revolt against Spanish rule—was even more remote and that much more mysterious.

By the time Leo heard about the Bayano, Yankee canal builders and an army of workers had been toiling in Panama for three years. The canal would fulfill a centuries-old dream of a shorter, faster route for global trade. For Washington, it was a strategic necessity as well. The restless, take-charge man in the White House, President Theodore Roosevelt, could barely wait for the day US warships could slip through the passage and assert the country's naval power wherever—and whenever—needed. Panama had been a province of neighboring Colombia, but Roosevelt had flexed his military muscle to get what he wanted. When Panamanian rebels overthrew the Colombian regime in 1903, a timely US blockade prevented Colombian troops from intervening. The newly independent Republic of Panama, roughly the size of South Carolina, promptly signed a treaty that allowed the United States to begin construction.

American businessmen, eager to exploit Central America's riches—coffee, bananas, minerals, timber—had imperial designs of their own. When United Fruit Company, the region's biggest player, was formed in 1899, it controlled large tracts in Honduras, Nicaragua, and Costa Rica. The Boston-based corporation was a force unto itself, employing fifteen thousand and operating a fleet of steamships and a rail network to carry bananas from plantation to market. It was becoming a force in Panama as well, with twenty-one thousand acres planted in bananas by 1903. "Whenever we see we can make a dollar," the firm's president, Andrew Preston, once noted, "we do it."

David Nieto had his own plan to cash in on this tropical bonanza. Leo met him through Daniel Belasco, Leo's law partner at the time. Nieto was a man of about forty, London born, who described himself as a merchant. He was Belasco's second or third cousin and of Portuguese or West Indian extraction—Leo was never sure which cousin or which nationality. Nieto had been of service to the Republic of Panama during the revolt, or so he claimed, and his reward was title to timberland on the Bayano River. He had come to Chicago to convince railroad executives to buy the wood and use it for rail ties. But he needed some up-front cash, say $10,000, to cut and deliver the timber to market.

That was a lot of money—$10,000 in 1907 would be $250,000 today—but Leo was confident he could scrape it together. The deal sounded like a sure thing. "I fell—fell hard," he would later say, "swallowed the bait, hook, line and sinker."

He passed the hat and in no time convinced nine friends and colleagues to join him, each putting up $1,000.

"I thought I was going to make a lot of coin out of it myself and for my friends," he recalled. Nieto, before he headed off to Panama, "assured us all of that." Leo advanced him enough money to pay for his passage and to buy the saws and axes needed "to clear away that timber and make us all rich."

Weeks passed. A cable arrived from Nieto, asking for more money. Leo sent it. More cables followed, each more urgent than the last, each requesting more money. "And when he became too insistent," as Leo told the story, "I began to get suspicious." It was time, he decided, for a trip to Panama, "to find out just what I had put my money into."

Leo bought a ticket on one of the steamships that made regular runs between New York City and Panama's Caribbean coast—vessels crowded with workers and supplies bound for the canal project. He arrived in early 1908, at the beginning of a four-month respite from the region's torrential rains and oppressive heat. Landfall was at Colón, a vice-filled boomtown at the Atlantic terminus of the half-built canal. He disembarked and boarded a train for the two-and-a-half-hour ride across the isthmus to Panama City, the republic's capital and largest city. From there, it was a thirty-mile cruise along the Pacific coast to the broad tidal flats at the mouth of the Bayano River.

The next stage of the journey, up the river itself and into the jungle, would not be as easy. Malaria, the scourge of the tropics, stalked newcomers; even in the Canal Zone, where improved sanitation kept the disease at bay, malaria killed more than two hundred workers that year. At least Leo had come in the dry season, when the mosquitoes

"On the Bayano River, interior Panama—Indians supplying Panama soldiers,"
undated stereographic image from a photograph taken in the early 1900s.

were less active. There were other dangers. The primitive tribes of the upper Bayano valley harbored "a hatred for all strangers," an American who studied Panama's aboriginal inhabitants observed only a few years later, and "it would not be safe for anybody to penetrate into their forests without a strong escort and continual watchfulness. Many instances of murders, some confirmed and others only suspected, are on record."

About the time of Leo's visit, a photographer was also journeying up the Bayano. He ascended from the river mouth in a small motor launch, alternatively battling and riding the shifting tidal current. Alligators, he reported, were "huge and numerous"—some eighteen feet long—and the riverbanks crawled with snakes "of most unattractive aspect." After twenty-four hours his party reached a military outpost. As villagers tied up their dugout canoes to trade bananas, he set up his camera and snapped a photo. It was published in the United States as a stereographic card, and in a note printed on the back of the image, the photographer doubted this land of alligators and snakes would ever amount to much. While the soil appeared fertile "and would without doubt produce crops of immense value if it could be worked by intelligent modern methods," he observed, "the difficulties in the way of its development are so vast, the district will probably long remain as it is now, a tropical wilderness."

Before Leo faced the snakes and alligators and ill-tempered natives, he had to find Nieto. He made inquiries around Panama City, but no one, it seemed, had heard of Nieto. Leo grew more suspicious and more worried. Then, by chance—and surely to the astonishment of both men—they met one day on the street. After what must have been an awkward conversation, Nieto agreed to take him to the property. But by the time they boarded a boat for the trip, Leo knew Nieto was lying. He had made more inquiries and had learned that Nieto was still trying to lease timberland in the region. Nieto took him to the Bayano and showed him land on the river.

Leo was unimpressed. There was no timber, "just a few quagmires and mudholes—worthless stuff," he recalled. "And no $10,000."

He was furious—"fighting mad," as he put it. "I knew I was duped." He confronted Nieto. It was a scam, Leo said, and he wanted the money back. No, Nieto insisted, the land was a good investment. He begged for more time and more money.

When Leo threatened to go to the authorities, Nieto became incensed. He had a threat of his own: Turn me in, Leo, and I'll kill you.

Leo backed down. He never went to the authorities. He had been played for a sucker and stung for a lot of cash, but he was determined to find some way to repay his friends. "It was my fool mistake," he scolded himself, "just my fool mistake."

He boarded the Royal Mail Lines steamer *Trent* in Colón on February 11, 1908, for the return trip to the United States. He could not stop thinking about how naive and foolish he had been, how easily Nieto had ripped off people who had trusted him.

When he stepped onto a New York pier nine days later, the city was paralyzed by a wintry blast of rain and wet snow and shrouded in a thick fog that perfectly matched his mood. But an idea—"the big idea," Leo would come to call it—had been planted in his mind.

THE BIG IDEA

Leo returned from Panama bitter and $1,000 poorer. David Nieto's scam had cost his fellow investors another $9,000. "It was a hard blow for Koretz," said Francis Matthews, a lawyer and close friend who had worked with Leo at Moran, Mayer, and Meyer. Leo scraped together enough money to pay everyone back, and said he had learned a valuable lesson: from now on he would avoid "wild-cat" schemes and "stick to legitimate enterprises."

His friends, of course, had no idea he was already a fraud artist in his own right and struggling to cover payments on a web of fake mortgages. Money seemed to be the least of his worries. In June 1908, only a few months after his return from Panama, he took Mae and her older sister, Etta Speyer, on a trip to California. They spent time in Los Angeles and stayed at the Hotel Del Monte, near the seaside town of Monterey. It was a posh resort where a millionaire railroad magnate showed up in his personal Pullman car to stay for the season and Presidents Rutherford B. Hayes and William McKinley came to escape the pressures of the White House.

Touring California and hobnobbing with the Del Monte crowd put a further strain on Leo's finances. He had new responsibilities in his personal life, too. Mae had quit her teaching job, and their first child—a son, Mentor Henry—had been born in September 1907. They had moved out of her parents' house and taken an apartment a few blocks away on South Michigan Avenue, an address that was still within the upscale Golden Ghetto.

"I got deeper in the hole," Leo explained years later. "You understand how it goes; one false step leads to another, until it is impossible to turn back. You must go on or face exposure."

As he looked for new ways to make money, construction of the canal unleashed a rush of land speculation in Panama. Fortifications being erected to protect the Canal Zone from attack, one writer noted, "made the whole country seem safe for American capital." An array of projects were in the works—sugar refineries, coffee plantations, farming colonies, sawmills to cut exotic woods for export. American lumbermen were startled to discover that the inhabitants were using mahogany logs worth thousands of dollars for dugout canoes and makeshift bridges over streams.

Even the Bayano region was in the news—and appeared poised to make real money for investors. At the beginning of 1909, the New York–based Bayano River Lumber Company floated a $500,000 bond issue to finance its operations. A year later, newspapers across the United States reported the purchase of a hundred thousand acres along the river with "vast supplies of timber." The buyers, a group of wealthy Los Angeles businessmen, planned to build a sawmill and plant sugarcane to produce rum. Both companies had snapped up at least some of the land Leo had thought would make *him* rich.

Then the idea that had been percolating in his mind since his return from Panama began to take shape. His friend and law partner Daniel Belasco had vouched for Nieto, and that had made the phantom Panamanian timber holdings seem plausible. That "stuck with me," Leo recalled, and "taught me how easy the suckers can be made to fall, and that the closer they are to you the harder they will fall." If a huckster like Nieto could do it, Leo could, too—only he would do it better. "I got to thinking about it and decided I could put it over, profiting by Nieto's mistakes." And "out of it all grew Bayano—the big idea."

Nieto's major mistake, as Leo saw it, was failing to keep his investors satisfied and under control. Nieto's eagerness to get his hands on the $10,000 seed money had raised suspicions about what he was up to in Panama. Leo would be patient. Nieto's scheme had fallen apart because Leo had gone to Panama to see the reputed holdings. He would make his Bayano enterprise a profitable and solid investment—so solid that no one would feel the need to travel south to take a look. And he would cultivate a reputation as a prudent and successful businessman. It was essential that he earn the trust—the absolute, unshakable trust—of everyone who bought into his Bayano dream. David Nieto had been fly by night; no one would ever have cause to doubt the word of Leo Koretz.

There was one more thing: the Big Idea would be meticulously planned.

SS *SANTA MARTA* EMERGED from a fogbank and eased against a New York pier on April 6, 1911, back from Panama via Jamaica. Fifty-three passengers were onboard, among them a couple from Chicago and their young son. Leo, Mae, and two-and-a-half-year-old Mentor had spent five days in Colón and Panama City. It had been a vacation, a $3,000 escape to the warmth and sun, but there had been another reason for Leo's return to Panama. He had told Mae a lie about looking after "vast timber interests" for a syndicate. He had ventured off a few times on his own, saying he had to attend to business. Leo had mentioned a man named Espinosa, describing him to Mae as a local banker. The details of the Big Idea, the facts and names he would need to make it believable, were beginning to coalesce in his mind. On this second Panama trip, as Francis Matthews would correctly surmise years later—and far too late—Leo had picked up the "local color" he needed to flesh out his new venture.

The next step was to put something on paper. Back in Chicago, Leo drafted a report extolling the resources of a Panamanian property ripe for development. Its size? He settled on an impressive five million acres—7,800 square miles of territory, as big as New Jersey. Like Nieto, he placed it on the Bayano River. "This region," Leo wrote, "besides being capable of production almost beyond the dreams of avarice, is blessed with an avenue of communication and transportation that is nowhere surpassed." The avenue was the Panama Canal, which would open within a few years and make the region and its resources readily accessible.

He appended a map and described the property as a paradise of thick forest and lush grassland. "There is scarcely a vegetable grown in the United States that will not grow here and produce to troublesome abundance," he wrote. Sugarcane, cocoa, bananas, pineapples, limes, cotton, corn, peanuts, yams, coffee—all were growing or would thrive there, along with rice, "the wheat of the tropics." Arkansas had taught Leo a lot about rice, but how could a Chicago lawyer know so much about the agricultural prospects of the remote Bayano?

To erase such doubt, he peppered the 150-page report with offhand remarks to create the impression that he had seen it for himself. The climate was "hot only in the direct rays of the sun," he noted, "but I have not found it sultry." Pineapples grown in the area "are large, sweet, and have a fine flavor," he assured readers, who would assume he had tasted them himself. "The quantity and profusion of the vegetation," he observed at another point in the report, "is such that no one, not having seen it and cut his way through it, can form an adequate idea of it." Perhaps not, but readers could picture Leo hacking his way through the jungle in his quest to unlock the secrets of the Bayano.

The report zeroed in on the most promising of the property's varied resources. There were hundreds of rubber and cocoa trees. Areas planted in sugarcane, Leo predicted, would yield about five tons of sugar per acre. Cattle would thrive. The property possessed so many resources, he cautioned, that "there is a real danger in the temptation to develop too many of them." One resource stood out: timber of "every grade of hardness," from lightweight balsa to dense, durable lignum vitae. While the up-front costs of planting sugarcane and introducing cattle were high, cutting and exporting timber would bring "immediate and large returns, with comparatively limited expenditures."

Construction of the canal was creating a market for lumber and railroad ties at the syndicate's doorstep. The timber was easily accessible and could be floated to the river during the rainy season via tributaries that crossed the syndicate's land.

Leo had done his homework, and if all this failed to satisfy the skeptics, he brazenly lifted a page straight from Nieto's scam. "I anticipate no trouble in disposing of the tie timber," he stated in the report's conclusion, "and in fact have received assurances from various railroads that they will buy all the ties which we can or care to sell to them annually."

The report was part fact, part embellishment, part pure imagination. Leo had gleaned enough information about the region during his Panama sojourns to make the venture sound plausible. Finding a name for the corporation that controlled this valuable, resource-rich property was the easy part, and the Bayano River Syndicate was born.

THE SYNDICATE

HENRY KLEIN KNEW a good deal when he saw one, and that's how he became a major player in the liquor industry in the Midwest. He bought out Chicago's bankrupt Liquor Dealers' Supply Company around 1910 and built it into a major wholesaler and distributor. By 1914 he had an extensive network of customers in six states and sold whiskey under the popular Century and Century Club labels. Bespectacled, thin faced, and big eared, Klein was upwardly mobile, too, having married well and joined Chicago's Standard Club, the Jewish community's leading social and benevolent organization. Klein's wife, Bertha, was one of the daughters of Philip Stein, a community leader and the first Jew elected to the bench in Illinois. Judge Stein was also wealthy, worth more than $1 million when he died in 1922.

But one of Klein's most astute moves—or so he thought—was teaming up with Leo Koretz. They had met around 1905, and although Klein was six years older, they shared a common heritage: Klein's parents were Bohemian Jews from Písek, not far from Rokycany. In their early business ventures, Klein and Leo went fifty-fifty to buy mortgages and other secured debt, no doubt including some of the fake ones Leo was selling to stay afloat. Klein found him easy to deal with and admired his head for business. Leo, he recalled, "met all obligations promptly." Klein never suspected, not for a single moment, that his partner was a liar and a thief.

Just before the outbreak of the First World War, they split the cost of buying about a thousand acres of rice land in Arkansas. In an era when the typical Chicago business turned an annual profit of 5 percent, Klein and other investors in Leo's Arkansas farms were earning double that, 10 percent. Klein never saw the deeds or mortgages for the Arkansas property. Leo handed over personal promissory notes as security for Klein's investments, saying he had stashed the original documents in his office for safekeeping. Klein never saw the books of the Arkansas farm corporations, either. Leo said they were in the hands of a Chicago auditing firm. These explanations were good enough for Klein. "I always made money in his ventures," he noted. "I believed in that man absolutely."

When Leo mentioned the Bayano Syndicate and its holdings in Panama, Klein was intrigued. The scam that had burned Leo and some of his friends became part of the sales pitch: In the course of exposing David Nieto's scam, Leo explained, he had been retained to survey the syndicate's property and prepare the prospectus. In return for his services, he had received $1 million worth of stock in the Bayano enterprise with an option to buy more, at $1,000 a share, and had been named to the board of directors. Contracts to supply timber for railroad ties, he said, would earn shareholders a 10 percent return.

Leo was tight lipped about the syndicate and the men behind it, but this came as no surprise to Klein—all his friend's business dealings, he found, were cloaked in secrecy. The Bayano Syndicate was made up of "immensely wealthy men," Leo told Klein, who relied on him to invest "huge sums of money" on their behalf. Eventually he confided their names: Al Bronson, Gustav Fischer, Al Watson, and the Panamanian connection, a man known only as Mr. A. Espinosa. Klein never met them, even though they often gathered in Chicago to talk business.

At one point, Klein asked to join one of the meetings. Sorry, Leo told him, the syndicate met in secret and late at night. Besides, he said, Klein—a millionaire and a successful businessman—was not "big enough" to merit a place at the table. Klein should have been insulted,

but the explanation only made him more confident that Leo was deal-
ing with the big boys and Bayano was a sound investment. Leo talked
about the syndicate's backers so often that it was as if they would walk
through the door at any moment.

"I'll consult Mr. Fischer about this," he told Klein as they discussed one transaction.

"I'll have to wire Bronson," he noted when a decision had to be
made.

"You remember Watson," he name-dropped on another occasion.
"I've told you about him."

Leo, as it turned out, had told him little about any of them. Klein
knew that Fischer was fifty years of age, Watson was sixty, and both
were retired businessmen. Other investors picked up tidbits about
them over the years. Watson was believed to live in suburban Wilmette
or Winnetka, home to many wealthy Chicagoans. Fischer "travelled
quite a bit," one investor was told, and was based in Milwaukee. Francis Matthews, who later bought shares, thought Fischer was a capital-
ist from New York. Bronson's background was a mystery, and all that
Leo's confidants knew about Espinosa was that he was rich and lived
in Panama. Even Josephine Schroeder, Leo's personal secretary, was
in the dark; she never met or spoke to Watson, Fischer, Bronson, or
Espinosa and she never handled correspondence involving any of them.

Leo made no secret of his own role, though: he rounded out what
came to be known as the Big Five, with each man holding an equal
stake in the syndicate and its prized lands in Panama.

AT FIRST, ONLY KLEIN, Matthews, and a few of Leo's
other close friends were told about Bayano. But people soon began
to take note of the charming young lawyer who was joining the right
clubs and socializing with the right crowd. Leo became a regular at
Metzger's, a downtown restaurant renowned as the place the wealthy
lunched. When it was time to pay for a meal or a new suit, he peeled
notes from a thick wad of cash. Leo rarely talked business, and that
made people curious about how he was making his money; perhaps,

Bayano River Syndicate stock certificate issued to Leo's sister-in-law, Etta Speyer, in 1922.

with his help, they could make some for themselves. He dropped "a hint here and a hint there," one man recalled. "He never discussed his affairs much," added a fellow lawyer, but "somehow or other the word was passed along."

And word was that Leo Koretz, the young man who had done well with rice in Arkansas, was making a killing in Panama.

The Big Idea was in play.

Leo was determined he would not sell shares in the Bayano River Syndicate—the shares would sell themselves. And the best way to stimulate demand was to restrict supply. He made stock certificates hard to get, which made people all the more desperate to get their hands on them. In the words of one investor, "he utilized to a weirdly elaborate degree the principle that a person will literally fight for something that is most difficult to get."

"I tried my best to buy some of his stock," complained the owner of a factory on Chicago's West Side, but even though he had known Leo since boyhood, "Koretz would not take my money." Anna Fox, a wealthy woman in Hyde Park, was among those shut out. "I have been trying to figure out some way of letting you have a little stock in the Bayano River tract, but up to date have been unable to do so," Leo consoled her in a letter. The more he said no, the harder Anna Fox, the factory owner, and other would-be investors pleaded for a sliver of the Bayano pie.

"I didn't go out after prospects, they actually begged to be let in on Bayano," Leo explained later in an interview with the *Chicago Daily News*. "Many a morning I have found wealthy friends and total strangers waiting to beg that I take and invest their money. Many a day I have put off one or another and advised delay in investing. They camped at the curb outside my home, and at my doorstep." When Leo did sell stock, it was always with a feigned reluctance that convinced buyers that he had done them a favor. And they paid extra for the privilege. Shares with a face value of $1,000 usually fetched a hefty premium: Arthur Mayer, an insurance broker and a close friend, paid $2,000 per share for three shares, and Samuel Richman, a lawyer who rented office space from Leo, forked over $38,000 for twenty-eight shares.

Leo was doing more than whipping up enthusiasm and driving up prices. Being selective meant every investor was handpicked. "I'm only letting my real friends in on this," he would say. Marcy Schoener, the son of a New York tobacco merchant who tried for more than a year to buy Bayano shares, eventually figured out why Leo played so hard to get. "Koretz was a brilliant student of psychology and he often told me that he never had dealings with a man before subjecting him to most searching scrutiny," Schoener would later explain. Leo's "ace in the hole," he continued, "was an attitude of refusing to let strangers into his schemes. . . . He was afraid they might be the kind who would investigate his projects." Many who bought stock were professionals and businessmen, people so tight with their money, a source told the

Chicago Evening American, they "would not lend you $5 to save your life without good collateral." It was a testament to Leo's powers of persuasion that he had them begging to open their wallets.

Investor by investor, he created an exclusive club of loyal, trusting insiders, each one carefully sized up in advance. At first, Bayano stockholders were drawn from the ranks of Leo's closest friends and his immediate family. Over time, he expanded the club to include friends of friends, in-laws, and the occasional legal or business colleague such as Samuel Richman. The list of investors included at least a half-dozen members of his synagogue, Emanuel Congregation, and the congregation's rabbi, Dr. Felix Levy.

"I never suspected him. Why should I?" remarked Charles Cohn, Arthur Mayer's partner in the insurance business and a friend of Leo's since their school days. "I had every confidence in the world." Cohn invested in the Arkansas properties and graduated to Bayano stock. John Irrmann, a lawyer and childhood friend who worked in Leo's law office for a few years, told a similar story. When he convinced Leo to sell him a single Bayano share, "I thought he was doing me a favor," he recalled. "I regarded him as a friend whom I could trust and to whom I would turn in time of need. And when I did turn to him, as I had occasion several times to do, he never failed me." Irrmann considered him "the very soul of honor," and plenty of investors would second the motion. "That is the whole secret of his tremendous operations," noted a Chicago financier who knew Leo but never got his hands on Bayano shares. "His stockholders were all hand-picked, guaranteed not to wilt, fade or doubt, absolutely trusting friends and relatives. An outsider couldn't get in."

His most loyal investors were his family. Leo's five brothers held stock. Julius, who sold women's hats to retail shops and was a couple of years younger than Leo, reaped steady returns of 10 percent a year. "Every time I would get a dividend," he said, "I would give the money right back to him for reinvestment." His stake in Bayano and Arkansas farms eventually reached $52,000. Emil, an older brother who ran a property rental business, was doing so well in Bayano stock that he was thinking of retiring at fifty to live off his dividends. "My money was Leo's any time," he said. "I turned over every cent I had to him. I thought he could handle it better than I could." Leo's father had died of heart failure in 1912, at age sixty-seven, and his mother, Marie, was living off the income from her Bayano investment. Leo gave his wife stock certificates as a gift, and Mae's stake eventually grew to eleven thousand shares.

Leo was just as generous to his in-laws. When Mae's father, Henry Mayer, died, leaving his widow, Bertha, $50,000 in life insurance and property, Leo acted as executor and obligingly invested the entire estate on her behalf. Mae's sisters Pearl Mayer and Maude Klein put their money into Bayano; when another sister, Aimee, married Milton Simon, Leo gave the couple a half share of Bayano as a wedding present; two weeks later, he was kind enough to sell Milton Simon the other half share at face value, $500.

Leo later claimed he took their money because he had no other choice. "I never wanted members of my family in," he contended, "and often I sought to persuade some friend or relative in all sincerity not to turn over their thousands." He relented and let them buy shares "only because their suspicions were beginning to be aroused."

His family's involvement, in turn, became another powerful recruiting tool. For some investors, it was all the proof they needed that Bayano was a solid investment and their money was in good hands. "The man had his own relatives investing in his company," Samuel Richman pointed out. "I did not suspect him in any way." And it never occurred to him to make inquiries about the syndicate, or Leo for that matter. "I didn't investigate," he explained, "because I didn't want to embarrass him."

WHAT WAS THERE FOR Richman or any other Bayano investor to investigate? Leo lived a millionaire's lifestyle—a suburban mansion, limousines, well-appointed offices. In 1916 he signed a ten-year, $300-a-month lease on an impressive residence at 2715 Sheridan Road in Evanston, a university town of about thirty thousand, north of the city, that one visitor touted as "the bedroom of Chicago," home to "the successful merchant and professional man."

The house was worth about $90,000—well over $1 million today—and sat on a landscaped one-acre plot with a hundred feet of lake frontage not far from the campus of Northwestern University. Clad in white stucco, topped with a high-pitched hipped roof, and as refined and grand as its tenant, it was "one of the show places of Evanston," according to a reporter who checked out the property. "Scornfully it turns its back on the passerby, so that the back yard, if it can be so termed, faces the street." The mansion—"for no other word will describe it," the newsman assured his readers—had a glass-enclosed room at the north end that captured the morning sun and framed a spectacular view of the lake. A pergola marched through the grounds to the shoreline.

Mae's budget for furnishing and decorating the home was $15,000, more than enough to assemble a collection of antiques and fine furniture, complete with a piano. Sèvres vases in blue porcelain, antique silver candelabras, statuettes, and other decorative pieces—many of them gifts Leo brought home from business trips—added richness to the decor. An autumn landscape by Bruce Crane, a sought-after American artist of the day, hung on a wall. In the drawing room, blue-green draperies framed the tall cathedral windows, and a davenport anchored the main sitting area. The reception room welcomed visitors with soft velvets and more of the antiques Leo loved to collect. The table in the billiard room was so large it would have cost a small fortune just to remove it from the house. Leo hired a staff of four to run the place, including a cook, a maid, and a houseman to tackle the chores. A German-born governess helped Mae look after the children—Mentor was nine when they moved in, and they now had a daughter, Mari, who was three.

And there was a library with an impressive collection of books, each volume containing a personal bookplate bearing the inscription "Mr. and Mrs. L. Koretz." Leo bought thousands of dollars' worth of books at a time, from valuable first editions to the latest two-dollar hardcover offerings by his favorite novelists. "Mr. Koretz was most sensitive to fine writing," in the opinion of Adolph Kroch, proprietor of the Michigan Avenue bookstore where Leo did much of his shopping. "He could talk of what he'd read, too; he appreciated it." Crime fiction was Leo's passion—he snapped up the adventures of gumshoes and crooks as soon as they appeared—but he also scoured the shelves of Kroch's store for literary works. One of his favorite authors was Joseph Conrad, a safe choice for a man who wanted to impress others with his taste in literature; *Time* magazine, which debuted in 1923, hailed Conrad as holding "probably the most exalted position in contemporary English letters." Leo knew *The Rubáiyát of Omar Khayyám* by heart and splurged on an $850 copy of the twelfth-century ode to living in the moment. Given his twisted sense of humor, he no doubt relished reciting the line, "A Hair perhaps divides the False and True."

The last word in opulence could be found in the two-car garage facing the street—"a building of no mean architecture or proportions," noted the newsman with the eye for real estate. It had a hipped roofline to match the mansion and housed those two Rolls-Royce limousines. Leo told friends he had answered the doorbell one evening and found one of them, a closed-cab model in tasteful maroon paint, idling in his driveway, with a thank-you note from "your grateful partners" on the steering wheel. It was a gift, he said, from Al Watson on behalf of the other members of the Bayano Syndicate. Leo had surprised Mae with the other Rolls, an open touring car, but she preferred to run around town in a more modest Packard, at least until she traded up to a snazzier Stevens-Duryea. Life in Evanston was good—and getting better every year. It became a tradition for Leo and Mae to invite the rest of the Koretz clan to the mansion to celebrate the holiday season.

Leo, who still dabbled in wills and divorce cases, ensured his downtown law offices were as impressive as his home. He rented space in the *Daily Tribune*'s skyscraper—located in the dead center of the Loop, at "the hub of business activity"—for six years, until 1912, when he traded up to a newer building, the Rector. "I always have had a beautiful suite of offices and at all times the very finest and most expensive engraved and embossed stationery," he would one day boast. "They never failed to make the right kind of impression."

By 1920 he was renting the entire third floor of the Majestic Theater Building at 22 West Monroe Street, a couple of blocks west of the Michigan Avenue lakefront. With a wedding-cake facade of gleaming white terra-cotta that soared twenty stories, the Majestic had been the city's tallest building when it opened in 1906 and was considered "a striking specimen of skyscraper architecture." The main-floor theater featured more than a dozen vaudeville shows and movies a day, and Leo could invite guests downstairs to enjoy topflight acts such as the escape artist Harry Houdini. The lease alone cost him more than $5,000 a year, and as usual, he did not scrimp on the decor.

The suite was expensively furnished, and each office featured a picture of Illinois's favorite son, Abraham Lincoln. An inner vault held a stash of hundreds of bottles of wine and liquor; although Leo drank little himself, he made sure he had plenty of booze to offer to clients and investors. His personal office was fitted with a wall-mounted electric cigar lighter, and visitors were surprised to see a Bible on his desk—until they discovered it was a cigarette holder. A quote in praise of "Honest Abe" claimed a prominent place near his desk, an appropriate office accessory for a man with such a solid reputation in business and finance. Leo rented space to Samuel Richman and other lawyers, injecting bustle and energy and disguising the fact that he only needed a staff of two—a secretary and an office boy—to run his law practice, his rice farms, and his Bayano holdings.

Leo hosted lavish dinners and parties at his mansion and was invited, in turn, into the homes of wealthy Chicagoans. He thought nothing of booking restaurants and nightclubs to entertain relatives, friends, and investors. Memberships in the city's best clubs expanded his social circle. Charming and funny, well read and sophisticated, he was also a bit of a dandy who was seen strutting around in checked sports coats and dangling a walking cane. When he dropped by Henry Heppner and Company's tailor shop on State Street, no one batted an eye if he ordered $1,000 worth of new suits and accessories. He had an unlimited charge account with Lewy Brothers Jewelers, at the corner of State and Adams, where he often bought pieces costing more than $5,000. He once ordered a pair of $1,500 cuff links from another jeweler but sent them back, complaining they were tawdry.

Leo gained a reputation around Evanston as generous and community-minded. He supported the Chicago Jewish war relief fund and other charity drives and served as vice-chair of the Evanston Council of Boy Scouts. In 1917, when his doctor and friend, Milton Mandel, was serving at a military hospital in France, Leo sent over money and asked that it be used to cheer up the patients. He dutifully filled out a draft card in September 1918, two months before the war ended, when the Selective Service Act was extended to cover men up to the age of forty-six; he had just turned thirty-nine and, under the heading "Present Occupation," described himself as an attorney "also engaged in rice growing in Arkansas."

Mae, too, was active in the community. She served on the executive committee of the mother's aid group at Chicago's Lying-In Hospital and Dispensary, which offered free prenatal and obstetrical care to residents of the Maxwell Street ghetto. Leon Klein, who was married to Mae's sister Maude, christened her "the most wonderful woman on the North Shore" and reckoned she donated more than $1,000 a month to a Jewish orphans' fund and other charities.

Down in the Loop, Evanston's model citizen, Leo Koretz, was generous in other ways. He was often seen escorting women to restaurants for lunch or dinner. "The women were crazy over Leo," exclaimed Anna Auerbach, a Bayano investor and close friend, but he never "played flappers and unmarried women." These rendezvous, she insisted, were innocent and aboveboard. "He specialized in the companionship of ladies who were safely married to sound business men," herself included, and "most of the times it was with the husband's knowledge." "They were glad that Koretz admired their wives," she said. Leo doted on his dining companions and never forgot a birthday, sending along a bouquet of roses or orchids or a diamond butterfly pin or other gift. His investors and associates, it seemed, trusted him with their wives as much as they trusted him with their money. "He was so sympathetic and kind," Auerbach gushed. "And so thoughtful." Mae knew of his many female friends—there are "many women in Leo's life," she often remarked to Auerbach—but since they were married and their husbands seemed to approve, she trusted him, too.

There could be a darker side to his attentiveness. He used at least one woman to lure her husband into the Bayano fold. She had met Leo at a party and accepted his invitation to lunch. He took her to a busy restaurant, to ensure they would be seen together, and asked her to persuade her husband to invest; otherwise, he warned, people might think their lunch date was about something other than business. "The poor woman," as the story was later told, "afraid of gossip though she had done nothing wrong, went home and told her husband that Koretz had tipped her off to a very good thing, and that he had better invest in it." Her husband did, and once again Leo had been able to make a sale without soliciting the buyer.

But not everyone was buying the dreams of easy money Leo was so adept at selling. Maurice Berkson, a lawyer who had attended school with Leo, insisted he "never liked or trusted the man." To some, Leo's reticence about his wealthy Bayano partners spoke of classiness and discretion. To Berkson, such secrecy was a red flag. "He was one of the mysterious sort," he said. "Always there seemed to be a mystery about him. He never was out in the open and nobody ever knew exactly what he was doing."

A few stockholders wondered whether Bayano's fat profits were simply too good to be true. "Now and then the thought did occur that we were being paid excessive dividends," noted Clara Philipsborn, "but somehow the man's personality and his standing in the community allayed our suspicions." She also took comfort in the fact that Leo had never asked her to invest a dime.

Those who doubted Leo's word or betrayed the slightest unease with his methods were quickly brought into line. At one point, several investors became troubled after taking a close look at the promissory notes they held as security for mortgages—fake mortgages, of course. The signatures on the notes were almost illegible, and a delegation was formed to ask for the proper documents. Leo, so the story went, "became indignant at their lack of confidence." He needed to keep the original records, he explained, to collect the interest payments on their behalf. The investors backed down, unaware how close they had come to discovering the truth.

Such suspicions were rare. People thought they were in on a good thing because, to all appearances, they were. Arkansas farms and Bayano stock paid dividends or interest of at least 10 percent a year, every year; a check for profits earned arrived on the first day of the month, every month. "It was like a hot tip on a horse race," noted one of Leo's relatives. "Everybody jumped on who could." Profits were high enough to attract investors but not large enough to make Bayano smack of a get-rich-quick scheme. A Chicago financier who never invested but watched closely from the wings believed Leo's business empire was real: "You could have told me he was a swindler, a robber and a bank bandit and produced a police photograph to prove it," he later told a reporter, "and I'd have laughed at you." Leo's reluctance to take money also silenced the doubters; by the time investors finally wore him down and got their hands on some Bayano shares, the possibility of being swindled was the last thing on their minds.

If anyone who held stock got cold feet or wanted out for any reason, Leo wrote a check on the spot. "The few investors who sought to withdraw always were given their money on a moment's notice," noted one press account, and this only enhanced his reputation for integrity.

When one man who sank $30,000 into Bayano became uneasy and asked for his money back, Leo said, "Sure thing," and wrote out a check for $40,000—the original investment plus a parting bonus. "Your stock really earned it," he said. "Nothing but fair to you."

It was not long before the man returned, chastened, with the uncashed check in hand. "Here, Leo, take back your check," he pleaded. "I think I made a mistake in getting out."

Other investors made it easy for Leo to meet his mounting obligations. Many followed the lead of his brother Julius and invested their profits in more Bayano stock. Milton Eisenstaedt, a doctor, earned a dividend every month for a decade—doubling his original investment—and reinvested every one. The family of Bessie Rosenthal, one of Mae's closest friends, invested $45,000 and never cashed a single dividend check. "I have never received a penny from him," Rosenthal once noted, "that I did not reinvest."

Rosenthal, Eisenstaedt, and other investors who used their imaginary profits to buy more imaginary Bayano shares became unwitting accomplices. Their votes of confidence freed up cash Leo could use to keep other investors happy. And as his moneymaking machine became more complex and more unwieldy, he needed all the help he could get. "There was no turning back," he later explained. "Men and women believed in Bayano even more than I did. . . . The Bayano bubble lifted me off my feet and swept me along."

Leo had been juggling people and numbers and spinning lies and half truths, day in and day out, for almost fifteen years. He kept hundreds of investors happy while constantly on the lookout for new ones. He fooled his wife and family, his closest friends, his fellow lawyers, his business associates, and everyone else. There were dividends to distribute and bills to pay. He had an expensive home and an opulent lifestyle to maintain. He was in far too deep to ever get out. Emil Koretz recalled watching his brother jot notes in a small black book and assumed he was keeping track of his financial affairs. He was—keeping track of the myriad details of a make-believe world of fat profits and Panama riches, of Arkansas rice farms and mysterious syndicates.

As the twenties were about to roar, Leo's investment juggernaut was running out of steam. Every month he needed to scrape together thousands of dollars to feed the insatiable appetite of the beast he had created. New investors and new money were not coming in fast enough; "business," as he put it, "was dull." To make matters worse, not everyone swapped their profits for more Bayano stock or wanted to stay in for the long haul. The only way he could continue to meet his obligations—and stave off a default that would expose his intricate fraud—was to bring in more money.

He needed a fresh angle, a new product from the Bayano River valley that would unleash a new scramble for shares in the syndicate— something so attractive and so lucrative that more people would camp out at his doorstep and beg him for a piece of the action.

And then it came to him—the perfect, irresistible product that would make 10 percent annual returns on Panamanian timber and Arkansas rice farms look like chump change. The Big Idea was about to become much, much bigger.

THE HANGING JUDGE

As Leo was plotting the next phase of his Bayano fraud, Chicagoans were fixated on the disappearance of a little girl. The neighbors called her Dolly, and there was no denying that the six-year-old with the bobbed blond hair and deep blue eyes looked like a China doll. In the photo that ran in the newspapers in the summer of 1919, Janet Wilkinson sat with her hands folded in her lap and her mouth caught midway between a pout and a smile.

ALL CHICAGO SEEKS SOLUTION OF MISSING CHILD MYSTERY, blared a headline. The *Daily Tribune* offered a reward to anyone who knew where she was. Police officers combed her North Side neighborhood, poking through basements, sewers, and garbage bins; even her classmates at Holy Name Cathedral School joined the search. Janet had disappeared at about noon on July 22 and was last seen speaking to a man who lived on the other side of her duplex, a hotel night watchman named Thomas Fitzgerald. He was an odd man, awkward around adults and known to offer candy and comic books to kids. He was the kind of man whom parents—including Janet's—warned their children to steer clear of.

Police took him in for questioning. For more than four days, as the search continued, Fitzgerald was interrogated around the clock. He finally cracked and confessed. He had grabbed Janet and hauled her into his apartment. She screamed. He panicked. "I grabbed her by the throat," he told the lead investigator, "and choked her to death." He led police to the basement of his building and showed them where he had hidden the girl's body. She was under a pile of coal that was wedged between a chimney and the foundation wall, a space so narrow no one had bothered to check it during the search. The autopsy added a gruesome coda to an already horrific crime: Janet was still alive when buried.

"Seldom has the populace been so aroused over a criminal case here," the *New York Times* reported. There were demands for a city-wide roundup of perverts and pedophiles—"morons," in the euphemism of the time—to prevent more outrages against Chicago's children. The prosecuting attorney, James O'Brien, who had sent enough murderers to the gallows to earn the nickname Ropes, vowed to seek the death penalty even if the defense pleaded insanity. The press egged him on. "There will be a general opinion," the *Tribune* asserted, "that he is sane enough to be hanged."

If it was revenge people wanted, Chief Justice Robert Crowe of the Cook County Criminal Court was determined to make sure they got it. When Fitzgerald pleaded guilty to murder in September 1919, Crowe offered him little hope for mercy. "If the evidence shows that hanging is proper," he announced, "there will be no turning aside." Fitzgerald had a history of exposing himself and was attracted to children; his wife, who was much younger, called him "subnormal" and, "knowing his weakness," said she had not been surprised to learn of his crime. Crowe, a father of three—his oldest, a daughter, was Janet Wilkinson's age—was sickened by what he heard. It was, he said later, "a dastardly crime," committed by a man who lacked "the decency or the heart to put a handkerchief over that little dead face as he heaped the coal upon it."

There was an unwritten rule in Cook County: murderers who pleaded guilty were sent to the state prison in Joliet, not to the gallows. It had been that way for decades. On September 23, 1919, before a packed courtroom, Crowe ordered Fitzgerald to stand and asked if he had anything to say.

"I'm sorry. I—I ask forgiveness."

"Is that all?" Crowe shot back.

"I ask God to forgive me."

Crowe sentenced him to hang the following month. Hundreds of people scrambled for tickets to attend the execution in the Cook County Jail. The *Daily Tribune* called it an "exact and just" sentence that sent a message to "all those musty minded perverts whose unprintable activities have long been beyond tolerance." The *Chicago Republican,* heartened to see justice "unmixed with mercy," declared that Crowe had not only "performed a plain duty, but also rendered society a service of inestimable value and benefit."

"What Chicago needs is not more law," the paper added, "but more judges of the Crowe type."

IN THE YEARS IT had taken Leo to create his phony empire of rice and mahogany, his colleague from their days as young lawyers had gone on to become a star in the legal profession and a man to watch in Chicago politics. Robert Crowe's early election to the bench—he was still in his thirties when he stopped arguing cases and began deciding them—was the product of political opportunism multiplied by personal ambition.

After leaving Moran, Mayer, and Meyer in 1903, Crowe opened a practice in downtown Chicago with his brother, Frank, and a classmate from Crowe's high school days, George Barrett. Barrett, a future judge, was active with his own brother, Charles, in Republican politics on Chicago's West Side. Frank Crowe was thirteen years Robert's senior and well established as a criminal lawyer; while his kid brother studied at Yale, Frank was sending bad guys to prison as an assistant state's attorney for Cook County.

Robert Crowe gravitated to criminal law, and it was a good fit. There was no murky middle ground, only absolutes: defendants were guilty or innocent, good or evil. He had absorbed his Yale teachings and saw a world where every fact, every action, was either right or wrong. And Crowe was always right. Contemporaries described him

*Robert Crowe, elected to the bench in 1916 at thirty-seven,
was a rising star in Chicago's Republican party. Crowe and Leo
began their legal careers together at a Chicago law firm.*

as "vigorous and quick-tongued," as "blunt, stormy, dangerous"—
a force to be reckoned with. He charged ahead like a prizefighter, at-
tacking opponents with a flurry of verbal punches. As his rhetoric and
blood pressure soared, his husky voice cracked; words tumbled out in
a high-pitched, nasal torrent that startled those who had only seen his
words in the newspapers.

There was no middle ground in politics, either, only Republicans
and Democrats, allies and enemies. It was another good fit for a man

with Crowe's confidence and certainty. The former leader of Yale's Young Republicans joined forces with the Barrett brothers to become a key player on the West Side. Political life in Chicago was not a matter of principle or public policy, the city's *Evening Post* once observed; it was "a professional occupation, carried out by men and women who expect to be compensated, not thru the indirect benefits of efficient government, but thru direct benefits in the form of jobs, contracts and other material gains." The city functioned as a democracy, but only on the surface.

The tactics were bare knuckle, the stakes winner-take-all. Voting fraud was commonplace, and hired thugs patrolled polling stations to intimidate or assault anyone who supported a rival candidate. Politicians raided the public treasury to reward the troops and buy their loyalty. The Irish, among the most adept players of the game, built powerful organizations at the ward level that left one observer in awe of "the wild doings of the political Irish gang." The system was thoroughly corrupt and impervious to civic reform, and it operated above the law. Only Cook County's judges and the state's attorney had the power to intervene, but they were elected on party tickets and as beholden to the political machines as everyone else in public life.

The state's attorney, equal parts lawman and politician, was perhaps the most powerful elected official in Cook County—a "dictator-like office," some observed. Crowe and his staff launched and shut down grand jury investigations into crime and corruption. They could target gangsters or crime bosses or political enemies, or choose to leave them alone. They could oppose a defendant's release on bail or put the suspect back on the street. Prosecutions could be delayed for months, even years. Charges could be pressed with vigor, withdrawn without comment, or plea-bargained down to minor offenses. It was easy to play favorites. Answerable only to political supporters and public opinion, the state's attorney pandered to both.

Crowe's rise to prominence began in this office where politics and the law collided. He campaigned for his friend John Wayman, who ran as the Republican candidate for state's attorney for Cook County in 1908. Wayman won, hired Crowe as one of his assistants, and took on the role of a reformer. But crime and vice flourished during Wayman's tenure as it had under his predecessors', until an exposé of Chicago's white slave traffic and the debauchery of the Levee forced his hand. Wayman ordered a roundup of pimps and madams in 1912, and within days, the district that had earned Chicago its reputation as the Wicked City was shut down. "Fallen is Babylon!" proclaimed one antivice activist.

Crowe, watching at close range, saw how Cook County's state's attorney balanced the zeal of reformers against corrupt forces as rooted in the city's landscape as its towering buildings. When Wayman mounted a failed bid for governor of Illinois, Maclay Hoyne took his place as state's attorney. Some of the Levee's brothels and gambling dens reopened, enough for Hoyne to mount his own well-publicized crusade to put them out of business in 1914. It was business as usual, with one exception. Hoyne was a Democrat. Crowe, a Republican appointee, knew his days as a prosecutor were numbered.

He continued to build a political base on the West Side. Crowe caught the eye of a University of Chicago professor who considered him a new type of Republican boss, "aggressive, but with more education and polish" than most of the city's ward heelers. Crowe's marriage in 1912 to Candida Cuneo, the daughter of an Italian grocer, extended his political reach into an immigrant community growing in size and clout.

The *Chicago Examiner* lauded his "brilliant record" as a prosecutor and lawyer. Judges spoke highly of his ability and integrity. Chicago's newly elected Republican mayor, Big Bill Thompson, took notice.

WILLIAM HALE THOMPSON IS a legendary figure in Chicago's politics, so brash and larger than life that the authors of an early biography feared their work would be considered fiction. "Once upon a time," they assured readers, "there really was a Big Bill Thompson." He was six feet tall, square faced, and solidly built, which accounted for his nickname; working on western ranches as a young man explained his showman's habit of turning up in downtown Chicago on horseback, wearing a Stetson.

Fred Lundin, the leader of the West Side Republicans, backed Thompson for mayor in 1915 and helped Big Bill win by a landslide. Crowe, a key player in Lundin's West Side machine, undoubtedly helped elect Thompson as well. The new mayor, who never left a favor unreturned, named Crowe to the city's legal staff in 1915, and soon he was defending Chicago police officers accused of misconduct. When elections to local and state offices rolled around in November 1916, Thompson and Lundin had the perfect candidate for a seat on the Illinois Circuit Court.

Crowe was thirty-seven when he was elected to the bench. Energetic and determined to make his mark, he heard cases and delivered verdicts faster than most of his colleagues. When America went to war in 1917, he stepped up as leader of a local branch of the Patriotic League and devoted several nights a week to helping the families of West Side men who were serving overseas. And when gangs began stealing automobiles at an alarming rate, Crowe pushed for a special court to hear only allegations of car theft. He presided in person, convicted nine out of every ten defendants, and was credited with cutting the theft rate in half. A Rolls-Royce limousine, Leo Koretz's vehicle of choice, "became as safe as the flivver on the streets of Chicago," Crowe later claimed. Here was a judge, the *Chicago Evening American* told its readers, who dispensed three kinds of justice: "swift, uncompromising and stern."

Chicago needed Crowe-style justice in the summer of 1919. Racial tensions erupted in violence after blacks strayed into a segregated area on a lakefront beach. In the confrontation that followed, a white man threw a stone that struck and killed Eugene Williams, a black teenager. Violence spread across the city, and four days of rioting left thirty-eight dead and hundreds injured.

Thompson stumbled in the face of the crisis and waited days to call in the National Guard to restore order. Crowe, in contrast, took decisive action. He publicly denounced the "anarchy" in the streets and promised speedy trials for those responsible. While more than half the dead and two-thirds of the injured were blacks, far more blacks than whites had been arrested and charged. Crowe acquitted many of the black defendants and won praise from a leading black newspaper as "the most fair-minded man who ever graced the Chicago Bench."

Weeks later, in September 1919, he was appointed to lead the Cook County Criminal Court, the youngest chief justice in the court's history. He was as imposing on the bench as he had been on the courtroom floor; the dark-rimmed glasses he now wore most of the time, with lenses thick as bottle bottoms, made him look more aloof and imperious than ever. Crowe hit the ground running, sending the child murderer Fitzgerald to the gallows and a loud and clear message to all criminals. He presided over a special grand jury that handed down more than a hundred indictments as part of a nationwide crackdown on Communist Party leaders and labor activists. He set up a special court in 1920 to process a backlog of more than forty murder cases. In ten months his court racked up a record number of convictions— almost two thousand—dispatched twelve hundred offenders to prison, and sent fifteen more to the gallows.

As Crowe emerged as a leader and a doer, Thompson foundered. There were rumblings of graft and patronage as he followed the time-honored practice of padding the city payroll with thousands of supporters. Thompson spoke out against America's entry into the war—Chicago was "the sixth largest German city in the world," he rationalized—and became a national embarrassment. He stood for reelection in April 1919 and limped back into office, his margin of victory slashed to a little more than twenty thousand votes.

Big Bill was vulnerable. It would soon be time for Robert Crowe to make his next move.

9

THE STING

SUITE 629 OF the Drake Hotel was the grand stage where Leo Koretz's grand scheme came to life. He had cleared out the standard-issue furnishings and forked over about $2,000—enough money to buy a pair of top-of-the-line Hudson Essex touring cars—to bring in his own. Visitors could relax in a red velour lounge chair or pull up an overstuffed armchair with matching ottoman. A phonograph stood ready to supply background music, and a risqué piece of green statuary depicted a man holding a scantily clad young woman. A framed photograph of Mae served as the centerpiece for a lamp table. Bookcases groaned under the weight of thousands of volumes, an imposing collection that ranged from the complete works of Mark Twain to the latest novels of 1921's Nobel Prize winner, Anatole France. A lineup of technical works on the petroleum industry, published in an array of languages sure to please supporters of the new League of Nations—French, Italian, Spanish, and German as well as English—hinted at the new source of wealth Leo had discovered in the jungles of Panama.

Only a select group of investors was invited to do business in these posh digs. When summoned, it was said, they felt "the same glow of pride" as "when gaining entry to an exclusive speak-easy." Their host held court behind a ten-foot-wide mahogany desk piled with more books and bearing an engraved brass plate that declared, MADE FROM

THE FIRST LOG CUT AT BAYANO. Guests chuckled when they saw a gold-framed sign hanging on one wall: YES, WE HAVE NO BAYANO TODAY, it said, a play on a wildly popular song of the day, "Yes! We Have No Bananas." Good old Lovable Lou—he never missed a chance to crack a joke.

From his windows, Leo could follow the shoreline of Lake Michigan as it faded from sight. On summer days, Oak Street Beach, a crescent of sand behind the Drake, was crammed with people escaping Chicago's blistering heat. In winter, Leo's windows often framed a sullen and brooding landscape of gray sky and grayer water. The hotel stood at the north end of fashionable Michigan Avenue, far enough from the Loop to be billed as one of America's first urban resorts. Guests could relax on the beach, swim, play tennis, or shoot a round of golf on a nearby course. The H-shaped building, its clean lines modeled on the Renaissance palaces of Rome and Florence, had cost $10 million to build, furnish, and decorate. "Each step you take in The Drake Hotel," the actor Peter Ustinov would one day declare, "is like walking on diamonds."

In the comfort of suite 629, after the checks were written or the hefty dividends had been reinvested, Bayano investors could thumb their noses at the Prohibition laws and celebrate with a shot of rye or bourbon or a few fingers of scotch, or maybe Leo could be persuaded to dust off a bottle of vintage wine from his stash. It all added up—the exclusive hotel, the opulent suite, the million-dollar view, the gracious host who was striking it rich and taking his friends and relatives along for the ride.

Only the Drake's bellboys seemed to think something was amiss. Leo always flipped them a silver fifty-cent piece, and this raised a few eyebrows. "Real millionaires," as one of them explained, "never tip more than a dime."

SOMETIME IN 1921, WHILE chatting with a friend, Leo dropped the bombshell—his new, even bigger Big Idea. "I casually mentioned that oil was discovered on this Bayano tract," he recalled.

And just as he had intended, "the news spread rapidly." The profitable Bayano timber syndicate was in the far more lucrative oil business.

There were a couple of versions of the story of how oil came to be discovered. He told Mae that a party of South American prospectors poking around Panama had sought permission to drill exploratory wells on the property. There was a more whimsical tale, however, that sounded like vintage Leo. A drilling crew traveling from California to South America along the Pacific coast was shipwrecked and came ashore on the syndicate's land. Bayano's local manager—the mysterious A. Espinosa, no doubt—gave them refuge. The crew's boss, with time on his hands, thought the region looked promising and sought permission to drill. The manager gave the go-ahead and the crew struck oil.

There was a rush for Bayano shares. "They began to besiege me with money for certificates," Leo said. "They thrust it on me . . . and refused to take it back." One man reputedly paid $30,000 for a single certificate.

Leo leaked more details to drive up prices and to lure in more buyers. He told Samuel Richman about the discovery and then, in the weeks that followed, mentioned more strikes and more crude. Soon he was assuring Richman he had forty wells in production, each spewing at least ten thousand barrels a day. He told his investment partner Henry Klein that Bayano was earning several million dollars a month. Telegrams arrived at social functions, informing Leo—and everyone around him—of new wells. Bayano's vast reserves, he bragged, were the envy of Standard Oil. Best of all, he announced, the days of 10 percent annual dividends were over. Oil would earn Bayano shareholders a 5 percent return *every month*—an astounding 60 percent a year. This was only the beginning; in time, Francis Matthews remembered being assured, "this amount would be doubled."

Then came what was perhaps his most brazen ploy. One day, with a close friend playing the role of witness, he produced a check—payment, presumably, for oil sold by the Bayano Syndicate. It was made out for $1 million. "Hooray! Look what I just got from the Standard Oil company," he shouted. "They're coming my way now."

The startled friend did the rest, and soon more people were clamoring for stock. Leo's theatrics, it was later reported, sold another $1 million worth of shares. But he continued to play hard to get. Isaac Fischel had been among the first investors in Bayano, buying $3,000 in shares in 1911, but he had sold them back to Koretz within a couple of years. When he heard that oil had been found, Fischel was desperate to get back in. After "much persuasion," he recalled, Leo sold him four shares.

One prominent Chicago banker who had long tried to buy stock cornered him in the midst of the oil frenzy and seized him by the lapels. "Now, look here, Leo," he begged. "Why not have a heart." Leo relented. A check for $40,000 soon arrived, but instead of cashing it, Leo showed it to potential investors, swearing them to secrecy. Impressed to learn that someone of the banker's stature was taking a big stake in Bayano, many of these confidants asked to buy shares as well. After getting mileage out of the check for a couple of weeks, he returned it to the banker. "I'm sorry," he said in an accompanying note, "but I can't spare you any Bayano just now." The banker refused to give up and ultimately bought $100,000 worth of shares.

Bayano's gushers tossed the lifeline Leo needed to stay afloat. But oil created new problems as well. He had more investors to keep happy and a host of new lies to keep straight. Cash was flowing in, but now he was committed to paying out much more each month in dividends. Many investors were eager to spend their inflated profits, and not even the smooth-talking Leo could persuade everyone to reinvest. Several families used their windfalls to ship sons and daughters east to expensive colleges. Others cashed their dividend checks so that they could enjoy the good life, among them an investor who moved from a modest flat to a luxury hotel suite and had enough money left over to dash around town in a chauffeur-driven car.

And investors were beginning to wonder what the syndicate

planned to do with its crude. How was it being stored and transported to market? Would all of it be sold to Standard Oil?

"Questions were asked of me," Leo recalled, "as to what I was to do with these immense holdings." His answer? Bayano, he declared, would no longer be merely a producer of oil. The syndicate was going into the petroleum business, and in a big way.

IT WAS A PERFECT time to be selling stock in an oil company—to be selling stock in anything, for that matter. The American economy, after a few postwar sputters, was booming; the "prosperity bandwagon rolled along," wrote Frederick Lewis Allen, the decade's finest chronicler, "with the throttle wide open and siren blaring." Consumer spending jumped $7 billion during 1922 alone, to $63 billion, at a time when Washington's total tax revenues were a modest $4.3 billion. In 1920 the first commercial radio broadcast ignited a new craze—the first of a decade remembered for its fads and crazes—and created a new industry almost overnight. Americans spent $136 million on radio sets, parts, and accessories in 1923, doubling sales in a year. "There is radio music in the air, every night, everywhere," noted a San Francisco newspaper inspired to rhyme.

But the driving force of the overheated economy was the automobile. Henry Ford produced his first Model T in 1908, the year General Motors was founded, and by 1915 there were 2.5 million cars and trucks on America's roads. The number quadrupled to more than 10 million in 1921. The construction of better highways and a switch to building closed cars, which could be driven in comfort year-round, further boosted auto sales.

Leo saw the results every time he ventured out in his maroon Rolls-Royce: Chicago's streets were jammed with Fords, Chevrolets, and lumbering Studebaker Big Sixes. The "new age of locomotion" had transformed the city into "a wild jungle," the *Daily Tribune* complained, and more than seven hundred people died in car or car-pedestrian crashes in 1922. A survey counted two cars for every three families in a typical American city and discovered that poor people were more likely to have a car than a bathtub. Horses were disappearing from the nation's streets and roads so quickly that in 1923 a paleontologist at the University of California predicted the animals would be extinct in a century or seen only in zoos.

Once there was a car in the driveway and a radio in the parlor, a lot of people had money left over to play the stock market. Stock mania was the defining feature of the decade, an investment frenzy that culminated in the crash of '29. A sign overlooking New York's Columbus Circle admonished passersby: YOU SHOULD HAVE $10,000 AT THE AGE OF 30; $25,000 AT THE AGE OF 40; $50,000 AT 50—a tall order in an era when four-fifths of the population made less than $3,000 a year.

To get there, and to get there as quickly as possible, more people than ever invaded the traditional preserve of the wealthy and put money into stocks. Million-share trading days on the New York Stock Exchange became common. Investors borrowed to buy shares and used them as collateral to buy more, or bought stock on margin from brokers, paying as little as 10 percent down. People were growing accustomed to buying cars and radios and other goods on credit, so why not stocks? As long as values rose, a lot of people made money. Even the gangster Al Capone, who made his money with threats and guns, was impressed: "It's a racket," he said. "Those stock market guys are crooked."

The stock market was not the only get-rich game to play. Investors put their money into Florida real estate, new inventions, mines, and a host of other risky ventures—anything that looked promising. Door-to-door salesmen and storefront operations known as bucket shops peddled stock in phony or dubious enterprises to gullible investors. The ease with which Charles Ponzi roped in the suckers with his bizarre postal-reply coupons scam said much about the investment-mad times.

One investment stood out above the others: oil. The automobile was a godsend for America's petroleum industry, which had watched nervously as electricity displaced its main product, illuminating oils such as kerosene. The engines puttering under the hoods of all those cars and trucks needed fuel, and gasoline, once considered a useless by-product of crude-oil refining, was in high demand. More than any other product, gasoline made Standard Oil's founder, John D. Rockefeller, the wealthiest man in the world.

An antitrust ruling had splintered Standard Oil into more than thirty companies in 1911—about the time gasoline sales eclipsed those of kerosene—but it remained one of the most powerful corporations on the planet. The largest of the stand-alone companies, Standard Oil of New Jersey, was the second-largest corporation in America in terms of assets, revenues, and profits, and three others—the Indiana, New York, and California divisions—would soon crack the top ten. It was little wonder that the mere mention of the company's name worked magic on Leo's investors.

By the 1920s, largely owing to the insatiable thirst for gasoline, US demand for oil reached almost a half-billion barrels a day, more than double the figure for 1914. The per-barrel price tripled. Even though the discovery of new oil fields in Texas, Oklahoma, and California brought more crude onstream, new reserves were needed. "America is running through her stores of domestic oil," a British magazine warned in 1919, "and is obliged to look abroad for future reserves." The discovery of new oil reserves in Venezuela at the end of 1922 eased fears of shortages—and, if there were any skeptics left in Chicago, made Leo's Panamanian oil fields seem that much more plausible.

Shares in Standard Oil and competitors such as Texas Corporation, Shell, Gulf, and Sinclair soared in value. Stock mania became oil-stock mania, and oil promoters—some legitimate, most not—were everywhere. The discovery of oil near Los Angeles in 1920 triggered a speculative boom in land and exploration leases that one journalist claimed turned Southern California "stark, staring, oil mad." Investors toured the fields, listened to the promoters' hype, and purchased a stake in a property or an exploratory well, often a one one-thousandth interest of little value, if any.

Not even Washington was immune to oil mania. Warren Harding, elected president in 1920 on a promise to return the country to "normalcy" after the disruption of war, oversaw an administration Frederick Lewis Allen blasted as responsible "for more concentrated robbery and rascality than any other in the whole history of the Federal Government." The biggest scandal was the secret transfer to private oil companies of US Navy oil reserves—including a field at Teapot Dome, Wyoming, which gave the scandal its name—in return for kickbacks to the secretary of the interior, Albert Fall.

Chicagoans—the in-crowd that knew Leo Koretz, at least—were in the grip of their own version of the stock-buying, oil-investing craze: Bayano mania.

THE CONFIDENCE MAN

CON MEN NEED a battery of traits to win their victims' trust and lighten their wallets. Leo Koretz had them all.

"They must, first of all, be good actors," able to play whatever role was required to pull off the scam, a career swindler explained to the criminologist Edwin Sutherland in the 1930s. Leo, acting the part of a savvy financier who hobnobbed with a mysterious syndicate of millionaires, delivered a magnificent performance. A winning personality, confidence, shrewdness, and the ability to think fast and improvise, this swindler added, were also essential. Con men "live a chameleon existence," adapting to the people and situations they encounter, noted Frank Abagnale, a master forger who impersonated a doctor, a lawyer, and an airline pilot before using his skills to battle fraud. His list of essential qualities included an eye for detail, a photographic memory, and "icy self-control."

Swindlers—the best ones, at least—tend to be well-read and knowledgeable on a wide range of subjects, allowing them to appear to be the smartest person in the room regardless of the topic being discussed. Leo's library shelves—crammed with everything from atlases and history books to Izaak Walton's seventeenth-century ode to fishing, *The Compleat Angler*—did double duty, impressing Bayano investors while providing the curriculum for his self-taught course in Swindling 101. David Maurer, who produced a definitive study of swindlers and their methods that became fodder for one of Hollywood's best-loved caper flicks, *The Sting,* found that the best ones possessed a keen sense of human nature. They knew how to read people and how to ingratiate themselves with their victims. A good con man, Maurer concluded, "must be able to make anyone like him, confide in him, trust him." Another of Sutherland's informants agreed, asserting that a swindler "must have something loveable about him." Everyone liked the generous, wisecracking, charming Leo, who always seemed to know the right thing to say. Luc Sante, a writer who has chronicled New York City's underworld, suggested that the best con men possessed skills and qualities that "would have propelled them to the top of any profession." Leo, whose ambition and self-confidence knew no bounds, could have been a top-flight lawyer, a business leader, or perhaps a powerful politician. He chose, instead, to become a master of promoting phony stocks.

THE TERM *CONFIDENCE MAN* was first used in 1849, when an enterprising New Yorker named William Thompson walked up to strangers on the street with a proposition: did they have the "confidence" in him, he asked, to entrust him with their watches overnight? Those who complied lost their timepieces and some of their faith in their fellow man. Eight years later, the term was in such common usage that Herman Melville published a novel about riverboat swindlers under the title *The Confidence-Man: His Masquerade.*

One scholar has discerned something quintessentially American about the con man, who reinvents himself to each new victim in the same way that America's early settlers reinvented themselves in a new land. The confidence man, argued Gary Lindberg, "is a covert cultural hero," an ingenious and enterprising figure who exposes the gap between "our stated ethics and our tolerated practices." America was built on dreams and promises, and dreams and promises are what a con man sells. One nineteenth-century commentator suggested that con men were a necessary evil, a species that survived and thrived only because people were inherently trustful. "It is a good thing, and speaks well for human nature, that . . . men *can be swindled.*"

Chicago's Joseph Weil, one of America's most famous con men

and a contemporary of Leo's, began taking advantage of people's trusting nature as a young man at the turn of the century, selling fake elixirs at medicine shows and imitation gold watches door-to-door. His nickname, the Yellow Kid, came from a popular comic-strip character of the time. He became an early master of "the wire," the delayed-race-results swindle popularized in *The Sting*. When that con became too well known, he posed as a mining engineer or financier and led his victims to believe he had the inside track on the stock market. Weil's props, like Leo's, were finely engraved share certificates, wads of cash, a millionaire's wardrobe, and a plausible-sounding story. Weil claimed there was one more weapon in any con man's arsenal: his victims' greed. "They wanted something for nothing," he explained. "I gave them nothing for something."

The Yellow Kid once offered Ben Hecht, one of the best Chicago journalists of the day, a few words of advice that Bayano investors would soon wish they had overheard. "Nobody," Weil said, "would ever be eager to share any good fortune with me. If I should ever meet any such philanthropic soul, I must know him at once as a crook."

In 1899, a few years before Leo began forging fake mortgages and selling worthless shares in rice farms as the opening acts to his Bayano main feature, a bookkeeper named William Franklin Miller had caused a stir in New York by offering to pay investors 10 percent interest. Not 10 percent a year—10 percent *every week,* more than quintupling their investment within a year. 520 Percent Miller, as he became known, claimed he would reap immense profits by playing the stock market. Even though Miller never invested a dime, there were plenty of believers, and he took in an average of $80,000 a week over the course of eleven months, paying enough back as interest to keep the scam afloat. He fled to Montreal with an estimated $2 million but returned to face charges and was sentenced to ten years in prison.

Then Charles Ponzi tried his hand at the game. An Italian immigrant, he had served time for forgery and smuggling illegal aliens before he turned up in Boston with a strategy to double investors' money in just ninety days. His plan was to buy international postal-reply coupons overseas, redeem them in the United States, and profit from fluctuating postwar exchange rates. The supply of coupons was limited, and they could be redeemed only for stamps, not cash, but none of that mattered because Ponzi never purchased a single coupon. Like Miller, he simply used investors' money to meet the inflated interest payments as they came due. "We all crave easy money," Ponzi noted. "If we didn't, no get-rich-quick scheme could be successful." Ponzi's was, for a short time at least. During the first seven months of 1920, he raked in more than $8 million from some thirty thousand investors before investigations and press revelations of his checkered past put him out of business. He pleaded guilty to charges of using the mail to defraud and was sentenced to five years in prison. Investors recovered barely a third of their money.

It was the template for the scam the Wall Street investment "wizard" Bernie Madoff used to deliver market-defying returns and rake in billions of dollars from investors before his massive fraud collapsed in 2008. The rob-Peter-to-pay-Paul fraud has become known as a Ponzi scheme, but by the time Ponzi came along, Leo Koretz had been perfecting the formula and duping investors for close to fifteen years. If Ponzi had not been exposed first, the financial press and Wall Street regulators might be cautioning today's investors to beware of Koretz schemes. As one 1920s newspaper headline concluded, PONZI HAD NOTHING ON LEO KORETZ.

Leo, the Bernie Madoff of the Roaring Twenties, operated his swindle for far longer and with more panache than his predecessor, Miller, or his contemporary, Ponzi. He was a better actor, a more adept liar, a shrewder salesman. The Miller and Ponzi scams collapsed within a year, while Leo kept his alive—and his investors none the wiser—for almost two decades. Their high-profile schemes attracted the attention of the press and the authorities, hastening their downfall. Leo operated in secrecy, promoting Bayano to a tight-knit group of people he could trust to keep their good fortune—and his dubious claims—under wraps. Miller made his pitch to New Yorkers of modest means, and most of Ponzi's victims were his fellow Italian immigrants.

Leo worked his magic on a tougher audience: businessmen, lawyers, doctors, insurance brokers, and other well-off, well-educated people who should have known better. Ponzi and Miller set up offices to take deposits, developed networks of agents to sell shares, and opened branch offices. Leo worked alone and handled every aspect of his swindle, from printing bogus stock certificates and luring in investors to keeping track of his obligations and cutting dividend checks.

But without a steady stream of new money coming in from new investors, his elaborate charades were doomed to collapse. That was why the Yellow Kid and other career con artists avoided the pay-dividends-from-capital scheme. "After a while," as one swindler explained to Sutherland, the criminologist, "the whole thing falls down." Charles Kindleberger, an economist who studied the psychology of financial panics and crashes, warned of the same inherent flaw. "There is never enough money for all . . . and the inflow of new money must ultimately dry up."

The Bayano bubble could not last forever. All Leo could do was delay, for as long as possible, the day of reckoning.

11

THE CRIME FIGHTER

THE PAMPHLET FEATURED a photograph of three young, wide-eyed children huddled with their mother. They looked fearful, as if seeking her protection. Above their heads ran a caption: "Four Reasons Why Judge Crowe Is Interested In Safeguarding Women and Children." The woman was Crowe's wife, Candida, and the children were the couple's two sons and daughter. The tough-on-crime judge was campaigning to be the next state's attorney for Cook County.

Crowe had been elected to the bench as an ally of Mayor Thompson and the Republican boss Fred Lundin and ran for state's attorney in 1920 on the same ticket. But rival Republican factions put forward their own candidate in the September primaries: David Matchett, a respected judge of the Illinois Appellate Court. Intraparty warfare broke out on voting day, as toughs armed with revolvers and clubs took to the streets to attack and intimidate opponents. One man died in a shootout with police officers guarding the polls, and party workers were roughed up in scuffles. Crowe won the real battle, the one at the ballot box, handily defeating Matchett for the nomination.

On Election Day, November 2, Chicago was spared the violence that had marred the primaries. Republican Warren Harding won the presidency by a landslide, and Thompson-Lundin candidates rode on his coattails. The state's attorney race was a rout: Crowe defeated his Democratic challenger by more than two hundred thousand votes.

WITHIN DAYS OF HIS election, Crowe had a chance to make good on his crime-fighting promises. A jury had been squeamish about imposing the death sentence on Carl Wanderer, a war veteran who confessed to murdering his pregnant wife in June 1920. At first he claimed that a robber had shot her as they returned home from a movie and that he had killed the assailant in self-defense. Then he admitted he had staged the whole thing; he had lured a homeless man to his doorstep with the promise of a job before shooting them both. "I was just tired of her," he explained to police. But when Wanderer recanted and accused the police of beating him until he confessed, the jury found him guilty of the lesser offense of manslaughter and sent him to prison for twenty-five years.

The presiding judge called the verdict a "regrettable error." To the prosecutor, Ropes O'Brien, denied another notch on his belt, it was "an asinine finding." Crowe, the new state's attorney, called the prison term "entirely unbefitting the atrocity of the crime." He ordered Wanderer to stand trial again, this time for the murder of the homeless man. The second jury brushed aside doubts about the confession and sentenced Wanderer to hang. Crowe pulled out a victory cigar when newsmen asked him to comment. "Justice has been done," he said, "and a great error has been corrected."

The Hanging Judge was now the Hanging Prosecutor and becoming one of America's leading advocates for capital punishment. "It is the finality of the death penalty which instils fear into the heart of every murderer," he argued in the pages of a respected national journal, the *Forum,* "and it is this fear of punishment which protects society." The country needed Old Testament, eye-for-an-eye justice to protect its citizens, the kind he was determined to deliver to the law-abiding people of Cook County. "I believe society should have no hesitancy," he wrote, "in springing the trap every time the noose can be put around a murderer's neck."

After Carl Wanderer came Harvey Church, a young man so obsessed with owning an expensive Packard Twin Six that he murdered two car salesmen to get one. He used a knife, a baseball bat, and his

Crowe and his wife, Candida, on a campaign platform in 1920 with his Republican allies Charles Barrett, left, and Chicago Mayor William "Big Bill" Thompson.

bare hands to dispatch his victims. Crowe orchestrated a crime-scene tour that scared and sickened Church into confessing. He was convicted in December 1921 and sentenced to hang. Crowe's statement to the press was published on Christmas Eve. "Cook County is extremely fortunate," he said, "in having twelve men who, despite the sentiment of Christmas, had the courage to find Harvey W. Church guilty of murder and fix his penalty at death."

When the new state's attorney appeared in public or in the courtroom, opposing counsel could not break the habit of referring to him as Judge Crowe. His combative style and tough talk soon earned him yet another nickname: Fighting Bob.

IN 1921, AT THE height of its power, the Thompson-Lundin political machine imploded. The *Daily Tribune* went on a mission to expose corruption at city hall and was so successful that Big Bill filed a libel suit seeking an unprecedented $10 million for damage to the city's reputation. The suit—"the most remarkable attempt to suppress free speech in the history of the American press," in the *Tribune*'s opinion—was thrown out of court, leaving the city and its mayor sullied. A bigger blow was the indictment of one of the mayor's closest allies, Governor Lennington Small, on charges of embezzling some $2 million in public funds in his former post as state treasurer. The *Tribune* was jubilant. "The end of the Lundin-Thompson tyranny," the paper declared, "looms in sight."

Crowe observed the mayor's troubles with a tactician's eye, waiting for the moment to strike. It came that fall, when Thompson's handpicked chief of police, Charles Fitzmorris, made a startling admission: his officers were so corrupt it was almost impossible to enforce Prohibition in Chicago. "Reports and rumors reaching me," he announced, "indicate that 50 percent of the men on the Chicago police force are involved seriously in the illegal sale or transportation of liquor." Fitzmorris transferred hundreds of officers in an effort to disrupt the illicit activities, but this was not enough for Crowe. He assembled his own force of sheriff's deputies and police officers to crack down on bootleggers and speakeasies, and invited newsmen and photographers along to publicize the raids. By the time Thompson ordered Fitzmorris to launch his own attack on the illegal liquor trade, the state's attorney had stolen his thunder.

Crowe broke ranks with Thompson and Lundin in 1922. He openly accused the mayor of meddling in the work of his office, of opposing "my efforts to close hell-holes of prostitution and vice." It was a messy divorce. Thompson began to refer to Crowe as "Bobby," as if he were scolding a wayward child, and called him a little rat. Crowe called Thompson a skunk and began probing corruption in the city's school system. By August, several school board officials faced charges of theft and fraud. A full-blown scandal broke in January 1923 when

Crowe indicted Lundin and more than a dozen others on charges of defrauding the board of at least $1 million through graft and kickbacks. Lundin was accused of pressuring school trustees to purchase supplies at inflated prices—a $133 potato peeler was just one example—and his own company had provided windows and doors for school buildings. With his political fixer exposed as corrupt and the mayoral election only months away, Thompson's political career appeared to be over. He announced he would not seek a third term.

Lundin and his codefendants stood trial in June but were acquitted, thanks largely to the formidable skills of the great defense lawyer Clarence Darrow, who dismissed the state's case as "suspicion and cobwebs." The verdict was a setback for Crowe, but the lengthy trial had exposed the extent of the corruption at city hall. With Thompson gone, Crowe could pursue his own political ambitions. Chicago elected a new mayor, Democrat William Dever, and Crowe looked like the Republicans' best hope to reclaim that prize in the next election, in 1927. Crowe's longtime ally, Charles Barrett, controlled the Board of Review, the body that set and adjusted property taxes, and this made him a political force. It was "difficult to refuse a favor," one observer noted, "asked by a man who might double your tax bill, or halve it at will." Crowe and Barrett, now the party's undisputed bosses on the West Side, became the most powerful Republicans in the city and would prove as corrupt as the Thompson-Lundin regime before them, conducting their own raids on the public treasury to reward followers with jobs and contracts.

A crime-fighting reputation and a timely prosecution had put the mayor's office within Crowe's grasp. After that, who knew? If he continued to play his cards right, he might be the party's best bet for governor.

The first step was winning reelection as state's attorney in the fall of 1924. But Chicago's criminals refused to cooperate. The number of murders in the city rose from fewer than 200 in 1921 to 1923's grim tally of 270. Crowe responded with a string of prosecutions he claimed would "call a halt to killing in this city." He took some killers off the streets but seemed powerless to stop a new wave of violence as well-organized gangs—including one led by a couple of transplanted New Yorkers, Johnny Torrio and Al Capone—fought for control of Chicago's liquor trade. Turf wars broke out. Beer shipments were hijacked. Crooks killed other crooks. There were ten gangland slayings in the fall of 1923, and they were only the beginning. The killers were rarely identified or charged. Crowe's promise to halt the bloodshed rang hollow.

The state's attorney turned his attention to easier targets. In June 1923 he launched a grand jury investigation into bucket shops. At least three dozen of the fly-by-night operations were active in the city, flogging worthless or watered-down shares to unsuspecting investors. His office oversaw well-publicized raids on several outfits and filed charges of operating a confidence game. Crowe's second-in-command, the prosecutor George Gorman, claimed the crackdown was driving the fraudsters out of town. Some had "caught fast trains back to New York," he told the papers, "where most of them came from only a few months ago."

Shareholders in the Bayano oil bonanza who heard the news must have shaken their heads, amazed at the gullibility of people who trusted their money to unscrupulous promoters.

THE BUBBLE

AT THE END of 1922, six months after Bayano's biggest investors hosted the banquet in his honor at the Drake Hotel, Leo returned the favor with a New Year's bash at his mansion. The invitation was a mock newspaper page that touted his latest project—a pipeline spanning the Isthmus of Panama, to carry Bayano crude to ocean terminals for shipment to the United States. The syndicate was jumping headlong into the oil business.

"We were told that the big five"—Leo, Espinosa, Fischer, and the two Als, Watson and Bronson—"were paying for the pipe line, which was to cost $5,000,000," Francis Matthews recalled. "With this line Koretz figured that the company would be earning about $100,000 a day." That was $36.5 million a year, or close to $500 million today. Leo's friends and family had hit the jackpot.

Each day seemed to bring more good news. Production reached 150,000 barrels a day and continued to rise. The workforce in Panama ballooned to five thousand employees. The syndicate had ordered a fleet of a dozen tankers to carry its oil to market, Leo said, and he produced the shipyard contracts to prove it. Standard Oil wanted to buy them out for $20 million, he told his investors, but he had turned them down. The oil giant had sweetened its offer to $25 million for just one thousand shares of Bayano, he claimed, and once again he had sent them packing.

He fed investors glowing reports on the syndicate's progress. "When you wish the Bayano a million barrels of oil a month you are a little bit behind the times," he assured Alex Fitzhugh of Des Moines, Iowa, in a June 1923 letter, "for out of 24 producing wells we are today getting a flush production of about a quarter million barrels per day." Fitzhugh was ecstatic: "That is simply astounding," he replied. "Here's hoping she goes bigger and bigger." Two months later, Dr. Milton Mandel and his sister, Sarah, who held a combined eleven thousand shares, were en route to a vacation in Hawaii when a telegram arrived at their San Francisco hotel:

> All our boats are in and unloaded. Some are already on the return to Panama. Additional barges have been sent for the surplus. Twenty-four wells are producing 10,000 barrels of oil daily each. Most of our deliveries are paid for. Dividend checks will be sent December 1.
> Much love.
> LEO

Visitors to Leo's offices in the Majestic Building could not help noticing a row of small bottles displayed on a table. Each one bore a label and a single word: OIL. The dark brown liquid inside, it turned out, was whiskey.

WHEN A MR. STEWART from the Fifth Avenue silversmiths Brand-Chatillon phoned in May 1923, seeking credit information on a guest who had just left the store, the cashier at the St. Regis Hotel was pleased to oblige. Yes, Basil Curran said, he had known this particular guest for many years. The man always stayed at the St. Regis when he was in New York and was prompt in paying his bills, which often ran as high as $5,000. Curran knew a few things about the guest's business affairs, too, from their chats over the years and from conversations he had overheard.

He "was interested in oil enterprises in Panama" and a millionaire many times over, Curran told Stewart, with a net worth of between $15 million and $20 million. Another guest, a Chicago banker, had vouched for the man, assuring Curran "he could borrow any amount of money he wished in Chicago on his own signature." One bank, in fact, had lent him $75,000—in today's terms, almost $1 million—without asking for collateral.

"I told Mr. Stewart that Mr. Koretz was a man of excellent financial standing," Curran recalled, "and that he was good for any credit he might want."

By mid-1923, Leo was visiting New York about once a month, and his home-away-from-home was a two-bedroom suite with sitting room at the St. Regis, an oasis of Old World elegance four blocks south of Central Park. Opened in 1904 at a cost of $6 million, it was built to the luxurious standards of John Jacob Astor IV and stood at the corner of Fifth Avenue and East Fifty-Fifth Street, a neighborhood of mansions, town houses, and upscale shops once known as Millionaires' Row. The eighteen-story hotel catered to those "who were rich, and who were or wanted to be fashionable," noted one study of New York's architecture—people who preferred to stay in a Parisian-style limestone tower and to be immersed in a world of Italian marble, English oak, gleaming brass, bronze grillwork, and Flemish tapestries. Resident families, including the piano-making Steinways and an heir to the Guggenheim fortune, moved in with servants in tow. After a tour in 1906, the Russian writer and revolutionary Maxim Gorky told a reporter that "neither the Grand Dukes, nor even the Czar, have anything like this." The upstart Drake Hotel in Chicago paled in comparison.

Leo chalked up his frequent New York trips to the demands of his burgeoning oil business and spoke of opening a branch office in the city. Freed from family obligations and the demands of his investors, he explored New York's nightlife and made new friends. He became close with Marcy Schoener and his wife, Mary, who lived at the Ansonia, a towering Beaux-Arts building on the Upper West Side. Schoener was a partner in his family's tobacco-wholesaling business, and like everyone else who befriended Leo, he was eager to buy shares in Bayano.

"He talked perpetually of the wonderful schemes he was interested in," Schoener recalled. "Finally I asked him if he wouldn't allow me to invest in them. He told me no stock was for sale." Leo also got to know Mary Schoener's sister, Millie, who was married to a professional golfer and lived in New Jersey. When Millie's husband died in a car crash in early 1923, leaving her to raise three young children alone, he sent her consoling letters and promised to find her a job in his planned New York office.

He was moving in other circles as well. Before the year was out, the former chauffeur for a wealthy Chicago family would tell of the many times he had driven Leo and female companions to train stations as they set off for getaways in New York; Yellowstone Park; Hot Springs, Arkansas; and other fashionable destinations. Leo had met his friend Anna Auerbach in Hot Springs in 1917, and it was easy to pass off a holiday at the resort town as a business trip to tour his nearby rice farms. Twice in the spring of 1923, the driver said, he saw off two couples—Leo and another man, escorting two women who were "the wives of wealthy husbands"—on trips out of town; the four returned, traveling separately, within a few days. No matter who accompanied him, the chauffeur said, Leo picked up the tab.

Isaac J. Wilbraham figured he was set for life. Eda Bergman, a widow, thought her nest egg was in good hands. Josephine Schroeder thought her boss was doing her a favor. And Alfred Lundborg? He had to buy his single $2,000 share by installments.

Wilbraham, a dining car steward on the Chicago, Burlington, and Quincy Railroad, was introduced to Leo in the summer of 1923 through his son, who was dating Leo's niece. He was among the privileged few invited to the Drake suite, where he handed over his life savings, $20,000, in exchange for shares in an Arkansas rice farm. Wilbraham never saw the stock—he naively accepted a receipt written on a scrap of paper—and quit his $143-a-month job within a few months to live off the profits he was certain were headed his way.

Bergman, who ran her late husband's store, invested $12,000

between 1919 and 1923. Leo allowed Schroeder, his secretary, to purchase two Bayano shares for $3,000—well below the inflated prices the
stock was fetching. "I thought he was just kind and generous to a girl
who had been conscientious in her work," she said later. Lundborg,
Leo's tailor, could scarcely believe his luck, either. "He was a very kind
man and one day asked me if I wanted to invest some money," he recalled. "I jumped at the chance."

For years, Leo had been selective about whose money he would
take. He preferred to deal with relatives and friends, or businessmen
and professionals who were already well off and had money to invest.
But by 1923 he was paying out so much money in sky-high dividends
that he could no longer afford to be choosy. A tailor's hard-earned
dollars and a dining car steward's life savings were too tempting to
pass up.

Then his reputation came under attack. He was hauled into court
by the relatives of the late Daniel Stern, a magazine publisher, and accused of abusing his position as trustee of the man's estate. The lawsuit
claimed Leo had induced Stern, who had died in 1920, to disinherit
his family and to direct that his $400,000 estate be used to build a
home for the elderly. The case went to trial in 1923, but a jury ruled
the will was valid. Within weeks of the verdict, the family leveled a
new allegation: about $90,000 in war bonds was missing from Stern's
estate.

Leo, who had sworn his investors to secrecy, faced another challenge. Word was getting around that he was building an oil company
and offering huge dividends. A fawning letter arrived one day from an
executive of a life insurance firm in Saint Louis, who had heard reports
"of the rosy outlook and assured big future of your Panama organization." Would Leo keep him in mind for an executive post?

People in the oil industry were catching on, too. Francis Loomis,
an official of Standard Oil of California, contacted Francis Matthews
in early June, to find out more about Bayano's operations and the
contract with Standard Oil of New York. How, Loomis wondered, was
the oil being shipped to market? What was the output of the wells?

If Matthews was troubled to discover that Bayano's operations were so little known within the oil industry, his mind was soon put to rest. Leo returned from New York a few weeks later with a supply contract; executives of Standard Oil of California might be in the dark, but Standard Oil of New York had agreed to buy Bayano's entire output for $1.37 a barrel. By August he was showing off a $300,000 check from Standard Oil—the initial payment, he said, under the supply contract.

Leo had bought himself more time.

"BY THE WAY, JUDGE, as I understand it, you have no means outside your $12,000 salary?" He was careful to frame his words as a question to remove a bit of their sting. "Why," he added, "you can't even keep a car on that." Not the kind of luxury cars Leo drove, anyway.

Harry Fisher was not sure where his host was going with this. They were enjoying an after-dinner smoke at the Koretz mansion on a May evening in 1923, and he did not know Leo well enough to feel comfortable discussing what he earned as a judge of the circuit court. Besides, he was supposed to be the one asking the questions. Fisher, a prominent figure in Chicago's Jewish community, was working on a charity drive, and Leo had agreed to contribute $15,000. The donation "was considered small for one of Koretz's supposed means," the judge recalled, "and I was delegated to ask him for more."

Fisher listened as Leo explained that he needed "somebody whose judgment he could absolutely rely upon to take an executive position with the Bayano company." A well-respected judge, perhaps. It was the beginning of a long, sometimes bizarre recruitment drive. Enticing someone of Fisher's stature and integrity into the Bayano fold promised to attract more investors; dropping the judge's name could be as good for business as waving around checks from prominent bankers and Standard Oil.

Leo invited the Fishers to dinner again in July. This time he was more specific. He wanted Fisher to resign from the bench to become the syndicate's in-house counsel. The salary was generous—$25,000 a

year, double his judge's salary. Fisher said he would need time to think
it over, and had one condition: he would have to inspect the Panama
facilities firsthand before he could agree to take the job.

"Of course," Leo replied, "we'll take a run down there together."

It was a tempting offer, and not only because the money was so
good. "I was more interested in the possibilities for the future," Fisher
recalled. At forty-one, he had been a judge since his election to Chicago's municipal court in 1912. He was in his third year on the more
prestigious circuit court, and a few months earlier an appeals court
had upheld the most important ruling of his career—his dismissal of
Mayor Thompson's libel suit against the *Daily Tribune*. Fisher was
being praised as a defender of "the fundamental right of the American citizen to cuss the government," and the lucrative post with the
Bayano Syndicate would allow him to leave the bench on a high note.

A round of negotiations followed. Leo offered a more generous
salary and stock options. Fisher insisted on the inspection trip. That
fall, Leo invited Fisher to join him in New York for a final meeting,
at his suite at the St. Regis. Leo reckoned he was now worth $100
million and said he wanted to give away a good chunk of his fortune.
Fisher's job, if he still wanted it, would be to oversee these philanthropic efforts. Leo also mentioned that he was on the hunt for wealthy
new investors and one prospect was Julius Rosenwald, president and
chairman of the Chicago-based mail-order giant Sears, Roebuck and
Company. Fisher got the impression that Leo was more interested in
one-upping Rosenwald than in helping others. Rosenwald's generosity
was legendary; a supporter of the University of Chicago and founder
of the city's Museum of Science and Industry, he donated millions of
dollars to fund Jewish war relief and to build schools for poor children
in the South. Leo vowed he would "make Julius Rosenwald look like
a piker when it came to philanthropies."

If Leo said he was worth $100 million—billionaire status today—
that was good enough for Fisher. His decision was made: as soon as he
saw Bayano's operations for himself, he would resign from the bench
and help Leo give away his money.

THE SYNDICATE'S RAPID TRANSFORMATION from timber exporter to petroleum producer had Leo talking bigger than ever. A new corporation would be formed on January 1, 1924, and Francis Matthews was preparing to leave his law firm to join Leo as a trustee of the renamed Bayano River Trust Company. Money was pouring in, investors were assured—$2.5 million in the month of October alone. There were plans to lease an entire floor of one of the new downtown skyscrapers—the thirty-story, gleaming-white Wrigley Building on Michigan Avenue was mentioned—for Bayano's headquarters. There would be a private office, its walls paneled in rich Panamanian hardwood, for the Oil King himself.

Leo recruited a team of executives to run it all, a small group of businessmen who would form the nucleus of the new, bigger Bayano Syndicate. "I want men of your conservative stamp and judgment," he told them. And he wanted them to travel to Panama, to "get on the ground to help in organizing this thing."

Perhaps Fisher's insistence on seeing Bayano's operations for himself had planted the idea in Leo's mind. The group—minus Fisher, for reasons that were never explained—would depart in late November to tour Bayano's impressive facilities. Leo handed them an additional assignment: they were to check out a million-acre tract bordering the syndicate's holdings to see if it was worth the two-dollar-an-acre asking price.

Why was Leo encouraging his new management team to travel to Panama? The moment the expedition arrived, everything he had said and done since he forged his first mortgage almost twenty years earlier would be exposed as a lie. It was as if he were pushing his scheme to the brink of disaster.

"I knew when they got there they would find nothing, no oil and no oil wells," he said later. Sometimes, though, it was difficult to separate the real world from the imaginary one he had been painstakingly creating for half his life—the world of rice and mahogany, of gushers and pipelines and tankers.

"It doesn't seem possible, but I came almost to believe in the proposition myself," he explained. "I talked Bayano, and planned Bayano, and dreamed Bayano, so that I actually believed the stuff. The idea grew and grew. Every day I spoke more of it until, finally, I was confident. It almost seemed that I had those thousands of acres and that oil down there in Panama."

Had the master swindler been seduced by his own con?

Not quite.

He scraped together about $50,000 to cover dividend payments due on December 1, but he was trapped in an endless cycle of hustling to find more investors and more money.

"I knew the bubble would burst," he confessed. "The losses had become so heavy that I saw there wasn't a chance for me ever to get straight again. I knew it was the end."

Leo was tired. He had turned forty-four that July, and lies and hustling were a young man's game. The stress and the fast living were taking a toll on his health. His doctor, Milton Mandel, had been treating him for diabetes since 1919. The prognosis for a man in his forties was grim; a study of diabetes deaths in New York City over a thirty-year period ending in the mid-1920s found that half of all victims were between the ages of forty-five and sixty-four. A team of Canadian researchers, led by Dr. Frederick Banting, had announced the discovery in 1922 of insulin to control the disease; until the drug was widely available, though, all Mandel could do was prescribe strict adherence to a low-carbohydrate diet, to ease the symptoms—fatigue, hunger, thirst, and frequent urination—and slow the progress of the disease.

Leo had spent most of his adult life exploiting the greed and dreams of others. He was fed up with the insatiable appetite for money he had inspired in so many people. "I was disgusted," he grumbled, unconsciously echoing Joseph Weil, the Yellow Kid, "with those seeming friends who wanted to get something for nothing."

He was running out of options. Sending his Bayano executives south on a wild-goose chase would get them out of town and buy him time to plan his next move.

LEO TOLD THE MAN at the counter he wanted to withdraw $3,500—every penny he had in his account. One of the bank's vice presidents soon got wind of the request. "Mr. Koretz," he sputtered, "we do not want to lose your patronage. If you are in need of money we shall be glad to advance you any amount you ask for." Leo declined the generous offer, pocketed his money, and left.

He had already asked the State Bank of Chicago to redeem almost $110,000 in Liberty Bonds and deposit the proceeds in his personal account. A brokerage account was closed as well, netting another $15,000. He sold off shares in a steel company for $17,000. The bank official so desperate to keep Leo's patronage was right: The Oil King was in need of cash. Lots of it.

Leo was withdrawing funds and cashing checks all over town. His secretary, Josephine Schroeder, reckoned the cash withdrawals in the weeks leading up to December 1923 totaled almost $300,000. Leo stuffed the money he was collecting into a briefcase and carried it back to the Drake. He asked the hotel staff to put it in their vault the first night. After that, to avoid suspicion, he took each day's haul to his suite and stashed it in a closet.

"I knew it was all over," he reflected later, "and I didn't have the courage to face the smash."

THE FLIGHT

SHE WAS AN attractive brunette—the kind of woman the newspaper guys liked to describe as "statuesque." Five foot four, mid twenties, George Hargrave noted as he sized her up, and elegantly dressed in a sealskin winter coat that opened to reveal a black, lace-trimmed crepe dress. A private detective like Hargrave made his living by noticing such things, and it didn't take Sherlock Holmes to figure out that this woman was rich as well as attractive. The "goodly retainer fee" she paid that day in late November and the fancy car waiting downstairs confirmed that. Hargrave was convinced she was using a fake name, but there was nothing mysterious about what she wanted done. It was the kind of assignment the Hargrave Detective Agency had taken on a thousand times.

"I want to know what women visit room 629 at the Drake," she said, "and what happens while they are there."

Hargrave posted men to keep an eye on the suite day and night. They were probably watching from the lobby or the hallway as Leo went inside to drop off some of the cash he was collecting from his bank accounts. The woman called every day for the next three days, and each time Hargrave provided the same progress report: "We told her that no women had gone into the place," he recalled, "only men."

"Men—I'm not interested in men," she snapped during one call. "It's the women I want to know about."

*A group of investors boarded a steamer for Panama in late November 1923,
eager to inspect the Bayano Syndicate's oil fields and timber holdings. Leo
"said we would be surprised," recalled Henry Klein, second from right.*

THE BAYANO SYNDICATE'S NEW executive team gathered
at the LaSalle Street Station. They would catch an overnight train to
New York and have a day in the city before catching the Grace Line
steamer *Santa Luisa* for Panama on November 29. The voyage would
take about a week and would be a respite from the freezing-point temperatures and overcast skies they were leaving behind.

Three of the six men waiting to board the train had resigned from
management posts at Wilson and Company, a meatpacking firm. Emil
Kitzinger had quit his $25,000-a-year job to become purchasing agent
for Bayano, at double the salary. Edwin Mayer, a twenty-five-year man
with Wilson and manager of its by-products plant before he left, held
$25,000 in Bayano stock and had been promised an executive post.
"I didn't know just what my official capacity was to be," he would
later admit. Wilson's former chief accountant, Milton Smith, had been
born, ironically, in Moravia, New York, boyhood home of one John D.

Rockefeller. Henry Klein was there, and even though he had spent almost his entire career in the liquor business, he had been tapped to be Bayano's head of engineering. Shandor Zinner, an accountant and until recently the secretary of the National Beverage Company, was Bayano's new sales manager. Rounding out the inspection team was a clerk, thirty-two-year-old Harry Boysen.

There was another man on the platform. Leo had come to see them off and handed each man a money clip crafted in gold. The company would cover all expenses, he reminded them, so be sure to "live like kings." He seemed glad they were finally going to see Bayano's oil fields. "He told us he wanted us to see things for ourselves, since we were to be the working organization of the corporation," Klein recalled. "He said we would be surprised."

Klein took Leo aside for a quick chat. They were working on a couple of deals unrelated to Bayano, and Klein handed over two checks. One was for $35,000—Klein's half of a $70,000 investment. He had signed the other check, but the amount was blank; he asked Leo to fill in the figure once he knew exactly how much money was needed.

AFTER BOARDING THE *Santa Luisa*, the Panama expedition received a cable from Leo.

BON VOYAGE, was all he wrote, signing off as THE BOSS.

The 4,900-ton ship, painted white for service in the tropics, cast off at ten o'clock in the morning under an overcast sky. The group set out, Edwin Mayer recalled, "fully confident that everything was as Koretz had represented it." Leo had furnished them with maps of the Bayano area "so skillfully drawn that there seemed to be no difficulty ahead in finding the district."

There was some oil play in Panama in the early 1920s, but the industry was a latecomer to the canal-induced gold rush. The republic appears to have granted its first oil concession in 1917, and by 1923 a handful of firms had exploration rights, including big names such as Gulf and Standard Oil of California. Some exploratory drilling was under way, but no one had found oil. Had Mayer or any other Bayano investor taken a few moments to thumb through the latest *Chicago Daily News Almanac and Year-Book,* they would have found a short entry for Panama. "The chief articles of export," it noted, "are bananas, rubber, coffee and pearls." No mention of oil. A little more digging would have turned up plenty of postcards that featured scenes on the Bayano River. There were photographs of big-game hunters posing on the riverbank with their trophies—giant alligators, their jaws propped open with sticks to show off rows of jagged teeth. One of the Bayano's chief exports, it seemed, was images of dead alligators. The syndicate's sprawling oil fields had escaped the notice of publishers of postcards and almanacs alike.

Before the ship cast off, Mayer huddled with his brother, who lived in New York, and worked out a coded signal. If the Panama oil fields were everything Leo said they were, Mayer would send back a one-word telegram: SHOOT. That was the cue for his brother to scrape together every penny he could and plow it into more stock.

BACK IN CHICAGO, Leo Kahnweiler, a diamond salesman, was pleased to see one of his best customers walk through the door on the first day of December, a Saturday. Leo had been buying jewelry from Lewy Brothers for years and could be counted on to spend thousands of dollars each time he visited. Kahnweiler invited him into a private room to inspect about a dozen bracelets arranged on a tray. Two caught Leo's eye. One sparkled with 218 diamonds set amid sapphire centers and crossbars. The price tag said $7,000. The other featured a one-carat emerald-cut diamond and twelve smaller hexagonal ones and sold for $7,500. Leo looked them over but could not make up his mind. Could he take home both, he asked, to see which one his wife liked best? Of course, said Kahnweiler. Another salesman, Louis Agatstein, slipped the bracelets into envelopes while Kahnweiler wrote up a slip to record the transaction. If Mae did not like either bracelet, he said before he left, "he would return both of them," Agatstein recalled; "it was entirely up to his wife."

Kahnweiler and Agatstein had no idea that Leo had been doing the rounds of jewelry stores in Chicago and New York, buying expensive pieces and taking home others on approval. Thanks in part to the accommodating folks at Lewy Brothers, he was amassing a small fortune in jewels.

EMIL KORETZ TURNED UP at his brother's suite at the Drake on Monday. Over dinner at a South Side hotel the previous evening, with most of the Koretz clan gathered around the table, Leo had made a surprising announcement: he had sold some of their stock at a good price. Emil, thin faced and nearly bald, had been instructed to drop by to pick up the proceeds. At the suite, Leo handed him a manila envelope.

"I have a little money here for you and the family," he said. "Here is $175,000. Count it."

Emil was speechless—"thunderstruck" was how he put it. "Just imagine how it feels to be handed $175,000 unexpectedly." He peered through his wire-rimmed glasses and counted out 172 $1,000 bills and six $500s. "I'd never seen so much money before." He was holding, in today's terms, more than $2 million.

A note written on the outside of the envelope explained how Leo wanted the cash to be distributed. Emil and their mother were each to have $50,000. The remainder was for Julius, Ferdinand, and Ludwig, who would get $25,000 each.

"He hoped we would approve of the deal," Emil recalled. Leo also told him that "if we wished the stock back he would be able to buy it for us at a profit later." At some point during the day, Leo arranged for similar cash payments to members of his wife's family. He summoned his brother-in-law Milton Simon, a business executive, and gave him $125,000. Mae's mother, Bertha, was to receive $50,000, and there was $25,000 each for three of Mae's sisters—Etta Speyer, Maude Klein, and Simon's wife, Aimee.

There was one more thing, Leo told Emil. None of the money should be deposited in a bank account. "Put it in a safety-deposit vault," he advised. "I'll tell you why later."

Leo sent Emil on his way and hailed a taxi outside the Drake. He was heading to New York, he said, on business. He carried a briefcase stuffed with the rest of the cash he had been collecting. The driver worked his way through Michigan Avenue traffic to the Majestic Building. Leo rummaged through his desk and destroyed as much evidence as he could—Bayano stock certificates and accounts, check stubs, letters, whatever he could find. He had already cleaned out his desk at the Drake.

Charles Cohn showed up at one point, almost out of breath; he had rushed over to make sure he caught Leo before he left. Cohn, already one of Bayano's major investors, wanted more shares. He handed over a check for $30,000.

SARAH MANDEL WAS AT home that Monday afternoon when the phone rang. An early Bayano investor along with her brother, Milton, Leo's doctor, she had quit her job as a teacher and was living off her Bayano profits. Leo was on the line. Meet me at the Majestic, he said, and come quickly. He was taking the 5:30 train to New York with Elias B. Woolf, a friend and Bayano investor. She arrived at ten minutes to five.

"I have just sold ten shares of my stock in the project to one of my associates," he said, handing her an envelope. "This is the dividend on it for you and your brother."

"Don't put it in a bank," he added, "put it in a safety deposit box."

She opened the envelope after he dashed off. Inside were twenty-five $1,000 bills.

NEXT, LEO GRABBED THE briefcase, a bit lighter but still crammed with $175,000 in $1,000, $500, and $100 notes. He was on his way out the door when Bertha and Pearl Mayer, Mae's mother and sister, showed up at his office. They wanted to show him photographs taken at the family's Thanksgiving dinner, but there was little time.

They tagged along as Leo and Woolf rushed to the LaSalle Street

Station, a half-dozen blocks away. It was getting dark and a light rain shimmered on the streets and sidewalks, the overture for a rainstorm moving in from the south. Pearl Mayer saw nothing strange in her brother-in-law's demeanor as he boarded the New York Central's Twentieth Century Limited, an express that would whisk him to New York in less than a day. "Leo bid us good-by," she said, "very affectionately and naturally."

MARCY AND MARY SCHOENER were delighted when Leo accepted their invitation to dine the next day at the Ansonia. After months of refusing to let the couple invest in Bayano, he had recently made an attractive offer. The Bayano Syndicate was opening a New York office, Leo said, and he wanted Schoener to be its general manager. The salary was $25,000—$10,000 more than Schoener earned at his father's tobacco-wholesaling firm—plus stock in the company. Schoener was elated; Bayano, he was convinced, "looked like a big thing." He handed in his resignation and was set to start running Bayano's local office in mid-December. He expected to sign a contract any day.

As they ate and talked, Mary thought Leo seemed "tired and discouraged." The couple knew he was a diabetic. "He was continually on a diet," Marcy recalled, "and had a fight for his life." When Marcy was called away to take a telephone call, Leo leaned over and confided to Mary that he had been to see a doctor.

"I have just six months to live."

She was too shocked to respond.

"I am going away," he added.

"Where?"

Leo wouldn't say. "No one will ever see me again."

"What are you going to do about my husband's position?" Mary asked. What about his contract with the Bayano Syndicate?

"He won't need me; he can sign up without me."

He had to rush off to a meeting, he said, to close a deal to buy a sugar refinery in Georgia. He jumped into a cab and disappeared.

JULIUS KORETZ WAS IN New York on business when Leo phoned his hotel on the following day, December 5. He was at the St. Regis, he said, with Woolf. Come over for the evening.

When he arrived, Leo suggested they see *Stepping Stones*, a musical-comedy version of "Little Red Riding Hood" that had opened on Broadway a few weeks earlier. Julius, relieved to find the rainy day had softened into a mild, foggy evening, made his way to the Globe Theater on West Forty-Sixth Street but returned with only two tickets. It was decided that Leo and Woolf would go and Julius would meet them later, back at the suite. After the show, the three men played cards until two in the morning. Pinochle was Leo's favorite game, and when he played with Mae, the usual stakes were five dollars a game. There was no trace of the downcast, six-months-to-live man who had dined with the Schoeners the previous day.

"Leo was happy and in high spirits," Julius recalled. "He wanted to sit up all night and play cards."

Julius, a man with a wide smile and a full head of hair that must have been the envy of his balding brothers, crashed at the suite for the night. Leo and Julius were close; there was barely two years between them, and they had shared a bedroom when they were boys.

"I want to tell you something, but keep it under your hat," Leo said before Julius left in the morning. "I sold one share of your Bayano oil stock for $25,000." It was an incredible return on a share with a face value of just $1,000. "Emil has the money," he continued. "When you get back you put that money in your safe deposit box until I tell you what to do with it."

Julius asked when Leo was heading home.

"I may leave for Boston tonight," he said, "and get to Chicago toward the last of the week." Julius offered to go with him to Boston.

"No," Leo said, "I've got a big deal on there and have to meet a lot of men." He promised to phone if he changed his mind and stayed in New York.

Julius went back to the St. Regis that evening. He had not heard from Leo, and he was surprised to learn he had checked out a few hours earlier, after a hotel clerk was kind enough to cash a check for several thousand dollars. He had told the hotel staff he was headed to Boston, and had last been seen slipping through one of the gazebo-shaped revolving doors that emptied onto East Fifty-Fifth Street.

MEANWHILE, AS *SANTA LUISA* neared the lush green Panamanian coast on December 5, Harry Boysen scribbled a brief progress report on a postcard. "We are in sight of land and will be in Colón before long," he advised his brother Louis, an official of Chicago's First Trust and Savings Bank. "Very successful trip so far."

The following morning, an American expert on tropical wood species boarded a boat in Panama City and struck out for the Bayano River. By a remarkable coincidence, Clayton Mell of Yale University was in Panama to survey the holdings of the Bayano River Lumber Company, the firm that had issued bonds in 1909, about the time Leo first envisioned his own timber empire. The company had done some cutting on its seventy-five-thousand-acre tract and had retained Mell to assess the feasibility of further logging or using the land for agriculture. He spent a week hiking the property, located about twelve miles upriver, and advised against further investment. The land was inaccessible by road and water, there was little good-quality timber left, labor was in short supply, and bananas or sugarcane could not be grown at a profit.

Mell filed a detailed report after his return to New York at the end of December. His conclusion was blunt: the information "promoters and would be experts" had disseminated about the region's agricultural potential and the "accessibility, vastness, richness, and wealth in fine and inexhaustible supply of timber" had been "greatly exaggerated," he wrote. It was as if he had read Leo's overblown, decade-old prospectus for the Bayano Syndicate. The hype, Mell added, "has already led to many investments and to the formation of innumerable enterprises among which the first one has yet to prove successful."

The Bayano executives reached Panama City at almost the same moment Mell was leaving the capital to begin his survey. Henry Klein and his group were about eighteen hours ahead of schedule, so no one was surprised when Mr. Espinosa or someone else connected with the syndicate was not at the dock to greet them. But as the hours passed, one of them admitted, "we began to worry a bit." Someone checked the phone directory. There were listings for Espinosa—the family, they discovered, was a wealthy and prominent one in Panama—but none for an A. Espinosa. Panama City was supposed to be the headquarters for the Bayano Syndicate, but they could find no trace of its offices. They went to the telegraph office and learned that the cable address Leo had given them for the Bayano Syndicate—"Koretz Panama"—did not exist.

"We were staggered . . . no one knew anything about a great Bayano syndicate," said Milton Smith, the accountant. "We inquired around, but no one had ever heard of Koretz or his oil company." They descended on the land registry office and combed through deeds but found no record of Leo's having bought or sold anything in Panama over the previous twenty years. The group gathered in Emil Kitzinger's room at the stately Tivoli Hotel, once the haunt of the higher-ups who built the canal, to discuss their next moves. "We began to suspect we had not inquired deeply enough," Mayer said.

They tracked down a Chicago man, C. L. Peck, the local representative of an American firm with a modest logging operation on the Bayano. They produced a map Leo had given them, showing the syndicate's properties and operations.

"The blueprint is a big fake," Peck exclaimed. "That land is ours." His company owned part of the syndicate's purported five million acres, and he assured them that other companies owned or controlled the rest. "Gentlemen," he announced, "I am of the opinion that you have been duped."

The group had come too far to take Peck's word for it. They hired a boat to take them to the Bayano River but abandoned the idea when port officials and other locals confirmed that Peck was right: they would find no oil fields. "Why," they were told, "that is where we go alligator hunting. There's nothing there but alligators and swamps—and plenty of each."

Urgent cables were sent to Chicago. The first was addressed to Leo: NO TRACE OF THE LAND OR THE COMPANY HERE.

Shandor Zinner directed the next message to Francis Matthews: CABLED LEO AT DRAKE HOTEL. CANNOT LOCATE PARTY OR PROPERTY HERE. NO ANSWER RECEIVED. WIRE ADVICE. There was no response.

The following day they tried again to reach Matthews: IS LEO AWAY? MADE INVESTIGATION AND PARTY AND COMPANY ARE NOT KNOWN HERE. Matthews was in New York, looking for Leo, as the messages piled up in Chicago. Harry Boysen finally got through to his brother Louis, the Chicago banker, with a terse summary of their findings: NO OIL, NO WELLS, NO PIPELINES, NO ORGANIZATION.

Louis Boysen finally tracked down Matthews in New York: NOTIFY KORETZ, he said, THAT THE PARTY HE HAD SENT TO LOOK OVER THE PROP-ERTY WAS RETURNING.

On December 10 the Bayano fact-finding team boarded SS *Santa Ana* for the return trip to New York. A last-minute decision was made to leave Harry Boysen behind to try to track down someone in the wealthy Espinosa clan, on the slim chance they had missed something. Henry Klein, Kitzinger, and the others passed the hat to cover Boysen's expenses, wished him well, and set off.

They knew what Boysen would find, though—another dead end. After five days of inquiries and poring over property records and phone books, "we were convinced there was nothing there and never had been," Klein acknowledged. The Bayano Syndicate, their investments, their new jobs as oil executives, their dreams of wealth—it was all a sham. The truth was perhaps most devastating for Klein, who had hundreds of thousands of dollars tied up in his good friend's investment schemes. He had been lied to. Used. They all had.

Klein remembered Leo's prediction that they would be surprised at what they found in Panama. They certainly were. Then he had a more sickening thought. What dollar figure did Leo write on that blank check?

LEO ASKED A LONG-DISTANCE operator to place two calls from New York to Chicago. One was to his wife. He said "nothing of importance," Mae recalled, other than mentioning he was making a side trip to Boston before heading home. The other call was to a Bayano investor, Sam Cohen. It was December 6, and he wondered whether Cohen had any news of the inspection group. Had they reached Panama City?

Yes, Cohen replied, they had.

Their early arrival seemed to catch Leo by surprise. He sounded "greatly upset," Cohen recalled, to learn they were on the ground in Panama.

14

THE SMASH

THE TWENTIETH CENTURY Limited hurtled westward at a mile a minute, charging into inky blackness. Fog and heavy drizzle clouded the locomotive's window and blinded the engineer, Charles Patterson, when he poked his head out to check the track ahead. A mile and a quarter outside Forsythe, New York, just shy of the Pennsylvania state line, a signal glowed red, warning Patterson to stop. A mile out, a second issued the same mute warning. Not far ahead, at the rear of a stopped passenger train, a brakeman's flare sent out a pinpoint of light.

Patterson hit the brakes; the locked wheels squealed. He hit the whistle; it let out a piercing shriek. To Robert Morton Lee, city editor of the *Chicago Daily Tribune* and a passenger on the train in Patterson's path, the oncoming locomotive emerged from the fog "like some horrifying monster of the fairy tales." It slammed into the rear observation car and "tore its way through wood and steel as if they had been paper and toothpicks." The car telescoped beneath the one ahead of it "with the swiftness of a rifle bullet," crushing nine sleeping compartments—all of them occupied—into a twisted mass. It lurched into the air and toppled onto its side. The next car was flipped from the tracks "as neatly as if a gigantic thumb and forefinger had plucked it out," Lee reported from the scene. Steel buckled with a throaty groan and windows exploded. Dazed passengers, half-dressed and badly banged up, stumbled into the fog. Porters struggled to pull the dead and injured from the wreckage.

The *Tribune*'s initial report pegged the death toll at fifteen, with eight more injured. Mae and the Koretz brothers began to worry. Leo should have been back from Boston via New York days ago. Had he been on the wrecked train? Emil feared the worst. "We thought he had been killed."

The Twentieth Century consisted of three separate trains, and the first two pulled into LaSalle Street Station by midday Sunday, after dropping off injured passengers at hospitals in Pennsylvania. The third section arrived five hours late with the bodies of the victims. "We met every section," Emil said, "thinking he might be on it."

The night before, as it turned out, a top executive of the Hearst newspaper chain had stood on the same platform, and he, too, had expected Leo to be on the ill-fated train. Victor Polachek, a former managing editor of the *Chicago Examiner*, held about $22,000 worth of Bayano stock and had been desperate to confront Leo. He had received a tip from federal agents that the scheme was about to collapse, and he hoped to get his money back before the swindle was exposed. Polachek had waited in vain and, to add professional insult to his financial injury, learned of the wreck when newsboys for the rival *Tribune* showed up, touting their scoop of every other paper in town.

When a list of victims was published on December 10, the death toll had been reduced to nine. More than twenty Chicagoans were injured, including Milton Cohn of the clothing firm Alfred Decker and Cohn, proud holder of $7,500 worth of Bayano stock. To the relief of Mae, Emil, Julius, and everyone else in the Koretz family, Leo's name was nowhere to be seen. Arrangements were made for a family member to view the victims' bodies, in case he had been misidentified. Still no Leo.

Where was he? Why did he not call?

Mae knew Leo often carried large sums of money. Had he been robbed? Was he just too busy with business to let her know where he was and when he would be home? She made frantic long-distance calls—eight of them—to New York. No luck. Julius and Milton Simon, the husband of Mae's sister Aimee, boarded a train for New York to see if they could track him down, thinking he must still be in that city. Aimee stayed with Mae in Evanston, offering what support she could. On December 11 a letter arrived for Milton Simon. It was from Leo. Inside were keys and a claim for baggage he had sent home from New York by train.

"Please go to the station and get the suit case," the letter said.

Aimee fetched the bag from Chicago's Union Station and took it to Mae's home. They opened it and found Leo's overcoat and a smaller case, which contained nine white envelopes. A jeweler's name was written on each one—Lewy Brothers and Tiffany and Company of Fifth Avenue, New York, were among those that stood out. The Lewy Brothers envelopes contained the diamond bracelets he had picked out for Mae. Another held a diamond ring worth $4,000; the various pieces in a third envelope were priced at $11,000. Each piece was accompanied by paperwork that confirmed the cache was worth about $75,000.

Leo knew his wife. Once she learned the truth, she would never keep his tainted money. The rest of his family and his in-laws had been reimbursed, and he hoped this would encourage them to help her. Selling the jewelry would provide something more for her and the children to live on.

Milton Mandel called on Mae that day. He had received an envelope from Leo, mailed in New York the previous day, with a letter inside addressed to Mentor. "If you think my son should have this letter," Leo had written in a covering note, "give it to him." Mandel thought Mae should decide.

"Dear son," she read:

This is probably the last communication you will have from me. I am a fugitive from justice, family and friends. I am a victim of idleness, selfishness and a desire for the acclaim of

friends. You have a wonderful mother and a fine sister. Be a
good boy, be straightforward and be honest. If you are ever
tempted, think of the fate that awaits me.
Your loving father.

The fortune in jewelry, the returned overcoat, the line about being
"a fugitive from justice"—it was all starting to make sense. Horrible,
unthinkable sense. Mae ripped the letter to shreds. She did not want
Mentor to see it, she told Mandel. It "might put bad thoughts into
her boy's head."

Events were moving fast. Harry Boysen's damning, eight-word
cable—NO OIL, NO WELLS, NO PIPELINES, NO ORGANIZATION—had reached
Chicago. Francis Matthews, back from New York, finally knew what
Henry Klein and the rest of the Bayano executive team had suspected
for days: Their good friend had absconded, taking their money with
him. Leo Koretz, the Oil King, was a fraud.

His siblings and in-laws finally understood why he had doled out
so much cash just before he left for New York. And now they knew
why he had urged them not to deposit their Bayano windfalls in a bank
account, where it could be found and seized.

Marie Koretz was sickened when she learned how her son had
made himself—and his family—rich. "I can't touch that money because it's stolen," she told Julius, who had just returned from his
search for Leo in New York. Julius, Emil, Ferdinand, and their wives
huddled to discuss what they should do with the $175,000 the family
had been given.

"We had a conference," Julius explained, "and we decided to give
the money back. We all felt the way mother did about it."

THAT AFTERNOON, WITH THE temperature well above freezing and the sky threatening rain, Matthews went to the office of the
Cook County state's attorney to file a formal complaint against his
friend and business partner. Robert Crowe could scarcely believe what
he was hearing. Panamanian oil fields, seven-figure buyout offers from

Standard Oil, 60 percent annual dividends—and all of it an elaborate hoax that had burned hundreds of investors. And the man behind the lies? That was the most incredible thing of all. He was a half-forgotten colleague from the state's attorney's early days in legal practice. Leo Koretz, the wisecracking clerk who had put himself through night school to earn a law degree, was a brazen swindler accused of stealing millions of dollars and skipping town.

Crowe assembled a team to search Leo's offices in the Majestic Building and personally led the raid. As he looked on, his assistant Stanley Klarkowski and three detectives rummaged through the books and files Leo had left behind. They found the little bottles labeled OIL that contained whiskey and the Bible that was really a cigarette holder. They found a travel guide to South America—a clue, perhaps, to Leo's whereabouts. They found a small safe, but it was empty. Law books, shipping registers, and magazines littered the floors. Ties and starched collars had been discarded in a corner, and the search also turned up a woman's slipper. When Crowe's team discovered the stash of booze, they called in Prohibition agents to seize hundreds of bottles of expensive wine and liquor. Letters, legal papers, and unpaid bills were gathered up. A truckload of documents was dispatched to the state's attorney's office for review.

As the raid was in progress, Mae and Aimee showed up with Leo's suitcase. They had contacted Matthews, and he had advised them to turn over the jewelry to the authorities. Klarkowski stopped his search long enough to examine each piece and to give each envelope an exhibit number. He arranged to have the jewelry secured in a safe-deposit box.

Then Klarkowski and two detectives headed to suite 629 at the Drake. There, they found more illegal liquor and more documents, including what appeared to be a list of investors, and the gold-framed sign on the wall, with its all-too-true slogan, YES, WE HAVE NO BAYANO TODAY. On Leo's desk was a book with the apt title, *Bunk*. They carted off three suitcases filled with records and receipts.

Crowe assembled a group of reporters and broke the news just in time to catch the late editions of the evening papers. "It looks like a serious case," he said. "Matthews charges that he lost $40,000 and that other friends of Koretz' were heavily hit." He would ask a grand jury for indictments on charges of grand larceny and operating a confidence game.

"There are a hundred other details," Crowe added. "It is impossible to enumerate them—almost impossible to imagine them."

Act 2

Cartoon published on the front page of the Chicago Daily News,
December 15, 1923.

THE SENSATION

The bold type at the top of page 1 screamed for Chicago's attention.

OIL SWINDLE NETS MILLIONS.

MILLION OIL BUBBLE BURSTS.

LAUNCH WORLD-WIDE HUNT FOR KORETZ, WHO SWINDLED CHICAGO BUSINESS MEN OUT OF MILLIONS.

Within hours of Crowe's announcement, the newspapers were dissecting the swindle and how it unraveled. "Koretz worked almost exactly opposite from the methods used by such con experts as 'Yellow Kid' Weil," the *Daily Tribune* explained. "He never solicited a sucker. He never urged one sucker to get another. He begged his prospective victims not to buy so much of his stock—but did it in such a way that they really were urged on. And once a sale was made the sucker was sworn to everlasting secrecy." A *Daily Journal* headline offered an eleven-word précis of Leo's methods: LAMBS SOUGHT OUT KORETZ AND BEGGED FOR A SHEARING; GOT IT.

Leo's photograph and description were plastered over the papers. So were photos of his abandoned wife and children and his mansion. The *Evening American* ran his mother's photo under the headline, DUPED BY SON. Crowe and his investigators paused as they rummaged through his office in the Majestic Building so that photographers could get their shots. Prohibition agents posed with the liquor cache.

The Bayano swindle was the big story in a town where every

The Chicago Daily Tribune*'s front-page coverage of the Bayano swindle
and Leo's disappearance, December 13, 1923.*

newspaper chased the big story. Chicagoans had their pick of six dailies. The largest, the *Tribune,* touted itself on its front page as the "World's Greatest Newspaper," and it *was* Chicago's greatest newspaper, in terms of circulation at least. In the early 1920s it was selling 500,000 copies on weekdays and more than 800,000 Sunday editions. The *Trib*'s only morning rival, William Randolph Hearst's *Herald and Examiner,* trailed by about 100,000 copies on both weekdays and Sundays but was keeping pace. The other papers—the *Daily News,* Hearst's *Evening American,* the *Daily Journal,* and the *Evening Post*—were vying for the attention of commuters heading home from work on trams and trains.

The *Tribune* was as powerful as it was immodest. It had campaigned to abolish slavery and had helped to put Lincoln in the White House. Its archrival, the *Daily News,* was one of the first papers in

America to target female readers and carried the most advertising of any of the six, making it immensely profitable. The *Journal*, the paper where a teenage Ben Hecht got his start, had been publishing since the 1840s. The veteran Chicago newsman John McPhaul remembered it as "wily, bold and imaginative in gathering and displaying the news." The *Post* billed itself as "the paper read by thinking people," but its shrinking circulation suggested that most thinking Chicagoans preferred to get their evening news from its competitors.

Hearst, the most powerful press mogul in America, had brought his brand of crime-and-scandal journalism to Chicago early in the century. While a Hearst paper should avoid "*coarseness* and *slang* and a *low tone*," he once instructed his editors, even the "most sensational news can be told if it is written properly." Professing the high road, he took the low one. His papers "'plugged' crime and scandal for circulation," observed W. A. Swanberg, Hearst's biographer. The *Evening American* proclaimed itself "A GOOD Newspaper . . . Clean and Wholesome" and "A Paper for the Family" above stories with lurid headlines such as KILLS MOTHER IN ROW OVER WIFE and HUNTS MATE WITH DEATH PISTOL. A photograph of a woman who was slugged by her husband and lost two teeth appeared with the caption, "Fist was her dentist." A Hearst newspaper, confessed Arthur Pegler, one of the chain's top Chicago journalists, was like "a screaming woman running down the street with her throat cut." Hearst could claim he was giving people what they wanted, and H. L. Mencken, the leading press critic of the day, was inclined to agree. Readers were only interested in "cheap, trashy and senseless stuff," he complained in 1924, "in bad English and with plenty of pictures."

Chicago's newsmen went to extraordinary lengths to scoop their rivals and score a "beat." With few of the ethical standards of today's journalists to rein them in, they thought nothing of breaking the law. Hecht's job title when he started at the *Journal* was "picture chaser," and his sole mission, he recalled, was "to unearth, snatch or wangle" photographs of people who had been murdered, committed suicide, or died in some other newsworthy fashion. He carried a pry bar, a file, and a pair of pliers in his pockets in case he needed to resort to burglary in his quest.

Legmen—frontline reporters who phoned in their findings to deskbound rewrite men, who then wrote and filed the finished story—impersonated police officers, coroners, gas-main inspectors, and other officials to pry information out of witnesses and gain access to crime scenes. They scooped up the letters and diaries of murder victims in search of anything incriminating or salacious. Police officers were bribed to look the other way or to tip off newsrooms before detectives carted off the goods as evidence. Some reporters—Hecht admitted he was one of them—resorted to making up names and quotes when sources could not be pressured or tricked into divulging information. Sob sisters—female reporters who could commiserate with widows, wronged wives, and spurned mistresses and loosen tongues in the process—were prized in Chicago newsrooms.

Hecht and a rival newspaperman, Charlie MacArthur, went on to cowrite a play based on their experiences as young reporters. When *The Front Page* was first staged in 1928, some critics dismissed the central characters—a loathsome band of unscrupulous, cynical, hard-drinking, poker-playing reporters—as too over-the-top to be real. Hecht and MacArthur, however, insisted they had toned down their portrayal of 1920s journalism, Chicago-style, for fear no one would believe the truth.

Leo, whether he liked it or not, had handed Chicago's journalists a story worthy of their talents for ferreting out the news.

FOUR OF THE KORETZ brothers—Emil, Julius, Ferdinand, and Ludwig—showed up at Robert Crowe's office on the morning of Friday, December 14. The family's lawyer, Leo Le Bosky, accompanied them, carrying a black briefcase. As detectives looked on, Le Bosky reached into the case and counted out $175,000, stacking the bills on Crowe's desk.

Newsmen were ushered in, and the brothers dutifully posed for photographs with Crowe's assistant Stanley Klarkowski. Emil did the talking, explaining the decision to hand over the money Leo had distributed before absconding, "so that the family would get nothing in excess of what any other creditor might get." Other relatives and friends who were reimbursed were expected to follow suit, and most did, bringing the amount recovered to more than $300,000. Crowe issued a statement praising Leo's relatives as "unusually honest." Chicago's press dropped its cynicism long enough to give credit where credit was due. The *Evening American* ran a photo lineup of eleven of Leo's siblings and in-laws—some gathered, no doubt, by intrepid picture chasers—below the headline KORETZ KIN WHO SCORNED TO TAKE "FAREWELL FORTUNE."

Emil had retired early from his property management firm, confident he could live off his Bayano dividends. "I thought I was rich," he told the reporters. "He took everything I had."

"Leo," he added, "is still our brother."

"You are not 'through with him'—disgusted, angry?" a newsman prodded.

Tears welled up in Emil's eyes. "No matter what has happened, and no matter what happens, we shall never forget that he tried to take care of us. . . . He has always been good to us. I assure you," he continued, "that none of us—no, not even his own wife—ever suspected his wealth was false."

The papers sought out other relatives. Julius's wife, Blanche, told one newsman that the Koretz brothers would be hard pressed to scrape together enough money to buy a postage stamp. "This—this isn't our shame," she said, sobbing as she spoke, "but our sorrow. We trusted Leo, we trusted him implicitly, for one doesn't—one doesn't suspect a brother. Every cent his brothers saved is gone with him. We are penniless." Adolph Koretz, eight years older than Leo and out $6,500, seemed to speak for the entire family when he told a reporter, "I was never so disappointed in my life."

The shock and scandal were almost too much for their seventy-six-year-old mother. It was widely reported that Marie was critically ill or near death. The family received another blow within days when a taxicab struck Ludwig as he crossed the street on his way home from a family gathering, no doubt convened to discuss the swindle. He escaped with a banged-up leg and bruises to his face and body.

Newsmen rehashed every detail of the sumptuous banquet Bayano's biggest shareholders had thrown in honor of their "Ponzi" at the Drake. "I cannot understand," Charles Cohn, one of the dinner's organizers, told the *Daily Tribune*, "how that man could have sat there and accepted the wholehearted hospitality of his lifelong friends and known all the time, as it would appear, that he was but a sham." Cohn lost big in the swindle—$55,000, including the $30,000 he handed over to boost his Bayano holdings the day Leo left Chicago. "That," Cohn said of the last-minute payment, "tells the story. . . . I had every confidence in the world."

Bayano investors were tracked down for comment. "It is amazing how he got by as long as he did," said a shaken Francis Matthews. "It was his personality, the confidence he inspired, which dispelled suspicion." Sidney Kahnweiler described Leo as "undoubtedly the cleverest Jeckyll-Hyde character ever uncovered." Clara Philipsborn suggested he "suffered from a sort of money mania." Another investor, who had retained Leo to draw up his will, managed to crack a joke despite his losses. "I am having the will changed today," he told the *Evening American*, "although I don't need a will so much anymore."

Some found it hard to accept the truth—that the kind, generous man they thought they knew was a liar and a thief. "It is like a nightmare," said John Irrmann, who had been friends with Leo for more than twenty-five years. "I can't understand it at all. In fact, I don't believe it yet." The president of Emanuel Congregation, Leo's synagogue, was also mystified. "It seems astounding," Samuel Weisberg said, "that a man of such charming personality as Leo Koretz should have done the things the newspapers say he did."

For a day or so, Harry Rosenhaupt of Spokane—a Washington state senator and Bayano investor and the husband of Mae's sister Estelle—clung to the possibility that Leo had been the victim of foul play or had succumbed to a mental disorder. "There are so many inexplicable circumstances in this case that I am not certain that I am going to lose any money at all." Judge Harry Fisher, who confirmed rumors of Leo's lucrative job offer, was prepared to give the benefit of the doubt. "I am still unable to decide whether the man was crooked or merely misled," he told the *Evening American*. Leo had not been to Panama in many years, he pointed out, and perhaps someone had played him as well.

Reporters surrounded the Evanston mansion, clamoring to interview Mae. A houseful of supportive relatives, friends, and neighbors kept them at bay. Mae sought refuge in a rocking chair in the butler's pantry. Beyond the kitchen's swinging door, wives chatted in one of the richly furnished rooms, husbands in another. Every few minutes, the phone in the kitchen rang.

"Everything is fine, just fine," Mae assured one caller who offered support, her voice breaking.

Nothing was fine. Her photo was in all the papers. The *Evening American* got its hands on a studio portrait—Mae, elegantly gowned, hair pulled back, a Mona Lisa smile on her lips—and ran it on the front page, under the headline WIFE SUFFERS, TOO. Other papers got plenty of mileage out of an old photo of her, beaming proudly as she clutched her children, taken when Mari, now ten, was a baby. LEFT DESTITUTE BY KORETZ was the *Herald and Examiner*'s caption.

The children were suffering, too. Mentor would have to quit school to find a job. Mari, too young to be told the truth, was upset that her father had not written to her. Someone offered to take the child to a vaudeville show, to get her out of the house, but one of the performers cracked a joke about Leo.

"Why," Mari asked, "are they talking about my daddy?"

Mae suffered a nervous breakdown, and there was a day when she was not up to seeing anyone, not even members of her family. A doctor was summoned to 2715 Sheridan Road. "She is a very sick woman," he told a reporter as he left, "but she is making a splendid battle."

When the fraud was exposed, Ben Hecht was publishing his own paper, the *Chicago Literary Times*, and he weighed in with a grandly titled piece, "An Investigation into the Inner Psychological Life of Leo Koretz, Swindler." Hecht considered Leo the "greatest rogue of modern times" and argued that, on some level, he had longed to be found out for all those years so that his victims and everyone else would appreciate his genius. An explanation for Leo's insatiable need for money, though, remained elusive. What had compelled him to steal from his family and friends, and even from his own mother? The *Evening Post* thought one possible explanation could be ruled out. "There was no other woman in his life, it is believed, nor was there any of the other reasons that ordinarily impel men to take money by hook or crook."

The *Evening Post* was about to discover that, like everyone else, it had misjudged Leo Koretz.

16

THE DOUBLE LIFE

ON THE OTHER side of town, south of the Loop, the staff and tenants of the Shirley Apartments on Drexel Boulevard were surprised to see the face of a man they knew well on the front pages. Funny thing was, the captions all said he was a missing lawyer who had bilked his friends in a massive con game.

"Koretz? Where do they get that name?" Charles Davidson, the janitor at the four-story apartment complex, wondered when he saw the photos. "Why, that's Al Bronson."

The Shirley's maid thought the same thing when she saw the photos. So did the woman who operated the switchboard. Someone tipped off the authorities, and Davidson was brought to the state's attorney's office in the middle of the night for questioning. Did he really know the man in the photos?

"Sure," he said, "that's Bronson."

Bronson had rented apartment number 200 for six years and had lived there with his wife, Alice Bronson, "a pretty brunette," until September 1923. The couple had been kind—Bronson tipped Davidson a dollar to fetch ice or milk—and he saw them arrive or leave by taxi two or three times a week. Bronson said he was a traveling salesman, which seemed to explain why he was often away from home. The couple also guarded their privacy, paying extra to install a private phone line instead of routing calls through the switchboard.

"I always thought it funny that they came only in the daytime, but that was none of my business," Davidson told a reporter after prosecutors took his statement. "It's strange," he added, "that a couple apparently as deeply in love with each other as these two should never stay at their home all night."

ANNA AUERBACH MET THE reporter for the Hearst papers at her home in the high-rise Webster Hotel, on the edge of Lincoln Park. Auerbach's husband of fifteen years, Salo, owned the seven-hundred-seat New Strand Theater, and selling dreams to moviegoers paid the rent on their sumptuous suite. There was money left over to invest, and that's why the newspaper had sent someone to wrangle an interview. The Auerbachs were Bayano stockholders and close friends of the missing swindler.

Yes, Anna Auerbach confirmed, the couple held $35,000 in shares. And of course, the news that Leo had swindled them and so many others was "a tremendous shock."

Auerbach was a "strikingly beautiful" brunette, tall and "vivacious and charming in her manners"—details the reporter carefully recorded as they spoke.

And yes, she continued, he was "a genius with the ladies." She spoke of how kind and thoughtful he was, how he pampered the wives of his business associates—taking them to lunch and buying them jewelry as birthday gifts. She suspected there was a "woman in the case."

"I know he would never become a fugitive, especially with half a million dollars maybe, without taking along somebody, some woman of whom he was fond."

The reporter took it all down and filed the story in time for the first run of the *Evening American*. It ran under the headline KORETZ LIKED THE LADIES, BUT LIKED 'EM SAFELY MARRIED.

Fake oil fields and timber holdings, bewildered investors, millions of missing dollars, an honest family spurning its ill-gotten gains—all took a backseat to the racier story behind the collapse of the Bayano swindle. Something stronger than greed had driven Leo to steal from his family and friends. "He was a Don Juan," declared assistant state's attorney Klarkowski, "as well as a Wallingford."

Detectives on Leo's trail and reporters pounding the pavement for beats had a new focus: find the woman. Breathless exposés of the swindler's double life soon filled the newspapers. Chicago editors, John McPhaul observed, subscribed to a time-honored axiom of journalism: "You can do well with a good crime story, but you can do better if you garnish it with sex."

George Hargrave told the police about the beautiful brunette who had hired his detective agency to find out if women visited Leo at the Drake. If one mistress had been trying to find out if she had rivals, just how many women were there in his life? Hargrave revealed an important clue to the woman's identity; he had traced the license plate of the car she had used to visit his office. The car was registered to Sylvia Schwartz, the young wife of Joseph Schwartz, a partner in a wholesale woolens business. The couple lived in the Webster Hotel, and Sylvia Schwartz's best friend was her neighbor Anna Auerbach.

Klarkowski issued subpoenas for both women to appear before a grand jury to reveal what they knew about Leo's private life and where he had fled.

Charles Davidson, the janitor at the Shirley Apartments, was shown another photograph, of a woman bundled in a sealskin coat. Was this Alice Bronson? Davidson said he could not be sure. "I never saw her," he pointed out, "except in a house dress."

Detectives took the photo to the maid and some of the Shirley's tenants. They were convinced it was Alice Bronson. Klarkowski was coy when reporters asked him to name the woman in the photo, but he left no doubt who she was.

"She lives in a fashionable north side hotel and her husband is a well-known and wealthy business man," he said, adding, "I don't want to cast odium on a woman . . . if she will tell the whole truth, her name still may be kept secret. But if she tries to hedge—well, we are trying to run down a man who swindled those closest to him, and none can stand in the way of justice."

The newspapers, handed a juicy new angle on the story, ran with it. BARE KORETZ'S DOUBLE LIFE, shouted a thick headline atop the front page of the *Chicago Daily Tribune*.

Al Bronson, readers learned, had done double duty—as a member of the phantom Bayano Syndicate and as a cover for Leo's philandering. Newsmen christened the apartment at the Shirley a love nest. The *Daily News* huffed with moral indignation: "Here . . . he passed his afternoons while his wife, in the luxurious home at 2715 Sheridan road, Evanston, was superintending the preparation of dinner against his return from 'business.'"

Klarkowski may have been reluctant to "cast odium" on the woman suspected of sharing the love nest; the newspapers were not.

Anna Auerbach, they speculated or outright reported, was Alice Bronson and the woman who had hired detectives to spy on Leo. Her name leaped out from bold headlines; she flashed a broad smile in a photo the papers ran alongside the latest news about Leo's disappearance and double life.

She hired a lawyer, who denied the allegations and said his client was too distraught to talk to anyone, even to the detectives camped in the hallway outside her suite, waiting to serve the grand jury subpoena. "She was not the woman of the Shirley apartments, not the woman who employed the Hargrave Secret Service agency to watch Koretz's suite in the Drake hotel," her lawyer insisted. "Implications that she was have caused her to become ill."

No one believed him.

Auerbach was hysterical. The policemen cooling their heels at the door heard her cry out: "I wasn't the only woman in Leo's life. Why do they pick on me?"

Hours later, when the detectives were allowed in to serve the summons, Salo Auerbach ran interference with the reporters who accompanied them. "I have absolute faith in my wife. I trust her and nothing can separate us," he said. "She had nothing but business relations with him."

No one believed him, either.

*Anna Auerbach, the wife of a theater owner, was identified
in the press as the woman who shared Leo's "love nest" on
Chicago's South Side. "I wasn't the only woman in Leo's life,"
she complained. "Why do they pick on me?"*

A HANDWRITTEN LETTER FOUND in Leo's Majestic Building offices offered fresh insights into his double life. It had been torn to bits, but a reporter for the *Daily News* scooped up the fragments and pieced them together. It was from a woman named Fraser and referred to another woman, "Alt," who was "heart-broken" by his disappearance. Fraser begged him to get in touch with them. "I would willingly come to Chicago if you want me to," she wrote. "I care a whole lot: you are the only friend I had. Please don't let anything come between us." There was a postscript in different handwriting, apparently from Fraser's friend Alt. "Please answer at once; I am so anxious."

The letter had been mailed on December 8—five days after Leo took the train from Chicago to New York—from Absecon, New Jersey. The *Daily News* imagined him meeting and charming the women as he strolled on the boardwalk in nearby Atlantic City during one of his trips to New York. "And now one woman writes for the other's broken heart," it noted, "while the second is too crushed to add more than a brief postscript." The paper published a photograph of the reconstructed letter under the headline TORN LETTER CLEW TO "OTHER" KORETZ LOVES.

Reporters soon tracked down both women. Fraser was Millie Fraser, the recent widow Leo had befriended and Mary Schoener's sister. A "motherly" and "not unattractive little woman," in the estimation of the Hearst reporter who turned up at her door, she insisted Leo had been a big brother to her, nothing more. She produced a letter he had written after her husband's death, offering her a job at the Bayano Syndicate's soon-to-be-opened New York office. She had begged Leo to invest $10,000 from her husband's life insurance settlement, but he had refused to take her money. "I shudder now to think what I might have done," she told another newsman. "I was so sure of his honesty."

The heartbroken "Alt" was Mary Schoener, one of the last people to see Leo in New York before he disappeared. At Robert Crowe's request, district attorneys in New York questioned her. Leo's startling announcement that he was ill with diabetes and had only months to live, Schoener claimed, had been the reason for her hysterics when he went missing. As far as she knew, he was not "mixed up" with any women in New York.

Back in Chicago, Klarkowski was confident Sylvia Schwartz could sort out what he termed "Koretz' complicated affairs with women." He became more confident after police tracked down Schwartz's former chauffeur, who described Leo's getaways to Hot Springs and other resorts, accompanied by other men's wives. "I drove a great part of the time for Mr. Koretz," he said, a job that included fetching women at Leo's request and delivering them to hotels and restaurants. Klarkowski was pleased to share these revelations with the press, as well as his suspicion that the frequent visits to New York on business or to Arkansas to inspect his rice lands were a cover for his affairs. Leo, he suggested, had maintained a series of "love nests" like the one at the Shirley Apartments—"a string of apartments and hotel suites from the Atlantic to the Pacific for the benefit of his many women friends."

"For four days we have followed the old French axiom of 'find the woman,'" Klarkowski added. "Now we have found not only a woman but perhaps half a dozen women."

Reporters jumped on the bandwagon with speculation of their own. The *Daily Tribune* concluded that much of the money Leo had swindled over the years had been frittered away on "the ancient triumvirate of wine, women and song." The "real cause of the swindler's flight," the paper concluded, was not the collapse of the Bayano bubble—it was "too many women." A story accusing him of kissing a woman named Eve "several times against her will" and making "improper advances" hit the front page of the *Daily Journal*. Hearst's *Herald and Examiner* and *Evening American* came up with a more intriguing explanation for what had happened to the money sunk into Bayano. A front-page story in both papers said police were looking into a tip that Leo had paid as much as a million dollars to blackmailers to conceal his love affairs.

Then Auerbach and Schwartz disappeared. They slipped out of the Webster Hotel late at night and were whisked away in Schwartz's Pierce-Arrow. Auerbach had suffered a nervous breakdown, Klarkowski was told, and had taken refuge in a sanatorium to avoid appearing before the grand jury.

"I want action," bellowed his boss, Robert Crowe. "Regardless of who it hits, get to the bottom of this."

Crowe put his best prosecutor on the case. John Sbarbaro, just thirty-three but touted as the ace of the state's attorney's staff, would work with Klarkowski to get the investigation back on track. Sbarbaro had joined Crowe's office in 1921, fresh out of law school, bringing with him a sly smile and loads of confidence. He may have known Leo—they were both members of the Illinois Athletic Club. Sbarbaro's first act was to secure a warrant for Auerbach's arrest on a charge of contempt of court. Chicago police searched her home at the Webster. Patrolmen who assembled for roll call at stations across the city were issued a copy of her photograph.

At ten o'clock that night, after reporters working the crime beat had gone home for the day or retired to a speakeasy, Auerbach and her lawyer turned up at the office of the state's attorney. She was questioned for three hours but could no longer offer the insights she had shared in her press interviews. "My only acquaintance with him was at functions which both my husband and I attended," she insisted. "I don't know where he is. I haven't heard from him since he disappeared."

Auerbach was free to go. She gave a brief, final interview to the ever receptive *Evening American.* "I knew and know nothing of any of Mr. Koretz' personal affairs," she said. "What's the good now in raking up all this personal stuff about him? It only breaks up families."

"We have no desire to subject this woman to humiliation," Sbarbaro told the press. "If she wishes to deny that she was the woman of the love nest she may do so. We are interested only in finding Koretz."

After days of chasing down witnesses who could link Leo and Auerbach to the Bronson apartment, Sbarbaro signaled a new approach. The investigation into the swindler's dalliances with women had produced lurid headlines and racy newspaper copy, but not a single clue to his whereabouts. Anna Auerbach, Millie Fraser, Mary Schoener—all were in the dark. Sylvia Schwartz was never questioned, but there was nothing to suggest she knew where he was, either. Klarkowski's "find the woman" strategy had failed. The *Evening Post* pointed out to the "thinking people" it courted as readers that the investigation had "concerned itself as much with inquiring about love nests" as with finding the fugitive swindler and his loot.

The office of the state's attorney switched into damage-control mode. Crowe issued a public apology to one of the women caught in Leo's web of lies. "We find that a grave injustice has been done Mrs. Schwartz," he announced. She had been an acquaintance of Leo's, nothing more. "She is absolutely innocent, I am convinced." There was no mention of Anna Auerbach and no apology for the relentless, humiliating effort to question her. If Leo had maintained a string of "love nests" across the country, nothing more was said about them. "The object of this investigation," Crowe reminded reporters—and, perhaps, his staff and himself—"is to turn up Leo Koretz."

*Mae Koretz, "dressed as a widow," waiting to testify
at the hearing into her husband's bankruptcy.*

THE VICTIMS

PHOTOGRAPHERS FOUND HER slumped on a wooden chair in the hallway, her arms limply folded as she stared blankly at the floor. A sitting duck. Mae made no attempt to hide her face or her sadness as shutters clicked and flash powder popped from all sides.

The newspapers were overflowing with allegations of her husband's infidelities, the South Side "love nest," the resort weekends with other men's wives. What was left to hide? Her husband of seventeen years, the father of her two children, the man she had trusted completely—lies, all lies. Leo's personal life had been as phony as his Bayano oil fields. His affairs and the parade of lurid, humiliating stories in the press left Mae numb. Discovering that her husband had orchestrated one of the biggest stock swindles in history had been devastating; this was worse.

She said nothing to the clutch of newsmen waiting to hear her testify at Leo's bankruptcy hearing. Her brother-in-law Leon Klein took a couple of the reporters aside. "Yes, it was a terrible surprise to Mrs. Koretz to find her husband had been going with other women," he told them. Even as the news was breaking in the papers, "she couldn't believe a word of it." "Now she knows the truth," he said, "and you can see how it has affected her."

She wore black from head to toe—"dressed as a widow," as one bystander put it. Her black, feather-trimmed felt hat was clamped on so tightly it almost touched the wire rims of her glasses. Bundled in a bulky, full-length winter coat even though it was warm outside for Chicago in mid-December, she looked like a helmeted soldier peering out at the enemy from a bunker.

Creditors—most of them Bayano investors—had petitioned Leo into bankruptcy. Mae was the first witness at a hearing convened to identify assets he had left behind. The referee assigned to the case, Harry Parkin, was a former US district attorney who, by coincidence, had once prosecuted Rockefeller's Standard Oil for violating antitrust laws. The Chicago Title and Trust Company, the receiver, hired the lawyer Maurice Berkson—Leo's childhood friend and one of the few people who had suspected his wealth was too good to be true—to spearhead the inquiry.

Her voice barely audible at times, Mae repeated what she had told a police sergeant who had visited her home a few days earlier: She had not spoken to her husband since December 6, when he phoned from New York and claimed to be headed to Boston. She could shed little light on the Bayano Syndicate or the Arkansas landholdings. She remembered the name Gustav Fischer, but she was not sure "whether he is real or just a figment of the imagination." Leo had given her six shares in Bayano in September, she acknowledged, which had earned her $550 a month until the swindle collapsed.

Mae was asked to account for every stick of furniture in her home, every gift he had given her, the $1,000 she had recently withdrawn from their joint account to cover household bills. She was asked about the assets she had already turned over to the receiver, including the two Rolls-Royce limousines. Her voice broke as she described handing over an emerald ring and diamond-studded hairpins—recent gifts from Leo. "I didn't think I had a right to them," she said. She had dismissed her maid, her cook, and Mari's governess and planned to move in the New Year, when the next rent payment on the Sheridan Road house came due. She had asked the superintendent of schools to renew her teaching certificate, so she could go to work as soon as possible.

Her ordeal lasted most of the day. When she was finally free to go, she paused for a brief word with Berkson. "My one regret," she told him, "is that I didn't save up money during the days when I was the wife of a wealthy man, so that I could help pay back some of these debts."

THE CUSTOMER WAS BEING picky. She wanted the perfect Christmas gift for her husband. "Yes madam," Mentor Koretz said as he produced another pile of shirts, "perhaps you would like this pattern better."

The day his mother's shattered world was dissected at the bankruptcy hearing was the sixteen-year-old's first as a clerk at the Rosenberg's department store in Evanston. Mentor withdrew from Lake Forest Academy within days of his father's disappearance. Mae could not afford his private school tuition, and the family needed his wages—eighteen dollars a week—to weather the tough times ahead.

A reporter watched him work. Mentor was tall with light brown hair and, *Evening American* readers would be told later in the day, had inherited "his father's engaging personality and winning smile." His light brown suit, camel's hair vest, and dark brown tie suggested he had Leo's eye for clothes as well. The reporter asked for a comment.

"Thumbs down on all interviews," he said, flashing one of those winning smiles. "Mother, you know." He turned his attention to another customer, a woman in search of the perfect necktie. "This," Mentor said, wrapping one around his fingers to display it, "is just the thing for a gentleman of refinement."

WHEN HENRY KLEIN AND the other would-be Bayano executives landed in Brooklyn in mid-December, the veteran reporter Sherman Duffy of the *Evening American* was among the reporters there to meet them. Edwin Mayer acted as spokesman. "We had heard about oil lands. We had heard about banks. We had heard about all sorts of valuable holdings Koretz controlled along the Bayano River," he said. "All that we found in Panama was the river, and Koretz had no claim on that."

Then Klein stepped up to the plate. "We talked to everybody and investigated every angle," he told Duffy. "It is a gigantic hoax. That is all. There isn't any oil, any land, anything. They don't even know anything about Koretz." The Panama excursion, they were convinced, had been a ploy to get them out of the way while Leo planned his escape.

There was one subject no one was eager to discuss: how much money they had invested. Klein would not confirm a rumor that he had given Leo a blank check, but the nudges and smiles his companions exchanged when they overheard the question convinced Duffy the story was true. "I don't want to talk about it," was all Klein would say. "A man that has been kicked doesn't like to talk about his injuries."

The inspection team became objects of derision. Duffy's report focused on how men convinced they had snagged "big paying jobs" had been forced "to hustle among their friends" for train fare back to Chicago. KORETZ DUPES FOUND A RIVER blared a headline in the *Herald and Examiner.* ARGONAUTS OF OIL RETURN, mocked another in the *Daily News,* BUT WITHOUT GOLDEN FLEECE.

By the time four of the five reached Chicago the following day, they were in no mood to take a further drubbing in the papers. Cameras snapped and questions flew as the men turned their backs to collect their baggage and greet their wives. "Haven't you fellows had enough?" Klein pleaded. "What more is there to say?"

"I have a lot of good pictures in my sachel," Emil Kitzinger joked to the photographers. "There are some excellent views of alligator swamps." Shandor Zinner, too, tried to lighten the mood. "Our offices are under our hats at present," he quipped. They were summoned to the state's attorney's office, where Sbarbaro said he needed statements from them to confirm "that Koretz' promotion was a fraud in its entirety."

Everyone who had sunk money into Bayano—not just the Panama adventurers—was ridiculed for their blind faith in Leo. Francis Matthews bore the brunt of the criticism. "You'd think that legal experience at least would have suggested investigation of a project which nicked him to the tune of $40,000," scoffed the Hearst columnist Herbert

Kaufman. Even Henry Platt, a member of Matthews's law firm, did him no favors. It was "incredible," Platt told reporters, that Leo had not been discovered sooner. "Just one small conversation by one of the victims with one real oil man," he said, "would have turned the trick—for any real oil man would have recognized the story as a myth."

Cartoonists were unforgiving. The *Daily News* splashed a front-page depiction of Chicago's skyline dotted with oil derricks and a stream of "Easy Money" flowing from a well labeled "Get-Rich-Quick Oil Co." A dapper-dressed man exclaimed "Another Gusher!" as he collected the money in a sack. The cartoon was captioned, "One of the richest oil fields of them all." The *Evening American* published a comic strip under the headline, "BUBBLE, BUBBLE, TOIL AND TROUBLE"—WHEN THE BUBBLE BURSTS. One panel depicted a flute-playing Leo as the Pied Piper leading a parade of eager followers. Even the highbrow *Evening Post* found it hard to resist having a laugh at the expense of the Bayano victims. Leo, it said, was the city's "leading financial laxative . . . he works while you sleep."

Laughter often erupted at Harry Parkin's bankruptcy hearing as witnesses struggled to explain why they had been so foolish. Lawyers and reporters shook their heads in disbelief as Samuel Richman explained that he never sought proof that the syndicate existed. "I did not think it strange that there was no big business organization here, because I thought the books of account were in Panama," he insisted. They were incredulous when Henry Klein described handing over the blank check; Leo, it turned out, had cashed it for $36,500.

Klein, desperate to downplay his losses, declared that he had never put a cent into Bayano—the bubble had burst before he had the chance. "I loaned a little money to Koretz," he testified.

"How much?" a lawyer asked.

"Well . . . in the neighborhood of $200,000." What Klein considered a little money would be more than $2.5 million today.

But the tone of the bankruptcy hearing often turned ugly as lawyers for the receiver, Chicago Title and Trust, searched for cash, jewels, furniture, and automobiles—anything of value—that would narrow the wide gap between Leo's assets and his massive liabilities. His relatives had been lionized in the press for returning their last-minute refunds, but it was soon discovered that some recipients felt entitled to keep their payments. Mae's sister Etta Speyer and their seventy-two-year-old mother, Bertha Mayer, refused to turn over the $75,000 he had left to them. They hired a lawyer to press their case.

"We will never give up the money until a court order demands it," Speyer told a Hearst reporter who showed up at her Hyde Park apartment. Her father and husband had died a dozen years earlier, Speyer explained, and Leo had handled the estates. "It was every cent we had in the world." The $75,000, she said, pausing to wipe away a tear, was money Leo owed to them. "These are the moneys mother and I have been living on."

The receiver and state's attorney disagreed. Chicago Title and Trust took legal action to recover the money; Crowe threatened to have Speyer and her mother—and anyone else who refused to return money received from Leo—indicted on charges of receiving stolen property. Despite the threats, other relatives were having second thoughts. The cash doled out before he disappeared, it could be argued, was a refund of their Bayano investments. Emil Koretz told the bankruptcy hearing his family had relinquished its $175,000 refund under pressure from the state's attorney. Leo's brother-in-law Leon Klein joined the refrain, telling Parkin he had felt "intimidated" into turning over his $25,000 share to Crowe.

Chicago Title and Trust demanded a grand jury investigation to determine if the Koretz and Mayer families were hiding additional refunds. A report in the *Evening American* suggesting relatives and friends had been refunded as much as $800,000—more than double the amount reported to the state's attorney—added to the suspicion. Crowe refused to intervene, announcing that Bertha Mayer and Etta Speyer would not be prosecuted for receiving stolen property. There was "nothing criminal" in their refusal to hand over their $75,000, he said, and whether they were entitled to keep it was a matter for the civil courts.

Even Mae became a target. Samuel Cohen, Leo's former lawyer, dragged her back into the headlines when he speculated that Mae had been left with more than a cache of expensive jewelry. "Knowing Leo Koretz as I did, I cannot doubt that Mrs. Koretz was provided for," he told Parkin. "It would be unlike him to go away without doing so." Mae, it appeared, might not be destitute after all. Attitudes hardened. Her cooperation with the receiver and her prompt return of the jewelry were forgotten. Parkin mused about recalling her to the witness stand for further questioning. A judge later rejected Mae's bid to recover one of the Rolls-Royces—the touring car that had been a gift from her husband—and artwork seized from her home. Both limousines were sold and fetched a total of $11,500 for creditors.

ESTIMATES OF HOW MUCH money had been stolen ballooned as quickly as the output of Bayano's make-believe oil fields. When the news broke in mid-December, the figure was pegged at between $3 million and $5 million. Within a day it was revised to $7 million, and on December 16 the lawyer for the receiver, Maurice Berkson, told the *Daily Tribune* that losses could reach $10 million. The following day the state's attorney's office, in a telegram asking New York prosecutors for assistance, revealed an official estimate of up to $20 million. The telegram, leaked to reporters, alleged that Leo had pocketed up to $10 million in Chicago and a similar amount from investors in New York and Denver and on the Pacific coast. In the weeks that followed, many press reports cited the $10 million figure, as either the total amount stolen or the losses of Chicago investors alone.

How much of this money was left after almost two decades of bogus dividends and Leo's free-spending ways was another question. Even after doling out some $400,000 to his relatives and a few close friends, Leo was believed to have fled with a substantial sum. Sam Cohen was convinced his good friend had made off with at least $1 million; an arrest bulletin issued by police shortly before Christmas put the figure at $2 million.

The press did its best to embarrass as many victims as possible, publishing the names and addresses of almost one hundred suspected investors within hours of their discovery on a typewritten list in Leo's offices. Rumors swirled that many more investors had been stung, but there was little incentive for victims to admit their folly. Filing a bankruptcy claim seemed futile, given the meager assets left behind. Many victims "swallowed their losses and said nothing," the *New York Times* reported, preferring the loss of money to the loss of their business and professional reputations.

After a week of interviewing victims and reviewing documents seized from Leo's offices, John Sbarbaro acknowledged the true scale of the fraud might never be known. Investigators could not find a complete record of the people who had invested in the complex Bayano, Arkansas, and fake-mortgage scams—a "sucker list," the press called it. The black books Leo used to record transactions were missing, and if a master list of investors existed, it had been carried off or destroyed. Crowe's prosecution team suspected one of the two hundred or so keys found among Leo's effects might unlock a safe-deposit box containing more records, but it was impossible to match every key to a lock.

"You can name your own figure," Sbarbaro told the *Daily Tribune*. "Personally, I think $15,000,000 would be very conservative. It may run double that." Sbarbaro had access to every piece of evidence the state's attorney's office had been able to find; if his worst-case scenario was on the mark, the swindle had netted as much as $400 million in today's dollars.

There were tantalizing clues to the identities of victims who preferred to remain in the shadows. Marcy Schoener, Leo's New York friend, told of a businessman in that city who sank $260,000 into Bayano stock but would not come forward, fearing the revelation would "ruin" him. LaSalle Street—Chicago's version of Wall Street—was "in an uproar," the *Evening American* claimed, as the fallout from the Bayano scam "hit right and left at bankers, insurance brokers, financiers, stock operators, commercial magnates and corporation officials." There was a rumor, one Leo would later deny, that the prominent

Jewish banker Oscar G. Foreman, chairman of two Loop banks, was among the victims. The state's attorney's office interviewed one bank president who lost $100,000 in the scam but refused to prosecute. The bank's directors would oust him if they found out, he said, even though the president suspected a couple of the directors had been burned as well. The president of another unidentified Chicago bank told the *Evening American* he had lost $75,000, but he insisted it was a personal loss that would not affect his bank.

Judge Harry Fisher's revelation that Leo had named Julius Rosenwald as a prospective partner in Bayano fueled suspicions that the high-profile head of Sears, Roebuck was among those nursing their financial wounds in silence. Decades later, Ben Hecht claimed in his autobiography that Arthur Brisbane, a confidant of William Randolph Hearst and a marquee columnist for the Hearst papers, had been among the "heaviest investors" in Bayano. Brisbane, whose *Today* column on politics and current events ran on the front page of the *Herald and Examiner*, was a millionaire who hobnobbed with the likes of Henry Ford and speculated in real estate. If the Hearst executive Victor Polachek could fall prey to Leo's charms, Brisbane may have as well.

Only Leo Koretz knew how many people he had swindled. And he was nowhere to be found.

The US Post Office advertised a $10,000 reward for Leo's "apprehension and return" to Chicago to face charges of using the mail to defraud.

THE MANHUNT

WHEN A PLANE landed unexpectedly at Key West in mid-December, a deputy US marshal named Lopez confronted two men onboard. One claimed to be a US senator from Pennsylvania; what he was, Lopez discovered, was drunk and in a hurry to get out of the country. Convinced the intoxicated man was Leo Koretz, Lopez wired the authorities in Chicago seeking the go-ahead to make an arrest. By the time a response reached Florida the following morning, asking that both men be detained, they were on their way to Cuba. Days later, Lopez was shown Leo's photograph and swore it was the drunken man. Had Chicago officials not dragged their heels, he complained, "these birds would now be where they belong."

It was one of many possible sightings as investigators mounted an international search for Chicago's fugitive swindler. Airfields in Chicago and Detroit were notified. Leo's description was broadcast on radio stations across North America and as far afield as Europe. Liners and steamships that had recently sailed from New York were hailed, in case he was onboard. Crowe's office fired off telegrams to police forces in dozens of US cities and to authorities in Canada and Central and South America, asking them to be on the lookout.

Tips flooded into police stations and the state's attorney's office. The owner of an airfield in Tessville, only a couple of miles from a certain lakeside estate in Evanston, insisted that Leo had tried to buy a plane or charter a flight out of the country. There were reports he had tried to purchase a high-speed yacht and escape to Europe. A woman who identified herself only as Ruth phoned John Sbarbaro to announce that he had fled to Cuba. The same day, Sbarbaro's colleague Stanley Klarkowski was arranging to meet a woman who was sure he was on his way to Morocco. An anonymous letter, neatly typewritten on the stationery of a hotel in Davenport, Iowa, asserted that he had been in Chicago as late as December 16—and, oddly, in attendance at a church service when his name was mentioned in the sermon. The letter was signed "One who has faith in Jesus Christ and Koretz." An anonymous caller claimed he was still in Chicago and had disguised himself as a woman. Chief of Police Morgan Collins assigned two officers to check into the dubious report. "This case is too big," he told a reporter, "to neglect any clue."

A week after Leo's disappearance, the authorities were no closer to finding him. For Crowe, the timing could not have been worse. Nineteen twenty-four was an election year, and Republicans loyal to Crowe's ally-turned-enemy, Mayor Thompson, were lining up possible candidates to run against him. Crowe fought back, touting his crime-fighting record. "I intend to keep my staff on its toes while I am state's attorney," he proclaimed, "and I hope to reduce crime to zero." But some wondered aloud how Crowe and his team had failed to detect such a massive swindle. Had the state's attorney been too busy hanging murderers, posing for photographers, and running for reelection? Crowe had mounted a crackdown on bucket shops back in June but had somehow overlooked Leo's phony stock empire. "Something's rotten in official Denmark," the Hearst columnist Herbert Kaufman weighed in, "when a swindler can indefinitely operate on such an extensive scale without exposure or interference." "Who was asleep?" demanded an editorial in the *Evening Post*. How had Leo been able to get away with it for so long?

Crowe, eager to silence his critics, secured an indictment charging Leo with theft, fraud, and operating a confidence game. Then federal authorities elbowed their way into the headlines with a grand jury indictment of their own and bold predictions that an arrest was imminent. Assistant US District Attorney Harry F. Hamlin issued an arrest warrant on December 18 on a charge of using the mail to defraud. The federal indictment was based on a letter Leo had written in June 1923 promising "huge returns" to the Chicago clothing merchant Alfred Decker. If convicted, Leo faced up to five years behind bars and a fine of $5,000. This, Hamlin stressed in press interviews, was only the beginning: his investigators had gathered enough letters to investors to support up to fifty counts. If convicted of every allegation, the swindler could face a cumulative penalty of a 250-year prison term and a $250,000 fine. Further indictments, Hamlin said, would be sought once Leo was in custody. "The main thing now is to apprehend Koretz."

The mail-fraud indictment elevated the "scope and dignity" of the manhunt, in the words of the *Daily News*. US marshals, postal inspectors, and other federal agents across the country were now on the case, and the State Department could ask foreign governments for assistance and seek Leo's extradition if he had fled the country. Federal investigators would cooperate with police and prosecutors at the state level, Hamlin promised, and would work out an arrangement to share evidence with the state's attorney, to avoid duplication of effort. But he was adamant on one point: the feds wanted first crack at prosecuting him even if Chicago police or Crowe's detectives arrested him first.

With the trail growing colder by the day, Crowe and his assistants were content to step back—for now, at least—to let the feds take the lead. "We hope that the federal officials, with their far reaching authority, may be able to act where we cannot," Sbarbaro told the *Daily Tribune*.

Hamlin and his investigators, though, fared no better than their Cook County counterparts. A tip that their quarry was on a steamer bound for South America prompted officials in Washington to issue a radio alert to ships heading in that direction. Nothing. Just before Christmas, postal officials distributed a bulletin bearing his photograph and description and offering a $1,000 reward—later increased to $10,000—for his arrest. "Dresses expensively," the bulletin noted, "is a liberal spender and undoubtedly has a large sum of money with him." The feds received their share of tips, some of them off the wall: one informant exposed Leo as the finance minister in Russia's fledging Soviet government; another was certain he was the king of Albania; a third pegged him as kingpin of a bootlegging operation. Hamlin claimed his staff was fielding enough bizarre leads "to supply several humorous magazines."

Then postal inspectors announced that Leo had been seen in New York with the actress Doris Keane, a glamorous forty-two-year-old who had recently played Catherine the Great on Broadway. A story linking Leo to another woman, and a famous one at that? The newspapers gave it top billing until a *Herald and Examiner* correspondent tracked down Keane at a cottage in the English countryside, where she was vacationing. She had been in Europe for weeks and had no idea what all the fuss was about. Not only had she never met Leo, but, she insisted, "I never heard the name Koretz in my life."

THE PRESS SCRAMBLED TO find adjectives to describe Leo's prowess as a fraud artist. With Charles Ponzi's scam fresh in readers' minds, there were references to "the super-Ponzi" and "the Panama Ponzi." The *Daily Tribune* even concocted a new word tailor-made for the swindle; his victims, the paper said, had been "Bayanoed." The *New York Times* considered Leo "the most resourceful confidence man in the United States." John Sbarbaro offered a superlative of his own. "This is the greatest swindle in the history of Cook County," he declared, "and people call Chicago the wickedest city in the world."

Leo was making headlines across North America. The Associated Press and United Press wire services distributed updates on the latest developments to readers in every major city, and he was big news from Zanesville, Ohio, to Casa Grande, Arizona. As news of the swindle spread, so did the purported sightings. The sheriff in a Michigan town on the main road between Chicago and Detroit reported that Leo had been seen in the backseat of a chauffeured limousine. A Chicago policeman was dispatched to Honolulu to follow up on a report that Leo had been found there. Another tip came from Texas, where a hotel guest in San Antonio was convinced she had spotted him asking the desk clerk for a room. Or perhaps Leo was the man who turned up at a public library in San Francisco and asked to see recent back issues of the Chicago papers.

Two days before Christmas, Sbarbaro and Klarkowski met with Mae. It was a long shot, but they wondered whether Leo had tried to contact her. "If I get any word from him my first act will be to tell you," she assured them. "I could never forgive him for leaving me destitute, with my children to support." Sbarbaro and Klarkowski suspected he was still in the country and lying low. When the news coverage subsided, he would pick his time and try to make his escape. A headline in the Christmas Eve edition of the *Daily News* summed up the situation in four words: KORETZ HUNT AT STANDSTILL. Klarkowski admitted the obvious: "We have pretty nearly run out of clews."

As leads were drying up and news of the Bayano swindle was fading from the front pages, a small blue envelope was delivered to Sidney Kahnweiler's home. Inside was a square greeting card. "If—On New Year's," it said. He opened it to find a simple verse:

If I could be transported
    This moment to your door.
        I'd bring you smiles by dozens
            And good wishes by the score.

Then he saw the signature at the bottom: "Leo Koretz."

About two hundred other Bayano investors received an identical card, rubbing salt into still-fresh wounds. "Leo's last line," the *Daily Tribune* called it, "his last joke on the men who made him millionaire and fugitive." Were they from Leo, or the work of a prankster? The handwriting and signature seemed to match dividend checks and other documents Leo had drafted, and the stunt smacked of his twisted sense of humor. But the postmark showed they had been mailed in Chicago on Christmas Eve; given the intense manhunt, it seemed unlikely that Leo had still been in town, and since he worked alone, it was just as unlikely he had enlisted someone to distribute them.

"Joke or not," said Kahnweiler, who had lost $4,400, toying with the card as he spoke to a reporter, "I only wish that greetings could come true—that Leo Koretz at this moment could be transported to my door."

THE ALIAS

TEMPLE SCOTT RECOGNIZED the bearded man who approached him that winter evening. Scott was teaching a course on bookselling at New York University and had spotted him in the audience at earlier classes. He stood out. Few men wore a beard anymore—it was a relic of the Victorian age. He introduced himself as Lou Keyte. Could they have a word after the lecture?

Scott was an authority on rare books and a well-known literary critic. Born Isaac Henry Solomon Isaacs in England, he was a graduate of the University of London who had spent much of his life in the publishing industry. Grant Richards, publisher of such luminaries as George Bernard Shaw and James Joyce, met him in London in the late 1890s and considered him a man with "hardly an equal for knowledge, intelligence and cunning in the whole publishing trade." Isaacs moved to New York at the turn of the century and adopted the pen name Temple Scott. He edited volumes of Jonathan Swift's prose and Oscar Wilde's poems, an anthology of garden-inspired poetry, and a guide to reading the Bible. In 1911 he released *The Friendship of Books,* a compilation of the thoughts of literary giants, from Saint Augustine to Robert Louis Stevenson, on the importance of books and reading. Literature "is one of the most potent teachers," Scott wrote in his introduction to the collection, allowing readers to learn life's lessons from the world's greatest minds. The timeless works of these masters should line the shelves of a truly great bookstore, Scott told his class at New York University, not the latest best sellers.

As they chatted after the lecture, Keyte told Scott he was interested in opening a bookstore. Scott said he knew of one for sale in a good location—the Neighborhood Book Shop at the corner of Madison Avenue and Seventy-Third Street on the Upper East Side, a block from Central Park. If it checked out and he bought it, Keyte asked, would Scott consider running it for him, for at least a year? Scott could put his theories of what made a great bookstore into action. He could turn it into "a model shop," Keyte suggested, "and then write a book about it."

Scott was intrigued—and soon was in awe of his new friend. Keyte, he recalled, "was one of the most interesting men I have ever known," a widely read, cultured man and "a brilliant conversationalist." Coming from someone as discriminating and well read as Scott, this was high praise indeed. In his introduction to *The Friendship of Books,* he had lamented how rare it was to encounter someone who read and appreciated great literature.

Scott did not know it yet, but he and Keyte had something in common besides a love of good books. Lou Keyte was not his new friend's real name, either.

WHILE CHICAGO POLICE AND federal agents chased down leads across the country, Leo Koretz was lying low in New York, getting used to his new name, and growing the beard as a disguise. After checking out of the St. Regis on the afternoon of December 6, he had rented a furnished apartment nearby at 4 East Forty-Eighth Street, a five-story building only a few steps from Fifth Avenue in a desirable and expensive neighborhood. The rent, $300 a month, was what he had been paying for his mansion, and New Yorkers instantly recognized the address as "off the Avenue." It was the city's most exclusive shopping district, lined with department stores, jewelers to rival the best of Paris, art galleries, and high-end furniture shops. Saks and Company, the famous department store, was barely a block from his front door.

Leo arrived in New York with $175,000 in cash, and he invested $69,000 of that in stocks and bonds. No risky, fly-by-night investments for Leo; he dealt only with blue-chip Wall Street brokers. The rest—some $90,000—never left the apartment. "I suppose I took some chance," he admitted later, but the need to have money close at hand for a quick escape outweighed the risk of losing his stash to a burglar.

Robbery was the least of his worries. He was uncomfortably close to a section of Fifth Avenue where a lot of people had known him as Leo Koretz—and now knew him, thanks to the widespread press coverage, as one of the greatest swindlers of all time. If he ventured too far north, he risked running into Basil Curran or someone else on the staff of the St. Regis. Salesclerks at Fifth Avenue jewelers who had trusted him to take home expensive pieces on approval would be on the lookout as well. There was one advantage to his Midtown location: if he needed to make a quick escape by train or to melt into a crowd, the nonstop bustle of Grand Central Terminal was only a few blocks away.

Leo checked the newspapers to make sure he was still a step ahead of the authorities, and he followed the bankruptcy proceedings under way in Chicago. He caught a break from the *New York Times*—the paper published a handful of reports that December on the Bayano swindle, but none included his photograph or description. He may have chuckled at a report that he was on a plane bound for Honduras, had crossed the border into Canada, or was on a boat setting sail from the West Coast. He would have been less pleased to see a reference in the *Times* to something his friend Mary Schoener had told investigators: Leo, she believed, was still in New York.

That, though, was akin to directing someone searching for a particular grain of sand to the nearest beach. With a population nearing the six million mark, New York was twice the size of Chicago, and that much more crowded and impersonal. It was "the metropolis of our planet . . . the culmination of twentieth-century civilization," Ernest Gruening, who edited the magazine the *Nation,* boasted in 1922, sounding as windy as Chicago's boosters. "Its high finance settles the fate of nations. Its shops display the rarest and costliest of the earth's goods. It assembles the brains and talent in business, invention, and the arts."

The skyscraper may have been invented in Chicago, but it was being perfected—over and over—in New York's skyline. The city claimed the world's tallest building, the fifty-seven-story Woolworth Building, and the humorist Will Rogers joked that builders seemed determined "to make the height of their buildings keep pace with their prices." The city was so big and so congested that people could come and go unnoticed. "In New York," noted Gruening, "one rarely seeks acquaintance with one's neighbor; it would be unusual, suspect." Strangers remained strangers. No one cared if the new tenant in the building was growing a beard and kept to himself. A fugitive could hide in plain sight.

And no one was looking for a man named Lou Keyte. Not even Leo was sure how he came up with the name. "It just occurred to me," he said later, when the question was asked. He thought it made sense to keep the initials LK, in case he still had some monogrammed clothing or belongings. People often called him "kite" but he corrected them: it was pronounced "keet."

At the beginning of 1924, the *Chicago Evening Post* published a list of New Year's predictions. One was that Leo would surrender to police in Brooklyn on April Fool's Day. "Prefers jail, he says," the paper wisecracked at Brooklyn's expense.

Brooklyn was as good a guess as any. By now, John Sbarbaro and Stanley Klarkowski suspected their prey was hiding in New York and waiting for a chance to flee the country. Harry Hamlin, the district attorney in charge of the federal investigation, suggested a reason the swindler was so elusive. "Koretz was an insatiable reader of detective stories," he noted, "and therefore probably is in disguise."

On January 3, the day archaeologists in Egypt uncovered the beautifully carved granite sarcophagus of King Tut, a Chicago locksmith was hired to search for treasure of a different sort. He spent two hours drilling into the steel case of box 4306 in the vault of the National Safety Deposit Company, as lawyers for the state's attorney and Chicago Title and Trust looked on. The box had been rented under the name Alice Bronson—of the Shirley Apartments love-nest fame—and investigators hoped it would yield clues to Leo's whereabouts. An *Evening Post* reporter was as disappointed as they were to discover it contained nothing of value.

Then Leo was linked to another woman—Jessie Taggart, a stenographer who had left Chicago in 1920 and was rumored to be traveling in the Middle East. She was traced to India after mysterious cables arrived at Leo's old law office, written in code and signed "Watson." A Hearst reporter cracked the code and discovered they were desperate pleas for Leo to respond. An even more enterprising *Daily Tribune* correspondent tracked down Taggart at a hotel in Calcutta. She was penniless and shocked to learn of the swindle and her sudden notoriety. Leo had sent her on a tour of the Orient, and she had been trying to contact him to send more money. "I regarded him as a clever, honest man," said Taggart, a stout, dark-haired woman in her midthirties. She was not asked why he had sent her away and had funded her travels, but after the revelations of affairs and love nests, the answer seemed obvious: other women had taken her place. And it was just like Leo to get more mileage out of the alias Watson, the name he had given to one of the Bayano Syndicate's shadowy millionaires.

LEO SETTLED IN FOR the winter in New York. He checked out the Neighborhood Book Shop and bought the business for $4,000, set aside $6,000 to buy books and cover the bills, and hired Temple Scott as manager. The store was more than a vehicle to launder some of the Bayano loot—Leo was free to indulge his love of books. He could browse the shelves and take home any title he chose. "All the books he took from the store or read while here were high class," Scott was pleased to note, "many of them classics, many by authors who are seldom read." As Leo explained it later, owning a bookshop added one more layer to the new persona he was creating—the wealthy, well-read Lou Keyte, writer, literary critic, and collector of rare books.

As an investment, the shop proved almost as ill advised as a stake in Panamanian oil wells. Scott's theories on what made a great bookstore did not translate into sales. The shop was "cozy rather than commercial," scoffed one journalist who stopped by, "one of those highbrow places, where best sellers are hidden and food for the discriminating few is given preference." Leo's own assessment was blunt. "It was a dud," he later grumbled. "New Yorkers don't spend their money for books."

When he grew tired of hanging around his money-pit bookstore, New York offered other diversions. It was "the city of the Good Time," said the visiting English novelist Ford Madox Ford, with the exuberance of "a storming-party hurrying towards an unknown goal." There were fifteen thousand drinking establishments in New York before Prohibition, it was said, and more than twice as many after liquor was outlawed. It was, Will Rogers joked, the "city of booze and bankrolls." It would have been impossible for the free-spending, fast-living Leo to resist the lure of the city's nightlife. The Cotton Club opened in Harlem in 1923, showcasing the music that would define the Jazz Age. A tune called "The Charleston" debuted in a Broadway show that fall, launching a hit song and igniting a dance craze. People packed New York's movie houses to see the biggest silent films of the year: *The Hunchback of Notre Dame,* starring Lon Chaney; *The Great White Way,* a romantic comedy set on Broadway that featured the Ziegfeld Follies; and Cecil B. DeMille's epic *The Ten Commandments.*

But Leo was not sure that New York was the best place to hide. He wanted something more remote, more secluded—"some place in the woods," as he put it. "I had been considering other possibilities in the states but they did not come up to expectations." In other words, none were far enough away from Chicago and New York to lessen the chances of someone figuring out who Lou Keyte really was.

One day, he ventured a few blocks south of his apartment, to the corner of Madison Avenue and Forty-Fifth Street, and walked into New York's most renowned sporting goods store, founded by David T. Abercrombie and Ezra H. Fitch. It was there that he learned about Nova Scotia and a secluded sportsman's retreat known as Pinehurst Lodge.

THE GUIDE

ABERCROMBIE AND FITCH catered to serious sportsmen, wealthy professionals, and businessmen who demanded the best hunting and fishing equipment. A "citadel of The Leisure Class," the *New York Times* called it, where "stylish sportsmen could count on finding the highest-grade rod and guns at the highest prices." When Theodore Roosevelt embarked on an African safari after leaving the White House in 1909, the store outfitted his entourage with snake-proof sleeping bags. It was where Presidents Taft and Harding bought their golf clubs and Woodrow Wilson went for his riding gear. In 1920 a customer inquired about a game she had seen while traveling in China, played with dice and tiles; Abercrombie and Fitch imported it, and soon mah-jongg mania was sweeping the country.

Leo had no need of a snake-proof sleeping bag, but someone on the staff might know where he could find a secluded property. He was referred to an employee in the fishing department on the eighth floor. Captain Laurie Mitchell was an accomplished hunter and deep-sea angler. An Englishman in his early fifties who hailed from Dorset, Mitchell was heavyset and chubby faced and sported a bushy mustache. His family had sent him to Oxford, but Mitchell had emigrated in the 1890s to Nova Scotia, where he found a wife and the wilderness life he craved. He once posed for a photograph with a rifle in one hand, a pipe in the other, and a hunting dog at his side, looking every inch the country gentleman transplanted to the colonial backwoods. He worked with local hunting and fishing guides and touted the woods and lakes of southwestern Nova Scotia as a "veritable paradise" for sportsmen.

In 1912, Mitchell established the Tuna Inn on a rocky island on the Atlantic coast. It was the first resort in the province to cater to deep-sea anglers who hoped to land giant tuna with rod and reel, and Mitchell promoted the lodge as an alternative to the popular sport-fishing grounds off California. "Here is the new field for tuna," he declared in an article in *Rod and Gun* magazine, claiming the fish swam so close to shore during the summer months that they had been spotted from the inn's veranda. In 1914, Mitchell backed up his claims by reeling in a 710-pounder, establishing a world's record for the largest fish caught using a fishing rod.

The war forced Mitchell to put his tuna venture on hold. He enlisted in the Royal Engineers and served on the Salonika Front in the mountains of Macedonia, emerging with the rank of captain. By the time he returned to Nova Scotia in 1920, a fire had destroyed the lodge and wiped out his livelihood. That was how he wound up behind the counter in the rod and tackle department at Abercrombie and Fitch, which only hired expert outdoorsmen to advise its discriminating clientele.

The latest customer seeking his advice introduced himself as Lou Keyte. "He was pleasant and agreeable and very much a gentleman," Mitchell would recall, though he noted that the man did not appear to be in good health. Leo must have found it intriguing that a central character in the novel *Nostromo* by his favorite author, Joseph Conrad, was named Captain Mitchell. Laurie Mitchell, for his part, was led to believe that Keyte was a wealthy real estate promoter in search of a refuge from the city. And he knew just the place.

Nova Scotia was less than five hundred miles northeast of New York, and no more than a day away by steamer and train, yet the Canadian province was a mystery to many Americans. A narrow peninsula—350 miles in length and as little as 50 wide—it was slightly larger than Massachusetts and Vermont combined and jutted from the Atlantic coast of North America as if the continent were dipping a foot into the Gulf Stream. The population stood at just over half a million; the capital and largest city, Halifax, was a historic port and had been a major naval base during the war. Ocean-cooled summers and a reputation for unspoiled, rustic beauty were just beginning to make the province a popular vacation destination.

American sportsmen were among the first to arrive in search of game and solitude, and Mitchell was not the only one plugging the tourism potential of the province's wilderness. "If one has never been in Nova Scotia," Byron McLeod of Boston, a former resident, wrote of a 1906 hunting trip in *National Sportsman* magazine, "then he can form no idea of how quickly, reasonably and conveniently he can be landed, say from Boston or New York, in a Sportsman's Paradise." In 1908, the New York writer Albert Bigelow Paine, Mark Twain's confidant and biographer, published an account of a camping trip by canoe across southwestern Nova Scotia. *The Tent Dwellers,* with its description of "fairy lakes, full of green islands" and "clear, black water" swarming with trout, helped to put Nova Scotia on the map for the well-heeled sportsmen who shopped at Abercrombie and Fitch. This was also "big game country," noted another American visitor, who wrote a glowing account of hunting moose "for fresh meat and dining-room trophies." Lodges sprang up to accommodate an influx of hunters, fishermen, and tourists. In the fall of 1916, John D. Rockefeller Jr., heir to his father's Standard Oil empire, made his third trip to the region to hunt moose.

If Nova Scotia's wilderness was good enough for a Rockefeller, it was good enough for the New Rockefeller. Mitchell told Leo about a lakeside lodge that might be the retreat he was seeking. Known as Pinehurst, it was located near the village of Caledonia in Queens County, in the heart of moose-hunting and trout-fishing country. Byron McLeod, the *National Sportsman* writer, had bought the ninety-five-acre property in 1905 and had built a two-story lodge with a long veranda overlooking First Christopher Lake. The lodge, which stood at the end of a long, curving driveway and was hidden from the main road, offered the privacy Leo needed. Pinehurst would be a good fit, too, for his new persona as a lover of books and literature: McLeod's uncle, Robert McLeod, had written an illustrated book filled with glowing praise for the "commodious lodge" set among the "green-robed senators of the mighty wood." The idyllic setting had inspired another local writer of note, William Marshall, to produce "Evening at Pinehurst," a short poem describing a sunset that transformed the lake into a "rose-tinted mirror."

Leo was interested but wanted to see the property for himself. Mitchell, who was about to move back to Nova Scotia for the summer, agreed to take him there. Before they set out from New York in mid-March, Leo dropped by the Neighborhood Book Shop and told Temple Scott he was going to Nova Scotia for his health. They worked out arrangements for Scott to oversee the shop in his absence.

Steamers ran from Boston to Yarmouth, a port near the southwestern tip of Nova Scotia. Leo appears to have had no problem crossing into Canada despite the alerts issued to border points when he fled Chicago in December. It may have helped to be traveling with Mitchell, a Canadian who knew the route and the drill at the border. At Yarmouth, travelers hopped aboard the Halifax and Southwestern Railway—local wags claimed the initials H&SW stood for "hellish, slow, and wobbly"—to continue on to Liverpool, a port town about a hundred miles west of Halifax. The bone-rattling ride took six hours.

The main road from Liverpool into the interior was still snow-covered and impassible by car. Mitchell rounded up a horse and sleigh for the twenty-five-mile trip through forests and farms to Pinehurst. The property bordered on two lakes, each a mile wide, and the snow gave the setting a Currier and Ives charm. The lodge was less than twenty years old, and its builders had sacrificed aesthetics for panoramic views; a row of second-floor windows ran above a long veranda facing the lake, creating a boxy facade but giving guests an unobstructed view of moonlit waters and "rose-tinted" sunsets. Inside, a massive brick fireplace stood ready to warm the large main-floor room where hunters and fishermen gathered to clink glasses and swap tales. There was no electricity, no central heating, and no modern plumbing, let alone the other comforts found in Leo's gilded world of hotel suites and limousines. But Pinehurst was remote and secluded, and that made it perfect. He told Mitchell it was exactly what he was looking for.

They returned to Liverpool, where Leo stayed with Mitchell and his wife, Elizabeth, at their home. His arrival made news in the provincial capital, with the *Halifax Herald* describing Keyte as "a writer of reputation" who intended to buy property in the area. Liverpool was one of the oldest towns in Nova Scotia, founded in the 1750s by a contingent of New Englanders that included a long list of *Mayflower* descendants. It bordered the broad mouth of a river christened, appropriately, the Mersey. The turrets and gingerbread trim of the oversize homes lining the main street, built by ship captains and lumber merchants, spoke of prosperous times long gone; by the 1920s the biggest industry in town was building and supplying the swift schooners and powerboats needed to smuggle liquor into the United States. Shady characters with New York accents and wads of cash turned up, eager to have boats built and outfitted or to hire skippers and crews to deliver crates of rum, whiskey, and champagne to "rum row," just outside US jurisdiction, for transfer to shore.

Leo was one of the few Americans in town with money to spend and no interest in smuggling booze. He got the lodge for a bargain price, $17,500, and a brief announcement of the lodge's sale to "L. Keyte, of New York, a critic of note in that city," appeared in a local paper at the beginning of April. Leo hired Mitchell to manage the place.

The arrangement was ideal for Mitchell, who had persuaded another well-heeled Abercrombie and Fitch customer to join him in Nova Scotia that summer to fish for tuna off Liverpool. He was Zane Grey, whose novels, with their gun-toting, trailblazing Old West characters, were enormously popular. Grey was the most successful author of the era; only two works outsold his many titles—the Bible and the *Boy*

Scout Handbook—and he earned almost $300,000 in royalties in 1924 alone. He was, in short, the kind of author Temple Scott despised.

When not churning out novels, Grey became an accomplished hunter and fisherman. He was a frequent visitor to California's Catalina Island, where he fished for tuna and swordfish, but his trophies were puny when compared to Mitchell's record 710-pound catch. Surrounded by the racks of fishing poles at Abercrombie and Fitch, Mitchell told Grey all about it, how the massive fish had dragged him "nine miles out to sea, and halfway back." Mitchell's record—and the prospect of beating it—"inspired me," Grey recalled. That winter they plotted strategy, discussing the rods, tackle, and boats best suited for fishing off Nova Scotia. They agreed to meet in Liverpool in August, when tuna began appearing in Nova Scotia waters.

Leo may have met Grey in New York through their mutual friend. They both spent time at Abercrombie and Fitch, getting to know Mitchell. A connection to Zane Grey through Mitchell might prove useful to Leo. Knowing—or claiming to know—the famous author would burnish Lou Keyte's credentials as a writer and literary critic.

THE HIDEAWAY

THOMAS RADDALL SAW him for the first time at a dance in Liverpool. In a town awash in lumbermen, fishermen, and rumrunners, this man was dressed like a dandy, in spats, a white vest, and a derby. "He was an odd sight," Raddall would recall, "obviously a city type."

The dance was in the Assembly Room on the second floor of Liverpool's town hall, a many-gabled, wood-frame building. The cavernous room, with its tin ceiling and dark Douglas fir woodwork, was a popular venue for banquets, teas, and other events. Dances were a big draw, and the Bambalinas, a group of young, tuxedo-clad local musicians who took their name from a popular fox-trot of the day, provided the music.

Someone introduced the newcomer in the derby to Raddall as Lou Keyte, the New Yorker the local papers said was looking for property in the area. He was clearly a man of means, and as if to prove it, he sent out to a restaurant for sandwiches, sweets, and coffee for everyone. "This," Raddall recalled, "made him popular at once." He catered the dance the following Saturday as well, and this time hit the dance floor. He proved to be an excellent dancer, and Raddall noted, soon "he was dancing with the prettiest girls in the room." Word quickly spread that the dapper, polite, and generous newcomer was a millionaire in his midforties who had just bought Pinehurst Lodge—and a bachelor to boot.

Raddall and Leo hit it off. Keyte, he recalled, was "a jolly good fellow." Raddall was much younger but mature and worldly for his age. He was short and stocky, with deep-set brown eyes capped by dark eyebrows—eyes that had seen a lot in just twenty years. Born in England, he had come to Canada in 1913. His father, a soldier in the Royal Marines, had died in the war, making Thomas the man of the house at an early age. When a munitions ship exploded in Halifax Harbor in 1917, leveling large sections of the city and killing almost two thousand people, Raddall had experienced the horror firsthand—he had been enlisted to help set up a temporary morgue. He had left school at fifteen, studied to be a wireless operator, and signed on to his first steamer in 1919. After a lonely year posted at a radio station on an island off the Nova Scotia coast, he had taken a bookkeeper's job at a pulp mill just upriver from Liverpool.

Leo promised to invite Raddall and his other new friends to parties at Pinehurst once his planned renovations were complete. In the meantime, he arranged a private dinner and dance at a hotel in Bridgewater, a riverside town northeast of Liverpool, and invited Raddall and a dozen other young people to join him. On the evening of May 26, the party set out in a fleet of six cars—Leo commandeered every taxi in town—for the thirty-mile trip. It was the Empire Day holiday in Canada, marking the birthday of Queen Victoria, and the weather was as warm as a summer evening. Leo hired the Bambalinas to play, and band members piled into the taxis as well. Raddall and his date had a car to themselves and found the backseat stocked with expensive chocolates and packs of cigarettes. Their destination was the Fairview Hotel, overlooking the town.

The entourage discovered that their host had thought of everything. He had reserved two upstairs rooms, one as a powder room for his female guests, the other stocked with whiskey and liqueurs for the men. At their tables in the wainscoted dining room, a printed menu card announced the meal to come. The appetizers were consommé and asparagus tips with celery, tomatoes, and olives. A choice of entrées followed: fried salmon with potatoes, or roasted stuffed chicken with cranberry sauce, mashed potatoes, and creamed peas. There was sponge cake, vanilla ice cream, and coffee for dessert. When the meal was over, just before the Bambalinas began to play and the group hit the dance floor, Raddall passed around his menu and asked everyone to sign the card as a souvenir of their memorable night. Everyone obliged except Leo. When Raddall insisted, he took the pen and scribbled "& Lou Keyte" beside the name of a young woman who had caught his eye.

After the dinner, as Raddall scanned the names on the back of the menu, he realized Keyte had not signed his name. He had printed it. Raddall was puzzled. It was as if his new friend, the American millionaire injecting life and glamour into his small-town world, was unaccustomed to writing his own name.

CALEDONIA, THE VILLAGE CLOSEST to Pinehurst Lodge, was located midway between Liverpool and Nova Scotia's Bay of Fundy coast. Home to a few hundred—disgruntled Bayano investors probably outnumbered Caledonia's residents—it was a cluster of stores and hotels lining the unpaved main road, with a sprinkling of churches and Victorian-style houses. The name of the local weekly paper, the *Gold Hunter and Farmers' Journal,* was a reminder of a gold rush that had drawn thousands to the area in the late nineteenth century. It was said to have begun when a couple of men hiding in the woods to escape the law—Leo could identify with that part of the story—spotted gold in a vein of quartz. Boomtowns had sprung up at mine sites, but the good times had ended in 1905, when the last major pit closed and the newcomers moved on.

Twenty years later, a wealthy American named Lou Keyte became the new gold rush. "Money was nothing to him," a local man, Walter Scott, said of Leo with considerable understatement. "He was a real big spender." Few people who encountered Keyte had seen such displays of extravagance. Waitresses who served him could count on a five-dollar tip, and according to a story told and retold in the area, he once bought ice cream, tendered a $100 American banknote, and left the shop without asking for change. Leo soon had two automobiles, a Chevrolet and an open-cabbed Franklin, a luxury car worth at least $1,500 with a distinctive engine hood that sloped like the tip of an upturned knife blade. He picked up the Chevy at a local garage, writing a check for the $850 asking price when almost everyone purchased such big-ticket items on a payment plan.

Then there was the small army of workmen hired to renovate Pinehurst. To furnish the place, Leo scoured stores and placed classified advertisements in the *Liverpool Advance* for antique furniture as well as the old books he needed to fill his latest library and bolster his literary credentials. He made the hundred-mile drive to Halifax on shopping trips; spotting a display of lamps in a shop window, he bought all six. Leo estimated he spent roughly $18,000 to renovate and furnish the lodge, which was more than he paid for the building and the surrounding woodlands. Renovations were still under way in mid-May when he moved in. The *Gold Hunter* made sure the entire community knew that Keyte "is now living at this beautiful summer home."

People were never quite clear how the newcomer had made his money. He rarely talked about himself, and when he did, it was only in vague terms. Some people were under the impression he was a retired New York financier. Others recalled his mentioning that he had made his money in real estate down south. "He spoke of the States with contempt," Raddall recalled, "and said he wanted to get away from it all." He seemed to be well traveled and claimed to one new friend that the few months he had spent in Nova Scotia was the longest he had been in one place in a decade.

As for what he did now, the *Halifax Herald* had introduced Keyte as "a writer of reputation" upon his arrival, and Leo did everything he could to play the part. He was spotted walking along Liverpool's streets with armloads of books. He styled himself as a literary and drama critic in search of a quiet place to work. He claimed to have written several plays, but it turned out none had been produced. He spoke of writing articles and book reviews for American magazines. W. B. McKay, a Liverpool businessman who spent a lot of time with

Secluded Pinehurst Lodge, near the village of Caledonia in southwestern Nova Scotia, after Leo's extensive upgrades and renovations.

him, often saw him jotting in a notebook. He was making notes about people he met and things he saw, he told McKay, material "to use later in his writings." Pinehurst's literary connections—Robert McLeod's book, William Marshall's poem—rubbed off on Leo as well. And he discovered, to his delight, that people often called him Keytes by mistake, adding an *s* to his new surname as if he were a distant relative of the famous poet John Keats.

Leo offered another explanation for his decision to put down roots in Nova Scotia—his health. When he arrived in March to check out Pinehurst, he was so pale that everyone he met assumed he was seriously ill. It must have been the effects of diabetes, but Leo brushed off questions with vague references to being on the mend after a long illness. His condition improved within a few weeks, and his health became a convenient way to explain why he had grown a beard. He was recovering, he said, from a serious infection of his teeth and jaw that had left his face temporarily deformed. The beard masked the effects, and the explanation encouraged the squeamish to quickly change the subject.

By THE TIME THE workmen declared victory and retreated from Pinehurst, the lodge had been transformed into a cross between a backwoods resort and a gentleman's country retreat. Pinehurst "was known as one of the best equipped hunting lodges in the eastern section of Canada," noted one visitor, but Leo "made it the best." Local people out for an evening drive sometimes ventured up the long driveway just to take a look.

The veranda that ran the length of the lodge—more than one hundred feet—had been widened from six to ten feet and enclosed in glass to keep out mosquitoes and blackflies. It was now an indoor space with a polished oak floor and a spectacular view of the lake. A main door off the veranda opened into a massive living room filled with both antiques and modern furniture. The music room, as Leo called it, housed a piano and a gramophone. The dining room easily accommodated a billiard table as well as a mahogany table and chairs; a silver tea service sat on a wagon in one corner, and a moose head glowered above the stone fireplace.

Upstairs were three guest bedrooms, each with its own bath. A fourth bedroom, Leo's, was on the second floor of an octagonal, three-level turret that rose like a silo from the north end of the lodge. It had two large windows to frame the view of the lake. He mounted a set of carpeted steps to climb into his four-poster bed and slept under a silk canopy. The comforter at the foot of the bed was silk as well and embroidered with Chinese dragons and serpents. The top floor of the turret had windows on all sides like a watchtower, ensuring he could spot any unwanted visitors who pulled up in the driveway. There were fifteen rooms in all, with seventeen fireplaces, enough decorative guns and swords to stock a small armory, and a herd of disembodied moose and other big game. Everything was "set in its place" and reeked "of newness," said one person who got a look inside, making the lodge feel more like "a salesroom in a department store" than a home.

Leo and his guests ate at a table set with fine china, walked on rich Axminster wool rugs imported from England, and sank into a plush chesterfield suite upholstered in Spanish leather. He upgraded the plumbing, ran a new telephone line, and erected a coal-fired plant to supply steam heat. The boiler also generated electricity, making Pinehurst the first dwelling in the immediate area to have electric lights. There was a garage for his cars, a tennis court, and a croquet lawn. Benches and observation platforms dotted the grounds. Several canoes bobbed at the lakeshore, and tons of sand had been trucked in to create a beach for bathing. Leo stabled a horse for saddle and buggy rides and had a French bulldog and an Airedale to greet visitors. Radios were still a novelty in the area—Alton House, Caledonia's largest hotel, had just installed one—but Leo insisted on the latest in receiving technology, a five-tube neutrodyne set that spared his guests the high-pitched squeals of older models.

It took a sizable staff to run it all. Laurie Mitchell was in charge; his wife, Elizabeth, ran the household; and a local man, Charles Kennedy, was hired as caretaker. Walter Scott of Caledonia, who had noted Leo's free-spending ways, was in his late twenties when he was put in charge of Leo's vehicles. "He was a real fussy man with his car," he recalled. "He wanted it perfect, everything from the inside to the tires." Leo disliked driving—he blamed his poor eyesight—and usually conscripted an employee such as Scott or a friend to act as his chauffeur.

Scott's younger brother, Maurice, who ran a barbershop and pool hall in Caledonia, was summoned to Pinehurst many times to cut Leo's thinning hair and trim his thick beard. "Getting me there to cut his hair was just a trick," he soon realized. He was really looking for someone to keep him company and put the billiard table to use. Maurice recalled, "We usually ended up playing pool," sometimes for the rest of the day. Leo would slip him four or five dollars and sometimes even a ten-dollar bill, a windfall to a man who charged twenty-five cents for a haircut.

Leo was as fussy about his dinner-table etiquette as he was about his cars. The evening meal was a formal affair, served by a young man dressed in a white jacket, black pants, and a black bow tie. As Leo and his guests ate, the server stood behind him like a footman in an English manor, ready to respond to his master's command.

As a final extravagance, Leo shelled out about $1,000 for a thirty-eight-foot motorboat, *Tuna II,* which was large enough to cruise the Nova Scotia coast and offered the comfort of a cabin with four sleeping berths. Leo kept it tied up in Liverpool and hired a local ship's captain as its skipper.

There was one thing the caretaker, Charles Kennedy, found odd about working at Pinehurst. Not a single photograph of Lou Keyte could be found anywhere in the lodge, and his boss refused to allow one to be taken.

THE PRINCE OF ENTERTAINERS

THE PARTIES BEGAN, as Leo had promised, as soon as the renovations to Pinehurst were complete. They became legendary affairs, growing grander and more decadent as stories spread of Lou Keyte's generosity and extravagance. He earned a reputation as a "prince of entertainers" who lived the "merry life" of a country squire. Some of his Pinehurst soirees, it was rumored, lasted up to four days or an entire week. He hired musicians to play and, according to one story, imported three members of the Boston Symphony Orchestra for a dinner-dance. Booze flowed in defiance of Canada's Prohibition laws.

He let his guests do most of the drinking. Eighteen people attended one of the parties, one guest claimed, "and seventeen were drunk." The sober one was Leo. While it was probably diabetes and not an aversion to alcohol that kept him from indulging, one observer later wondered whether he stayed sober "for fear he'd talk too much if he got drunk." Pinehurst became a northern version of the Long Island estate that F. Scott Fitzgerald imagined for Jay Gatsby, the title character of his classic novel written that year—a blaze of lights to all hours, guests filling the rooms and wandering the grounds in the moonlight, an endless supply of liquor, an orchestra providing the sound track. Leo was as gracious a host as the enigmatic Gatsby, flitting from guest to guest, drinking little or nothing, keeping his head as his new friends swapped theories about how he had made his fortune.

A cartoonist's view of Leo's busy social life in Nova Scotia in 1924 while posing as bearded literary critic Lou Keyte: sailing with the yacht-club set; conveying guests to hotel dinners in hired cars; showering gifts on young women.

Fitzgerald's Gatsby had eyes for only one woman—his old flame Daisy Buchanan. Not Keyte, who seemed to have an eye for every young, attractive woman he met in Nova Scotia. "Everyone liked him, especially the women," noted Walter Scott, the man in charge of the Pinehurst motor pool, and he "liked the women in turn." It was obvious to everyone who met him more than once that he dyed his beard to make himself look younger; one day it was black, another it could be reddish or auburn. Scott chalked up his popularity with women to his prowess on the dance floor. To others, including Scott's brother, Maurice, the attraction was obvious. "He was a rich bachelor," Maurice recalled. "Most of the girls in Caledonia and vicinity were struck on him."

That summer "a succession of dear friends," as Thomas Raddall termed them, visited Leo at Pinehurst. All were "goodlooking and most of them were American show-girl types," and he suspected one or more might be a prostitute "well paid for her 'holiday.'" One attractive young woman was a waitress he had met in Halifax; she took up residence at Pinehurst until a woman named Frances White showed up and sent her packing. Leo introduced White as the daughter of one of his publishers in New York—or was it Boston? No one was quite sure who the women were or where they were from, and usually they stayed for only a week or so.

White was said to have stayed the longest, but even her reign at Pinehurst was temporary. In Raddall's opinion, the women quickly grew tired of the isolation and solitude at Pinehurst, and Leo soon grew tired of them. "Keyte had a fickle and insatiable appetite for women," he noted, looking back on that summer many years later. "Sometimes a new 'friend' arrived while the 'old' one was still there—but the old one invariably departed promptly."

Leo, who was extremely good at pretending, pretended he did nothing to encourage his female admirers. "They send me urgent telegrams asking me to invite them up to my place," he once announced to his dinner guests. "I never answer them and that usually cures them."

"I am always indifferent to them," he continued, apparently with a straight face, "and sometimes I am downright rude, but it just seems to make them want me more than ever. I don't know what I do to make them behave so foolishly." It was the same reverse psychology he had used so effectively to sell millions of dollars' worth of bogus stocks.

THE GRANDEST PINEHURST EVENT of the summer was Keyte's housewarming bash at the end of August. It was, Laurie Mitchell said, "a brilliant party that astonished every one." About 125 people showed up, including some of the area's most prominent businessmen and politicians. Thomas Raddall's date was an American girl staying at a summer home nearby, and they thundered up the driveway in style, in her family's sleek and expensive Winton Six.

The weather was perfect. A hurricane that had swept across the province the previous night—guests picked their way to Pinehurst along roads littered with broken branches and downed wires—left a hot, sunny afternoon in its wake. Leo brought in an orchestra from a resort near the seaside town of Digby. "Dancing," the *Halifax Herald* noted in a brief account of the festivities, "was the chief entertainment." Some people commandeered canoes and ventured onto the lake. Inside the lodge, guests gathered around a large punch bowl—most likely the Willow-patterned, washbasin-size one Leo had picked up at an antique store for such occasions. A bigger draw was the bar set up in his bedroom in the turret, stocked with liquor and wine.

Raddall spotted an attractive woman seated at the far end of the large living room, "dressed in white," he recalled, "from head to foot." Leo introduced her as "a dear friend of mine," then seemed at a loss for words. He finally blurted out "Miss White," as if her attire had been the cue he needed to remember the name of the latest woman in his life—Frances White. "She made a little conversation and seemed a quiet and intelligent person," Raddall noted, "but she kept in the background during the party."

The party wound down around one in the morning. A group of drunken Liverpool businessmen emerged from the turret room. Guests stumbled off to their cars after saluting their host with a chorus of "For He's a Jolly Good Fellow." Raddall and his date were about to join the exodus when Leo pulled them aside. He was alone. The standoffish Miss White, Raddall thought, must have turned in for the night.

"Don't go," he pleaded. "It's a lovely night. Stay and talk with me for a while."

They sat on the veranda steps overlooking the lake and chatted for another hour. It was small talk, mostly, and they compared notes on who had done what during the party. The lodge windows sent shafts of light into the gloom, glistening on the water and casting deep shadows into the surrounding trees. The acid-sweet scent of pine drifted in the night air. Loons often called to each other from somewhere out on the lake, and perhaps one broke the stillness with its haunting, warbled cry. Leo, as usual, had had little to drink, but something loosened his tongue. Raddall, who knew him as well as anyone in Nova Scotia, suspected it was loneliness: "he felt himself far up in the wilds of Canada an enormous distance away from home."

Whatever the reason, he began to talk about the one subject he studiously avoided: himself. "I come from Chicago, and I made most of my money in land deals," he said. "My first big profit came from a large area of swamp land on the Mississippi. An engineer looked it over for me, and said it could be drained. The soil was deep and black, the very finest kind of soil for rice-growing. So I raised the money to drain it, and two or three years later I was able to sell it at a whale of a profit for myself and for the people who lent me the money."

A note of bitterness crept into his voice. "Then everybody wanted me to find another piece of land like that and make another haul," he continued. "They pushed their money at me. Well, I couldn't find another place like that, anywhere in the States. However I did find one, down on the Bayano River in Panama. After that I retired. I had enough, and I didn't want people pestering me any more."

Leo had often claimed to have made his fortune in real estate, but this was the first time Raddall had heard the details. A savvy businessman from Chicago who speculated in rice farms. A promoter who struck it rich with property on the Bayano River in Panama and made huge profits for investors. None of it meant anything to Raddall. Leo might as well have said he made a fortune mining green cheese on the moon. He did not know, would never have suspected, the significance of what he was hearing.

It was the closest Leo had come, in the many months since his arrival in Nova Scotia, to telling the truth.

THE CRIME
OF THE CENTURY

THE BOY'S NAKED body was found stuffed into a culvert on the outskirts of Chicago, and only by chance. A factory worker walking along a rail line happened to look down at the right moment and spotted the boy's feet floating in the water. A pair of horn-rimmed glasses had been discarded nearby.

The victim, Bobby Franks, was just fourteen and the son of wealthy parents. He had been badly beaten and had died of asphyxiation, not drowning—he was dead before he wound up facedown in the culvert. It was a brutal murder, even by Chicago's brutal standards, and the boy's age and his family's stature made it an instant sensation. Robert Crowe ranked it as "the most cruel, cowardly, dastardly murder" in American history. The judge who had sent the killer of little Janet Wilkinson to the gallows was now the prosecutor determined to avenge the death of young Bobby Franks. Those responsible, he assured shocked and outraged Chicagoans, would be found and punished.

By the time Franks's parents received a note demanding a $10,000 ransom, they knew their boy was dead. The kidnappers had not counted on the body's being found so quickly, within a day of his death. Police rounded up an array of suspects, from the boy's male teachers to the owners of cars like one seen near his school, but the eyeglasses were the clue that cracked the case. The frames were unusual; only one optician in Chicago sold them, and only one customer who bought them could not find his pair when police showed up at his door. He was Nathan Leopold, a nineteen-year-old university student and the son of a prosperous factory owner. Leopold's best friend, Richard Loeb, eighteen, was a neighbor of the Frankses and well off, too—his father was a top executive with Sears, Roebuck. Both were brought in for questioning.

Crowe took charge of the marathon interrogations. The alibis the pair had concocted for the day of the kidnapping crumbled. Loeb, caught in too many lies, finally confessed to John Sbarbaro that they had hatched a scheme to kidnap and kill a kid from a rich family, hide the body, and demand a ransom. Loeb claimed Leopold had inflicted the fatal blows with a chisel. Confronted with his friend's admission, Leopold said Loeb was the murderer. The motive? Not the ransom, Leopold insisted. They already had plenty of money. They had pulled off a string of petty crimes—vandalism, a break-in, car theft—and the kidnapping and murder were supposed to be their criminal masterpiece, the perfect crime. They did it, Leopold said, for the "love of thrills." They killed for kicks.

Nineteen twenty-four was the year Vladimir Lenin died. Adolf Hitler, jailed for his role in the failed Beer Hall Putsch, had time on his hands and started to write *Mein Kampf.* Four intrepid US Army pilots in two planes recorded the first round-the-world flight, a marathon that took 175 days to complete. But for millions of newspaper readers that year, in Chicago and across North America, only one story mattered—the Franks murder soon claimed the title of "crime of the century."

Near daybreak on the last day of May, with the confessions recorded and witnessed, Crowe emerged from his offices to declare victory. Little more than a week after the boy's body was found, the state's attorney had cracked the case. Jubilation overcame his exhaustion. "The Franks murder mystery has been solved," he announced. "Nathan Leopold and Richard Loeb have completely and voluntarily confessed." He was confident he had the evidence needed to punish the pair to the full extent of the law. "I have a hanging case."

THE DEATH PENALTY BECAME the only issue. The Leopold and Loeb families hired Clarence Darrow, the most vocal opponent of capital punishment in America, to lead the defense. Crowe's belief that fear of the noose was enough to prevent people from killing each other was, to Darrow's mind, nonsense. Most murderers acted on impulse, lashing out at their victims in a sudden rage fueled by fear or jealousy; murder tended to be a crime of emotion, not calculation. He condemned the death penalty as a "barbarous practice" that did nothing to prevent crime or to protect society. The state "continues to kill its victims," he argued, "not so much to defend society against them—it could do that equally well by imprisonment—but to appease the mob's emotions of hatred and revenge."

Leopold and Loeb had not acted on impulse, though; they were cold, calculating killers. And since they had confessed, Darrow's options for saving them from the gallows were limited. The crime was so horrible that it suggested some form of mental illness, and their youth offered another compelling argument for a prison term instead of a death sentence. Darrow entered guilty pleas and threw his clients on the mercy of the court.

That summer, Crowe and Darrow squared off in a month-long sentencing hearing before Chief Justice John Caverly of the criminal court. The courtroom was packed every day, and the heat was stifling. The state's attorney, with all Chicago watching, produced more than eighty witnesses to describe every detail of the crime. Darrow's defense relied on the testimony of eminent psychiatrists who explored deep-rooted mental problems that might help to explain an inexplicable crime. Crowe accused the defense of trying to have things both ways—admitting guilt while pleading insanity—and produced experts of his own, who found no evidence of mental illness.

The closing arguments dragged on for days. Darrow, hulking and rumpled, his hound-dog jowls rippling with every word, accused the state's attorney of seeking vengeance, not justice. Crowe mustered his indignation and tore into Darrow's portrayal of the killers as "poor sons of millionaires . . . mere infants wandering around in dreamland."

They were "perverts"—lovers as well as friends—and Crowe accused them of sexually abusing Bobby Franks before killing him. One of their motives, he told the judge, was "a desire to satisfy unnatural lust."

"They are as much entitled to the sympathy and the mercy of this court as a couple of rattlesnakes flushed with venom, coiled, ready to strike," he thundered. "They are a disgrace to their honored families, and they are a menace to this community. The only useful thing that remains for them now is to go out of this life and to go out of it as quickly as possible."

Crowe detected another motive that proved the murder was a deliberate, rational act, not the product of mental illness. He seized on a reference to the Bayano swindle buried in one of the psychologists' reports. Loeb, driven by greed, had killed Franks for the ransom. "Money, money, money," he shouted, "not thrill, not excitement." Loeb had talked of becoming "a clever financial criminal" and had dreamed of pulling off "crimes similar to that of Koretz, who had put through a gigantic stock swindle." Crowe wondered aloud why Darrow was not blaming Koretz for the murder.

Judge Caverly announced his decision on September 10. The Franks murder was "a crime of singular atrocity," he acknowledged, "executed with every feature of callousness and cruelty." But he believed Leopold and Loeb were too young to hang. "Life imprisonment may not, at the moment, strike the public imagination as forcibly as would death by hanging," he explained, but "the prolonged suffering of years of confinement may well be the severer form of retribution and expiation." He sentenced them to ninety-nine years for kidnapping and life terms for murder and advised the parole authorities to reject any application for parole.

For Crowe, the sentence was a repudiation of his hang-'em-high brand of justice. Darrow, whose successful defense of Fred Lundin on corruption charges had humbled the state's attorney in 1922, had won another round.

• • •

WHILE LEOPOLD AND LOEB grabbed the headlines, lawyers and courts continued to pick away at the financial mess Leo had left behind. The bankruptcy referee Harry Parkin's investigation plodded along, earning brief mentions in the press. Leo, it was discovered, had been paying about $50,000 a year in interest on mortgages taken out on Arkansas land worth, at best, $25,000. His rice farms were as much an illusion as Bayano oil.

Parkin's preliminary findings pegged investors' losses at just shy of $1.5 million with another $2 million in claims to be assessed. The figures—millions of dollars less than some of the estimates coming from the state's attorney's office—seemed to confirm that many victims had refused to come forward. The dividends investors had earned before Leo's scams collapsed offset their losses and reduced the amount they could claim in bankruptcy court. By April 1924, Chicago Title and Trust had recovered about $500,000 in assets, including the $175,000 turned in by the Koretz family. A sale of some of the seized property—ten thousand books, the phonograph from the suite at the Drake, items of clothing that included red morocco slippers and a purple silk dressing gown—drew hundreds to a Loop auction house at the end of April. Crowds "mobbed the place all day," the *Daily Tribune* reported, looking for deals or a souvenir of the sensational Bayano swindle. "Everybody thinks he was a rich feller an' the stuff must be good," one bidder told the paper. The sale netted $7,000.

As Leo lived the high life in Nova Scotia, his wife struggled. Mae and the children had moved into a modest, five-room home on a quiet side street in Winnetka, a suburb north of Evanston. Mae did not return to teaching and instead found a job selling coal for Edinger and Sons and did clerical work—addressing and stuffing envelopes—at night. She learned to distinguish between grades of coal and their heat content, and her knowledge of the business was said to match that of "any other salesman in the city." There was some irony in the fact that the wife of a man who sold dreams of oil riches to wealthy Chicagoans had been reduced to selling coal to suburban housewives.

"That woman is a brick," said one family friend who lost thousands in the Bayano swindle. "I should think her courage would shame Leo—if anything can." Julius's wife, Blanche, was equally impressed: "She has been remarkable in her ability to stand blows."

Even with Mentor out of school and working, the family could not get by. Mae refused offers of financial help from Leo's brothers but accepted it from an unlikely quarter. Henry Klein, the man who fell hardest for her husband's lies, bought the Winnetka house for her. She refused to live rent-free, however, and paid a reduced rate, about seventy dollars a month. A long friendship between Mae and Klein's wife, Bertha, survived the humiliation and financial devastation Leo had wrought.

A scaled-down manhunt continued. After the discovery of Bobby Franks's body, Crowe and Sbarbaro were preoccupied with trying to send Leopold and Loeb to the gallows. But twice during 1924, the state's attorney almost dispatched men to Paris based on tips that Leo was there and spending money freely. An Evanston shop owner told her hometown paper she was certain she had seen him in a hotel lobby while she was vacationing in California. Investigators used Leo's illness to track his movements. Insulin, the new diabetes wonder drug, was expensive but easily within the reach of a man flush with cash. Leo was traced, Sbarbaro later claimed, to a sanatorium in Montreal, where he had sought treatment at some point before his arrival in Nova Scotia. If the patient was indeed Leo, he was long gone by the time word reached Chicago.

The master swindler, it seemed, was an accomplished escape artist as well. By the summer of 1924, more than six months after he walked out of the St. Regis Hotel, Leo's whereabouts remained "a matter of conjecture," noted the *Daily Tribune*. While rumors and reported sightings continued to trickle in, "not a single clew has resulted in any definite information regarding him."

Some Bayano victims took matters into their own hands, retaining private detectives to join in the search. Others took up a collection and approached Chicago Title and Trust with enough money to increase the reward for his arrest from $1,000 to $10,000. Henry Klein provided a personal guarantee to cover the full amount of the reward. The Chicago office of the United States Post Office, as the agency responsible for prosecuting charges of using the mail to defraud, issued a poster announcing the new reward. It featured Leo's photo and a sample of his handwriting and signature. A detailed and less-than-flattering description followed: Leo was forty-five, Jewish, five foot ten, 180 pounds, with a "distinct paunch" and "slightly stooped" shoulders, light brown hair "thin on top," gray-blue eyes, a round face, and a pasty complexion. The fugitive "cannot get along without glasses," had a scar or birthmark on the palm of his left hand, was a lawyer by profession, and spoke fluent German. "Suffers from headaches," the description continued, "and has a habit of removing glasses for a short time to obtain relief." The reward would stand for a year, until the first day of July 1925. Chicago Title and Trust was soon receiving several letters a day from people with tips or theories on Leo's new identity or where he was hiding. The poster was distributed throughout the United States and Canada. Copies may have made their way east to Nova Scotia.

A train rider who passed through hot, muggy Chicago that summer described it as "an infernal place of noise and fury and gasoline." The passenger was headed east and looking forward "with thrilling zest," as he put it—and as only a writer of adventure stories would put it—to spending the next few weeks trying to outmuscle the giant bluefin tuna.

The man's destination was the South Shore of Nova Scotia, the prime fishing grounds he had heard so much about from his contact at Abercrombie and Fitch, Laurie Mitchell. He was a famous author, and many of his fellow passengers would have recognized him from his picture in the newspapers or on the dust jackets of his books. His name was Zane Grey.

24

THE PARIAH

WHEN ZANE GREY reached Liverpool at the end of July, his boats and fishing gear were waiting for him. Mitchell had seen to that. He was grateful for the work—and even more grateful to be rid of Lou Keyte.

Mitchell was no longer in charge at Pinehurst; he had quit after a dispute over wages. Keyte enjoyed spending money "just to make a splurge," Mitchell noted with bitterness, but he could be stingy with his employees. "He didn't pay me all he promised and when I asked for the money he made things so unpleasant that I left." He was fed up, too, with his employer's temper and moodiness. He "was all right when he was well," Mitchell told W. B. McKay, a Pinehurst regular, but "when he was feeling badly he was finicky and nasty . . . he didn't have the breeding a gentleman would have."

Leo had changed. It was as if someone had kidnapped the genial boss Charles Kennedy and the Scott brothers were so delighted to work for, and replaced him with Ebenezer Scrooge. Elizabeth Mitchell, who had never liked the man, had urged her husband to quit and was pleased to give up her job as Pinehurst's housekeeper. The break, to McKay's mind, left bad feelings on both sides. From then on, Leo "always seemed suspicious of Mitchell," he recalled, "and I'm sure that in some way Mitchell had become convinced there was something wrong." Money may not have been the sole reason for the Mitchells' departure; later, a story emerged that they had caught Leo sending letters and expensive gifts to their sixteen-year-old daughter, Elizabeth, a student at a private school in Halifax.

Richard Abbott, like the Mitchells, saw Leo's dark side and came to regret his decision to join the staff at Pinehurst. He was a seventeen-year-old stock boy at a Liverpool grocery store where Leo was a regular customer. One day, when a man came into the store to solicit donations for a local baseball team, Leo obliged to the tune of $200. Abbott could scarcely believe his eyes. "I figured if this man could write out a $200 cheque just like that, then he would be able to pay a man real well for working for him." Abbott took him aside, asked for a job, and was hired on the spot. They never discussed salary, but Abbott expected a fat paycheck—"maybe even as much as $50 a week."

Once at Pinehurst, though, he soon wished he were back stocking shelves. His new boss was prone to "violent headaches" that made him "hateful"; when stricken, he would flee to his bedroom and lock himself inside. And there was the backbreaking work: Abbott rose at five each morning to light the fire in a steam engine that pumped lake water to the lodge. He chopped firewood and carried it to the fireplaces—all seventeen of them. Then he had to scramble to clean up, shave, and put on a "monkey suit" to serve the evening meal. "I worked my backside off," Abbott grumbled, for what turned out to be just four dollars a week.

Leo was obsessed with loyalty and secrecy. There was the no-photograph rule, the reluctance to sign his name, and the vague references to his past, to his health, to his writing. He seemed to fear someone might spy on him, and on one occasion, when he was staying at a hotel in Halifax, he made a frantic long-distance call to the lodge. He thought he had left a trunk in his bedroom unlocked, and he was desperate to know whether the maid had entered the room in his absence. The trunk was locked, but upon his return, he fired the woman anyway, saying she was "too big-eyed." The trunk may have contained something that would reveal his true identity, or perhaps he was becoming paranoid. A fugitive who feared exposure could not afford to take chances.

Zane Grey's arrival put Leo in a far more uncomfortable position. He had led his Nova Scotia friends to believe he had "practically made Zane Grey," taking credit for bringing his work to the attention of New York publishers. He had talked of entertaining him at Pinehurst during his stay in Nova Scotia, of heading to sea aboard *Tuna II* to join the author's quest for the giant fish. And Grey was a key figure in a plan that Leo—ever the promoter—was touting to develop a high-end Nova Scotia resort. The idea was to transform Pinehurst from a private retreat into an exclusive club where wealthy sportsmen could hunt, fish, and play golf on the championship course he would build on the property.

"I'll show you how we can make some easy money," he had said when he broached the idea to Mitchell. "We will incorporate and sell stock for a million. . . . I will get wealthy New Yorkers if you can interest the Nova Scotians and Newfoundlanders." That's where the famous writer and sportsman came in. "I planned to make Zane Grey . . . one of the honorary directors of the corporation," Leo explained later, using Grey's star power to attract investors.

Now that Leo was on the outs with Grey's host and guide, the chances of a visit—let alone an invitation to go fishing or to lend his name to a resort-investment scheme—had evaporated. To cover his tracks, he concocted a story about a falling-out with Grey. He had "ripped" into the author "pretty hard" in a recent book review, he explained to W. B. McKay, and Grey was "raising hell about it" and "causing a lot of trouble."

Grey was on the water with Mitchell and other fishing companions by the first day of August. He landed a 684-pounder that came tantalizingly close to Mitchell's record catch. On August 22 he battled another giant for more than three hours before bringing it alongside. It was more than eight and a half feet long and tipped the scales at 758 pounds, a new record. The fish was hoisted aloft on a Liverpool dock so that Grey could pose for photographs with his prize. "If it were possible for a man to fall in love with a fish," he declared, "that was what happened to me."

One Sunday in mid-August, when it was too foggy and rainy to fish, Grey drove from Liverpool to Annapolis Royal to inspect a three-masted schooner he was thinking of buying. He was already planning his next fishing expedition, to the Galápagos Islands, and needed a large seaworthy craft to take through the Panama Canal. Grey ultimately bought the vessel, renamed it *Fisherman,* and had it moved to a shipyard in Lunenburg, where Mitchell oversaw a major refit that included building a main cabin large enough to display both of Grey's newly caught tuna. The drive to and from Annapolis Royal took Grey past the driveway leading to Pinehurst Lodge, and his party appears to have stayed overnight at a Caledonia hotel, but there is no record of a visit with the area's best-known man of letters. Leo, for his part, made no effort to seek out Grey before the author returned to the States in early September. The whole time the author was in the Liverpool area, some residents noted, Lou Keyte remained hunkered down at Pinehurst.

And there were growing suspicions about his claims to be a writer and critic, let alone his claim to have "made" Zane Grey. Leo had fooled Temple Scott, but he proved no match for Dr. John D. Logan, a lecturer on Canadian literature at Nova Scotia's Acadia University and one of Canada's leading literary critics. Logan sought out Leo after hearing stories about his collection of rare books and called on him at Pinehurst, hoping to add to his own library of early American humor. The visit was a waste of time. "He didn't know a good book from a bale of hay," Logan later scoffed. "I found right away he was only bluffing. I mentioned title after title that every book collector should know and he was not familiar with any of them." Another visitor thought the books scattered about at Pinehurst were meant only for show; many had never been opened, and for every work of Robert Louis Stevenson and Edgar Allan Poe, there were plenty of "cheap mystery and detective stories."

The goodwill Leo had earned when he arrived in Queens County—from the dances and dinners he hosted, the donations to community groups, and the money he pumped into the local economy—was fading. His reputation for being a lavish entertainer with a well-stocked bar did not sit well with some of his neighbors. The Baptist Church, a major force in the area, had condemned drunkenness and rowdiness during the gold-rush days and had objected to miners working on Sundays. The tourism industry of the new century brought new fears. The minister of the Caledonia Baptist Church warned in 1913 that the American sportsmen flocking to the area brought with them ideas and influences that "have a tendency to demoralize these communities."

Some thought Lou Keyte posed a new threat to community morals. His housewarming party was "the talk of the district" for weeks, as one newspaper noted, and not all the talk was positive. Wives whose husbands were frequent visitors to Pinehurst were said to be considering lodging a complaint with local Prohibition agents. Tongues wagged about the young women he was inviting to Pinehurst. The era of the liberated flapper had dawned in the big cities, but not in rural Nova Scotia. Local families, by one account, "forbade their daughters attending his parties and entertainments." Neighbors "soon had no use for him," Mitchell later claimed, "because of the number of young girls who went to his house at night." Mitchell had lived at Pinehurst long enough to know who visited the lodge—and if the rumor about Leo's infatuation with his daughter was true, he had ample proof of his former boss's eye for young girls.

Leo's wealth and generosity had won him a few loyal friends, but it could not buy him approval. His behavior was too brash, his lifestyle too racy. People began to decline invitations to Pinehurst and offered few in return. Social life in Caledonia was a community and a family affair—a succession of church events, sewing circles, citizens' band concerts, and drama club plays. Leo's no-expense-spared, booze-fueled, orchestra-serenaded Pinehurst parties would have been a hit back in Chicago. Here, they were as out of place as the derby on his head.

As summer turned to fall, Leo no longer seemed to care what people in Queens County thought of him. He was spending most of his weekends away from Pinehurst, in Nova Scotia's largest city.

THE WOMANIZER

LEO CALLED HER Topsy, and she was young enough to be his daughter. Mabelle Gene Banks was twenty-five, a petite brunette with bobbed hair and a broad smile. They were often seen together in Halifax at restaurants, theaters, and dance halls or poking through shops and strolling along the downtown streets. He showered her with presents, including, it was said, a pearl necklace and clothes from Jensen and Mills, one of the city's most exclusive stores. When he offered to buy her anything she wanted as they browsed in another store, she chose a paisley shawl with a $100 price tag. That was tip money to Leo.

Banks was "pretty and slim," Thomas Raddall recalled, "and avid for a good time." Her father, George Banks, was editor of Caledonia's newspaper, the *Gold Hunter*. Leo became a frequent visitor to the Banks home, and when others in the small community were shunning him or locking up their daughters, Banks and his wife were inviting him to dinner and encouraging the relationship. George Banks, like Leo, was an outsider. He had been born in New Jersey, and his father had moved the family to Caledonia in 1888, at the height of the gold rush, to establish the paper. Banks inherited the business and had little patience for his complacent and conservative neighbors. "Stop knocking, you pessimists and join the procession for a bigger, better and brighter Caledonia," he railed in one editorial. "The men and women who are lifting the world upward and onward are those who encourage

*The Halifax Hotel, Lou Keyte's home-away-from-home
in the Nova Scotia capital.*

and boost." Leo, who was doing his bit to boost the local economy, would have struck Banks as the kind of person the community needed. He would also be a good catch. Banks and his wife, Raddall believed, were "flattered with the notion" of Mabelle's "marrying a millionaire," and "there was talk of a honeymoon in the West Indies, where they would spend the winter."

Leo often climbed into his flashy Franklin for the hours-long, hundred-mile drive from Pinehurst to Halifax on twisting, graveled roads. George Banks was usually at the wheel and did double duty as chaperone if his daughter was along for the trip. Leo had visited the provincial capital soon after his arrival and usually stayed at the Halifax Hotel, a venerable establishment with a marble-tiled lobby, cherry woodwork, a rooftop promenade, and a dining room big enough to double as a ballroom. Soon he was almost as well known at the hotel and around the city as he was in Queens County. When Temple Scott took time off from managing the New York bookstore and visited Pinehurst that August, Leo whisked him off to Halifax. They arrived in time to see the battleship HMS *Hood,* the largest warship afloat, steam into the harbor to mark the 175th anniversary of the city's founding.

Halifax's population stood at less than sixty thousand in the 1920s—hardly a decent-size suburb by Chicago standards. Cobblestone streets and refined Georgian architecture gave the city an Old World feel. "Visitors from England," reported Phyllis Blakeley, a local historian, "commented on the striking similarity of Halifax in appearance and social life to the small garrison towns in England." And it was a thoroughly British town, where people still played cricket, paused for afternoon tea, and remembered the not-too-distant days when redcoats paraded through the streets, and dashing officers—including the occasional royal prince—were feted at dinners and balls. Nova Scotia had been a province of Canada for almost sixty years but remained, in spirit and in outlook, a cast-off fragment of the British Empire.

Leo's favorite Halifax hotel turned its four-floor, shingle-clad face to the street. It was no St. Regis, but it was the best Leo could do in his Canadian refuge. It stood on Hollis Street in the heart of the city, midway up a checkerboard of streets that clung to a steep slope rising from the waterfront wharves to a hilltop citadel. Leo entertained as often and as flamboyantly in Halifax as he did at Pinehurst. He took guests to the Hollis Sea Grill, dispensing charm and picking up tabs. Waiters at one tearoom knew him only as the "foreign Johnny with pots of money." He frequented the Green Lantern, considered the city's best restaurant, which offered home-cooked fare and an orchestra that played dance music every evening. It was there that Leo met the waitress who lived with him at Pinehurst before Frances White's arrival.

Leo hobnobbed with the city's elite at the prestigious Royal Nova Scotia Yacht Squadron. Almost a century old, the club had earned the right to call itself "royal" through the good graces of King Edward VII, an avid yachtsman who visited Halifax as Prince of Wales in 1860. The clubhouse stood at the tip of a stone breakwater south of the city center, affording members quick access to the open water at the harbor's mouth and the ocean beyond. It was a genteel place, where meals were served on china bearing the club crest, and boatmen clad in blue sweaters and white cotton trousers ferried crews to and from their vessels.

Members—more than three hundred of Halifax's leading businessmen and professionals—were elected, and the management committee had endorsed Lou Keyte's candidacy at its April meeting. Leo joined ten other members who preferred powerboats to sailing craft, and he cruised to the city from Liverpool once or twice that summer with a boatload of guests. On one trip, *Tuna II* slipped into the Northwest Arm, a three-mile-long inlet lined with rowing and canoe clubs and some of the city's poshest estates. Leo, according to one account, picked the grandest mansion of all—Thornvale, the ivy-draped home of William Webster, who made his fortune selling china—and asked permission to use the wharf. Webster welcomed his visitor and offered one of his custom-made cigars; Leo, displaying his usual chutzpah, declined.

"No," he replied, "you take one of mine, they are better. You can't get this kind down here."

The squadron hosted dances, teas, dinners, and picnics during the year, and more were added in 1924 as part of Halifax's anniversary celebrations. This was Leo's element, and he was said to have attended his share of social events with guests in tow. At one dinner-dance, sometime in October, he was introduced to Joseph Connolly, the newest member of a leading Halifax law firm.

"I noticed this very distinguished looking gentleman, and presently I was presented to him," Connolly recalled. "He was delightful." They would soon meet again.

MABELLE BANKS—TOPSY—WAS NOT THE only woman in Leo's new life. Gossip linked him to a succession of Halifax women "of all classes and standing in society"—from the Green Lantern waitress to store clerks, from maids to wealthy widows. What people found most surprising was the way he flaunted Banks and his other female admirers, escorting them around town as if he were oblivious to what others might say or think. Even Raddall, who was well aware of his friend's fondness for women and parties, thought he was living "at a furious pace . . . passing from one woman to another like a humming-bird in a flower bed."

Leo's over-the-top style and his roving eye seemed to repel as many people as they attracted, just as they had in Queens County, and the fact that he was an American—and a vulgar, flashy one at that—was enough to keep his name off guest lists. Many of Halifax's leading families were descendants of Americans who had remained loyal to Britain during the revolution; bitterness toward the upstart Yankees had been handed down through the generations, like a gene. It was "as if the American Revolution had happened yesterday," noted Charles Ritchie, a future diplomat who grew up in Halifax. "All our friends and relations are very much against the Americans." An American who favored the company of young women? That was worse.

There was one more thing about Leo that, had it been known, would have made his social circle that much smaller. No one in Nova Scotia seemed to suspect he was Jewish. Canada's Jewish community was small and scattered in the 1920s—there were almost twice as many Jews in Chicago as in the entire country—and faced discrimination and exclusion. There were fewer than six hundred in Halifax in the early 1920s and barely two thousand in all of Nova Scotia. The province's banks and many companies would not hire them, a Jewish businessman recalled of those days, and they were shut out of many

Halifax clubs, among them the yacht club that welcomed Lou Keyte as a member.

PINEHURST HAD BEEN BUILT as a moose-hunting lodge, and when the season opened on the first day of October, local guides insisted Leo should try to bag a trophy. Raddall soon heard all about the expedition.

He turned up, in Raddall's retelling of the story, dressed "as if he were going for a stroll down Madison Avenue." During the canoe trip to the hunting grounds, he huddled in a fur coat and buried his nose in a book of poetry, still playing the role of a man of letters. When a guide made moose calls, using a cone-shaped birch bark horn to mimic the bellows of a female seeking a mate, a large bull lumbered into view.

"There he is!" one of the guides shouted. "There he is, Mister Keet!"

Leo looked up.

"Ah! So that's a moose, eh? Well, well."

"There's the rifle, sir. Shoot! Shoot!"

Leo had already turned his attention back to his poems.

"Hell, I don't want to kill the damned thing. Let him go."

GEORGE BANKS POINTED THE sleek nose of Leo's Franklin in the direction of Halifax. It was November 21, a Friday, and he had volunteered to drive Leo and his daughter, Mabelle, into the city. The sky was overcast as they left Pinehurst, and a recent cold snap must have made Leo wish he had shelled out a few extra dollars for a closed car. "Jack Frost made his appearance this week in real shape," Banks commiserated with his readers in that day's edition of the *Gold Hunter*.

Weekend getaways to the city had become part of Leo's routine, and the following afternoon, he took Mabelle shopping. She picked out two dresses, and Leo dropped by the Robert Stanford Limited tailor shop to pick up clothes he had left for repair and pressing and to order an expensive new suit—the material alone cost fifty dollars. Leo seemed to be everywhere that day. He was spotted at the yacht

squadron, with a bevy of young women at the Hollis Sea Grill, dining at the Green Lantern. Later he hit the floor of a popular dance
hall. The Halifax papers routinely published lists of hotel guests, and
that day's edition of the *Acadian Recorder* noted that "Lou Keyte,
Pinehurst" was in town and staying, as usual, at the Halifax Hotel.
This tidbit would have been of particular interest to two men who
checked in to the Carleton, a couple of blocks away, that night. They
had rushed east by train from a major city in the American Midwest.
To make sure no one suspected who they were and why they were in
town, they signed the register as visitors from Montreal.

On Sunday, Leo attended church in the morning with Harriet
Schon, the widow of a wealthy merchant. Why he was escorting her
to Sunday services was never explained. His church-attendance record
back in Queens County was described as somewhere between "seldom" and "never," which was not surprising given his Jewish heritage
and the local backlash against his lifestyle. Not so in Halifax. Despite
the gossip swirling around him in the city, he was said to have been
invited to speak at an upcoming church service. The subject? Success.

Sunday evening, Leo entertained Mabelle and other guests in the
dining room of the Halifax Hotel. He donned a brown suit for the occasion, matched with a light green vest and gray suede-topped shoes.
His beard, some of his friends may have noted, had been lightened to
an auburn shade. Outside, the cobblestones of Hollis Street were still
wet from the day's showers. The sky was dark and brooding. Gusts
of wind rattled windows as they ratcheted up to gale force, ahead of
an approaching storm. The Franklin was parked out front, squeezed
between the curb and the trolleys that clattered past.

About half past eight, Leo retreated to his room with Mabelle.
They had a little time to spare before their next engagement, a birthday party at a home in the city's fashionable South End. They had
been inside only a matter of minutes when someone knocked on the
door.

Act 3

The front page of the Halifax Morning Chronicle,
November 24, 1924.

THE TRAP

Francis Hiltz, the owner of Robert Stanford Limited, Halifax's best tailor shop, was repairing the lining of a suit jacket for a customer, Lou Keyte, when he noticed the maker's label: "Henry Heppner and Co.," it read, "Chicago, Illinois." The name of the jacket's owner was on the label as well, only the name was not Lou Keyte—it was Leo Koretz.

Hiltz was puzzled. Why was a wealthy man wearing someone else's clothes? And the name, Koretz, sounded familiar. Someone connected to the Leopold and Loeb case, perhaps? The trial had been big news in the Halifax papers, and Hiltz wondered whether that was where he had seen the name. Exposure of the Bayano swindle eleven months earlier had received little coverage in the Halifax press—only an article or two—but the Franks murder was fresh in Hiltz's mind.

Keyte had opened an account with Stanford's and given the Bank of Nova Scotia as a reference. Hiltz figured someone at the bank could clear up the mystery. He called on Horace Flemming, the longtime manager of the Halifax branch and secretary to the bank's board of directors. Since Keyte did his business at the branch in Liverpool, Flemming knew little of his financial affairs. Hiltz described how he had found the tailor's label and the name Leo Koretz and mentioned his suspicion of a connection to the Leopold-Loeb case. The name meant nothing to Flemming. A wealthy man who wore secondhand clothing, or went by two names? Flemming, who had the poker face of someone accustomed to being discreet, said he would make a few inquiries.

He began with William H. Davies, manager of the Bank of Nova Scotia's Chicago branch. Since there seemed to be no urgency in clearing up the confusion, Flemming sent a letter to the bank's address in the Loop, 105 West Monroe Street. It was little more than a block away from the former law office of a swindler who had gone missing almost a year earlier. Could Davies provide any information about a man named Lou Keyte? Flemming asked. Or a Leo Koretz?

Davies received the letter at the end of October. He immediately contacted the bank's Chicago lawyer, Jacob Newman. Newman, in turn, notified Abel Davis, vice president of Chicago Title and Trust, the bankruptcy receivers. "You can imagine," Davis would later reveal, "the excitement that letter caused."

After almost a year of rumors, dubious tips, and false sightings, was it possible Leo had been found? The three men devised a plan to find out more before they alerted the authorities.

Davies replied to Flemming by telegram, with a synopsis of the swindle and Leo's disappearance. To prevent the news from being leaked to the press, he wrote the message in a code the bank had developed to protect confidential information. He also mailed Flemming a copy of the wanted poster, which included Leo's signature, a sample of his handwriting, and his photograph and description. Newman and Davis, meanwhile, boned up on Canada's extradition laws.

Flemming responded on November 18, in code. The photograph and description "absolutely" matched Keyte, he reported. Leo, who was "now wearing a full beard," he added, "was in Halifax last week." On November 20, a Thursday, Robert Crowe was notified.

"When we were absolutely sure of everything—when we had Koretz positively identified and his movements under observation," Abel Davis said, "we called upon State's Attorney Crowe to make the arrest."

"WHAT'S WANTED?" LEO CALLED out, after hearing the knock on the door.

As he turned the knob, two men burst into the hotel room.

"You are wanted—in Chicago," one said as the other seized Leo by the wrists and clapped on a set of handcuffs. The square-jawed man who had spoken was Rainard Scriven, deputy sheriff for Halifax County. The shorter man with the triangle mustache, Malcolm Mitchell, the one working the cuffs, was a former police officer now in charge of the county jail.

Leo knew who they were and why they had come. He had been expecting them for a long time.

"Sit down," Scriven ordered, needlessly. Leo's legs buckled as he sank into a chair.

"All right, boys, you don't have to worry with me," he said at last. "I'll go quietly. I'll give you no trouble."

They showed him the wanted poster. He admitted he was Leo Koretz. They produced an extradition warrant, based on one of Crowe's indictments, which accused him of defrauding $38,400 from his former law-office tenant, Samuel J. Richman.

A search of his pockets produced $450 in cash. Then they turned their attention to Banks. Who was she? By one account, she gave them a false name.

"For God's sake," Leo pleaded, "don't get her name into this." After a few more questions, she was allowed to leave.

Scriven and Mitchell marched their prisoner a few blocks up the hill to the county jail. He was taken to a room where assistant state's attorneys John Sbarbaro and William McSwiggin—the men who had arrived from Chicago via Montreal the night before—were waiting to interview him.

Leo was surprisingly upbeat. Sbarbaro later offered the press a brief summary of their discussion. "He was very calm about it all," he told one Chicago paper. "As he talked to us about his finances, he merely expressed surprise that he had not been caught sooner." He

*Leo outside the Halifax County Jail the morning after his capture
with Malcolm Mitchell, one of the men who arrested him.*

also dropped a bombshell: he was eager to return to Chicago to face
charges, he said, and would not fight extradition.

At about eleven that night, Sbarbaro and McSwiggin returned to
their rooms to notify Crowe and spread the news of the arrest. A reporter for Halifax's *Morning Chronicle* tracked them down that night
and left with a headline-worthy quote: they had captured "the greatest

confidence man in the history of the United States." Leo settled in for his first night behind bars.

CHICAGOANS AWOKE ON MONDAY, November 24, to below-freezing temperatures—their first taste of winter—and a banner head-line about a half-forgotten financial scam.

ARREST KORETZ IN CANADA, screamed the front page of the *Daily Tribune,* exulting in a rare scoop of its morning rival, the *Herald and Examiner.* That day's *New York Times* carried the story, and the news was all over Chicago's evening papers. Hearst's *American* led the charge with an avalanche of stories and photographs and stressed that Leo had been arrested "with a beautiful woman as his compan-ion." Articles on Koretz's capture and the effort to bring him back to Chicago would elbow their way onto the front pages all week, upstaging the death of the opera legend Giacomo Puccini as well as Charlie Chaplin's marriage to his eighteen-year-old leading lady, Lita Grey.

The arrest made headlines across America and around the world. In Canada, Leo was front-page news from Wolfville, Nova Scotia, to the Rocky Mountain community of Blairmore, Alberta. Overseas, newspaper junkies in Paris were able to tell their friends about the cap-ture of a swindler from faraway Chicago. Singapore's English-language newspaper, the *Straits Times,* ran a long piece on America's "newest criminal sensation" and considered Leo "one of the outstanding ex-amples of the type of swindler who exploits the get-rich-quick pas-sions of his friends and acquaintances." News of Leo's exploits and his downfall even reached readers in Brisbane, Australia, and in the town of Burnie, at the northern tip of Tasmania.

In Chicago, a reporter traced Mae to her new address in Win-netka. She was not home, but a peek through the windows confirmed she had salvaged some of the expensive furnishings—mahogany pieces and Oriental rugs—from her former home. Leo's abandoned wife, the *Daily News* sniffed, was "far from destitute." Once again her photo was splashed across the papers. She was tracked down at Mercy

Hospital, where Mentor, now seventeen, was recovering from a hernia operation.

"The children and I want only to fade out of the scene—we want to be just nobody," she told a reporter as she sat at Mentor's bedside. "You can't imagine how hard it is on them." The reporter suggested Leo might plead guilty and spare them the spectacle of a lengthy trial. "I hope so," she said.

So did his immediate family and his wide circle of in-laws and cousins. "The family had hoped that Leo would kill himself, or that he would die," one unnamed relative said coldly, "to avoid the disgrace of his capture." The only question in their minds was how soon Mae would file for divorce. "It doesn't matter what Leo had done," the relative added. "Mae would have forgiven him if he had not been untrue to her. That's the thing that has rankled." It had been bad enough when he was linked to Auerbach, the South Side "love nest," the globe-trotting Jessie Taggart, and all the rest; every day the papers were exposing tales of his new round of womanizing in Nova Scotia. He had picked up where he left off in Chicago.

The immediate concern was finding a way to break the news to Leo's mother. Leo had always been her favorite, but she had told a friend, only a few days earlier, "I pray every night that Leo will not be found while I still live." Family members avoided mentioning his name in her presence.

SOME BAYANO VICTIMS WERE glad to hear he was in custody, but sorry to be reminded of their folly. "It's been a pleasant day until now. Why spoil my dinner by reminding me of Koretz?" Arthur Mayer said when the *Daily Tribune* phoned. "I'll have to admit that I am not crying because he was caught."

"Me one of his investors?" exclaimed Milton Mandel, Leo's former doctor. "I was not. I was one of his boobs. I'm glad he's caught."

Tribune reporters tried to contact, in all, fifty victims for comment. Ten were out of town on business, and the reporters discovered that several of those who had lost heavily were wintering in California or

Florida. There will be "no hunger ravaged faces of starving dupes" to greet Leo upon his return, the paper concluded, and "none of them is in want as the result of Mr. Koretz's fleecing."

Even if few Bayano victims were starving, Chicago Title and Trust was determined to recover as much money as possible to reduce their losses. The receivers sent three lawyers to Halifax to take custody of Leo's assets in Nova Scotia. They found a cache of stocks and bonds in a safe-deposit box in a Liverpool bank. Pinehurst and its furnishings, thanks to Leo's extensive renovations and shopping sprees, were worth an estimated $35,000. Cars, cash, the motorboat, and other assets added several thousand dollars to the tally. In New York, the Neighborhood Book Shop was valued at $5,000, and Leo revealed he had another $48,000 stashed in one of the city's banks.

The taxman, however, was threatening to take away every penny recovered. Coincidentally, a few weeks before the arrest, the US government had filed a claim for $753,067—almost $10 million in today's dollars—in unpaid income tax for 1921, 1922, and 1923, the years the Bayano swindle was in full swing. It would take precedence over all other claims and threatened to leave nothing for Bayano investors. The wife of one victim, Grace Katz, was so incensed that she fired off a blunt letter to US Attorney General Harlan F. Stone asking the government to withdraw the claim so that the money recovered could be returned "to the *people from whom it was stolen*." Chicago Title and Trust vowed to oppose the claim on the creditors' behalf, arguing that money obtained illegally was not taxable.

At the New York bookshop, Temple Scott took the news of his boss's real identity in stride. "May be the joke's on me. We'll see," he told a reporter. "Possession is nine points of the law, they tell me," he added, and the store remained in his possession, "at least until the Chicago authorities indicate what they intend to do." But Zane Grey saw nothing amusing about being linked to Leo's alter ego, Lou Keyte. The *Herald and Examiner* published his photo and reported Leo's boasts about entertaining the author at Pinehurst. "Mr. Grey," it reported, "was very much perturbed by this unsought publicity."

In Nova Scotia, reaction to Lou Keyte's true identity ranged from disbelief to bemusement. The *Morning Chronicle* marveled at how easily he had masqueraded "as a respectable person" and how he had used his wealth "to flutter various sensitive hearts and silly minds." Liverpool, too, was said to have its share of people "who could have been knocked down with the proverbial straw." Leo had "flashed across the skyline of the social life of Queens" like a meteor, the *Liverpool Advance* acknowledged, and "no one suspected that he was what after events proved him to be."

People who knew or had befriended the fictional Lou Keyte scrambled to distance themselves from the real-life con man. "The few Halifax people who knew him say that their acquaintance was very casual," the *Morning Chronicle* noted in a feeble attempt to rewrite history. "They always thought there was something 'fishy' about him." Leo "was never received with open arms by the best people of the town," insisted a dispatch out of Liverpool.

For George Banks, the news was "a bolt from the blue." With the Franklin impounded to cover Leo's hotel bills, Banks and his daughter caught a train back to Caledonia to face choruses of "I told you so's" from their less trusting friends. Thomas Raddall was astonished to discover his friend the "jolly millionaire" was a notorious con man. He also remembered how Leo had talked, at the Pinehurst housewarming party, of making his fortune speculating in rice farms and "down on the Bayano River" in Panama. Most of what Leo told him that night, he realized, had been true.

The question on many minds was why a fugitive from justice would make such a spectacle of himself. Had Leo chosen to live a quiet life instead of spending freely and living large, noted a writer for the *Morning Chronicle,* his real identity might never have been discovered.

THE GANG WAR

Robert Crowe broke the news to the Chicago press and issued a statement taking credit for nabbing the elusive swindler. The *Daily Tribune* ran his photograph on page 1 and described how "Crowe's men" had tracked Leo to the east coast of Canada. It was, a prominent attorney told the paper, "a notable achievement for law enforcement in Chicago." The *Evening American* was in booster mode as well, attributing the capture "to the fact that State's Attorney Crowe would not permit himself to 'pass up' any kind of clue." The *Daily News,* however, gave credit where credit was due, to the detective work of Chicago Title and Trust's Abel Davis and his legal team. The state's attorney, the paper pointed out, "merely had to make the arrest."

In the dying days of 1924, Crowe needed a "notable achievement" and good-news headlines. His bid to send Leopold and Loeb to the gallows had been a spectacular failure. He had been elected only weeks earlier to a second term as state's attorney but faced a sudden surge in gangland violence.

Chicago was caught in the crossfire as gangs battled for control of bootlegging, gambling, and prostitution, and the deadly war was heating up. Al Capone had emerged from the shadow of his former boss, Johnny Torrio, and had seized control of suburban Cicero. Delivery trucks loaded with illegal beer were routinely hijacked. Crooks were killing other crooks in the speakeasies and on the streets. Less than two weeks before Leo's capture, a major underworld player, Dion O'Banion—"Chicago's arch-criminal," in the opinion of Police Chief Morgan Collins, and suspected of committing or ordering at least twenty-five murders—had been shot to death in his North Side flower shop. The prime suspects were O'Banion's bitter gangland enemies, Torrio and Capone, and their Sicilian allies, the Genna brothers. The day Leo was arrested in Halifax, the boxer-turned-saloon-operator Eddie Tancl was gunned down in his Cicero bar for refusing to buy beer from one of the gangs jockeying for control of his part of town.

Guns and gangs and revolving-door justice seemed woven into the fabric of life in wicked, brawling Chicago: "They tell me you are crooked," Carl Sandburg wrote in "Chicago," his ode to the city, "and I answer: Yes, it is true I have seen the gunman kill and go free to kill again."

Shooting victims who survived attacks refused to cooperate; witnesses dropped out of sight or were too scared to testify; gangsters thumbed their noses at the law and got on with the business of selling vice and shooting rivals. Gangs and guns had transformed the Wicked City into Murder City, and the state's attorney and the police seemed powerless to stop the bloodshed. Chicagoans fought back. Leading businessmen and citizens formed a watchdog group, the Chicago Crime Commission, and demanded better cooperation among law enforcement agencies. The *Daily News* issued an ultimatum: "Either the gunman or the decent citizen is going to run Chicago."

There seemed to be little difference between law enforcers and lawbreakers. Police officers took bribes to tip off the targets of impending raids or arrests. When charges were filed, delays and outright corruption prevented many from ever being aired in a courtroom. In 1923 alone, Crowe's staff withdrew or plea-bargained an astounding twenty-four thousand felony charges and sent fewer than two thousand offenders to prison. There were allegations of payoffs to fix cases. US District Attorney Edwin Olson, Chicago's top federal prosecutor and one of Crowe's Republican rivals, made headlines around the time of Leo's arrest by alleging that bribery was as much a fixture in Cook County's courts as the daily ritual of calling the first case.

In one courtroom, it was claimed, a system had been worked out: if a bailiff stationed in a back room knocked on the wall when a defendant's case was called, it was a signal to the prosecutor and judge that payment had been received and charges should be withdrawn or dismissed. So many judges were turning up at the funerals of slain gang leaders—including O'Banion's send-off, which drew twenty thousand mourners and was described as "the gaudiest of all gangland's burials"—that in late November a senior jurist made a public plea for them to stop. "Familiarity between judges and gangsters," he warned, "has lowered the courts and the law in the eyes of the public."

There were disturbing links, too, between the gangs and the state's attorney's office. O'Banion had helped to deliver two crucial North Side wards to Republican candidates, including Crowe, in the November 1924 elections. Not long before his death, he had led his thugs on an Election Day tour of polling stations, buying drinks for the converted and threatening those inclined to vote for the Democrats. "We're going to have a Republican victory celebration tonight," he declared in one saloon. "Anybody who votes Democratic ain't going to be there," he added menacingly, "or anywhere else."

When old age or a bullet ended the life of a prominent underworld figure, the funeral home operated by John Sbarbaro's family usually handled the arrangements—and, again, O'Banion's funeral had been no exception. One chronicler of crime in Chicago called it "a gangland favorite," and Sbarbaro personally barred reporters and photographers from the chapel during services for one prominent gangster. Only in 1920s Chicago could a public official prosecute criminals at his day job and in his spare time prepare the dead ones to face their final judgment. William McSwiggin, who had accompanied Sbarbaro to Halifax to catch Leo, was no better at hiding his underworld connections. He was a police sergeant's son but hung around with a group of boyhood pals that included members of the O'Donnell gang, West Side beer runners who would soon be at war with Capone.

The press demanded action. "The gunmen merely take advantage of official weakness and widespread corruption," the *Daily News* chided. The *Evening Post* said it was time for Crowe and the police to "teach the masters of crime that the law is not to be bought or sold, cajoled or threatened." When Crowe was formally sworn in for his second term, he dispensed with the usual ceremonies and floral tributes. The *Herald and Examiner* thought it the prudent thing to do. "With the community aroused over gangster murders, gambling, bootlegging and other crimes in Cook County, a celebration of Mr. Crowe's continuance in office might be misunderstood," an editorial writer remarked. "The public might not appreciate clearly who was doing the celebrating."

The state's attorney got the blunt message. Within hours of taking credit for Leo's capture, he opened a grand jury investigation into the Tancl shooting and a possible link to O'Banion's murder. The following day, detectives under his command and squads of city police raided illegal bars and gambling dens around the city, including Capone's flagship operation, the Four Deuces saloon. It was touted in the papers as "the biggest smash at the forces of gangland in the history of Cook County," and Crowe ordered the officers "to bring in every gangster, gunman, beer runner, gambler and vice lord they could find."

Leo's capture could not have come at a better time for Crowe. Prosecuting a swindler would be far easier than taking on Capone and his fellow mobsters. Leo's extradition from Canada and his trial on fraud charges would give the legmen, sob sisters, and rewrite men a juicy story to keep them busy. Headlines and editorials about a master con man and his gullible investors would divert attention, for a while at least, from the surge in gang violence and allegations of corruption in Cook County's justice system. It was the kind of high-profile case that would help Crowe restore his tarnished reputation as a crime fighter. All he had to do was get Leo Koretz back to Chicago.

28

THE PRISONER

LEO STOOD WITH his hands in his pockets, looking relaxed and slightly bemused. It was Monday, November 24—the morning after his capture—and the man making headlines around the world posed for news photographers in front of the Halifax County Jail. He had exchanged the brown suit he was wearing when arrested for a new outfit: green suit, white vest, polka-dot bow tie, topped with a derby. He was the "last word in style," a reporter noted, except for the trousers, which had lost their razor-sharp crease. Malcolm Mitchell, the jailer, stood beside him, holding his pipe at his side and striking a dignified pose.

Once Leo was back inside, a barber was summoned. The beard, Leo said, had served its purpose and he wanted a shave. "I want to go back to Chicago clean—like I left there." His face emerged, pale and glistening, for the first time in almost a year.

"Feels odd. Do I look any better?" he joked, rubbing his cheeks. "Well, now my troubles are just starting. I will have to shave all over again." Whether he looked better was debatable; the ravages of diabetes and a year of being the life of the party had left his face thinner and jowly. His troubles, without a doubt, were just starting.

He was taken next door to the courthouse at eleven in the morning to be arraigned. The lobby and broad staircase leading to the

Leo, minus the beard that had helped to mask his identity for almost a year, agreed to be extradited from Canada to face prosecution.

second-floor courtrooms were lined with spectators. Some were there for a murder trial, but many hoped to catch a glimpse of the swindler who had fooled almost as many people in Nova Scotia as he had in Chicago. The Koretz watchers were out of luck—he was whisked into the office of Judge William B. Wallace for a private hearing.

"Can I waive my right to fight extradition without making a statement?" Leo asked after the judge read aloud the allegations of defrauding Samuel Richman. Wallace said he could, but extradition could not be ordered without supporting evidence. He suggested Leo sign a written statement denying guilt but conceding that the State of Illinois had established a prima facie case—that the charges, on their face, had merit. Sbarbaro announced he would take steps to speed up the extradition process, as Leo wished.

Joseph Connolly, the young lawyer Leo had met at a Royal Nova Scotia Yacht Squadron dance a few weeks earlier, sat in on the hearing and agreed to serve as his defense counsel. Just twenty-nine and in his third year of legal practice, Connolly had served in a machine-gun battalion and won the Military Cross for bravery at the Battle of the Somme. Dublin-born and long-faced, with a close-cropped mop of thick curls, he had been admitted to the Nova Scotia bar without writing the entrance exams, thanks to a waiver available to former servicemen. Like Leo, he had parlayed a job as office boy at a top law firm—Henry, Rogers, Harris, and Stewart's clients included many of the region's major corporations—into a legal career. He was "a witty, big-hearted, flamboyant yarn spinner," a colleague recalled, who "embellished everything, including the truth." It was little wonder he and Leo had hit it off.

Nova Scotia's attorney general, Walter O'Hearn, a law-and-order man in the Robert Crowe mold, was wary of Leo's eagerness to leave. Was he trying to escape before he could be charged with swindles or other offences committed in Nova Scotia? There was "something sinister," Halifax's *Evening Mail* cautioned, in the desire of such a "daring, unscrupulous and oily gentlemen" to make a hasty exit.

O'Hearn was not about to let a slick-talking American con man get away with a crime committed on his watch. Extradition would only proceed, he announced, when "we are certain his record here is clear."

THE CHICAGO PAPERS DISPATCHED five reporters to cover the story. It would take them two days to reach Halifax by train; in the meantime, editors relied on material picked up from the Nova Scotia papers to chronicle Leo's exploits while on the lam. His fast-paced life in Nova Scotia was dissected in minute detail. He had spent money "like water," Chicagoans learned. One-hundred-dollar tips. Cars purchased with cash. His secluded lodge transformed into a mansion as posh as his old one in Evanston, and every paper had the photos to prove it. "His dances, his dinners, his house parties," the *Daily News* reported, "were done deftly and with no care for expense." Laurie Mitchell, interviewed just before sailing south on Zane Grey's new schooner, described the boozy housewarming bash and the many women Leo had courted and entertained.

Sbarbaro was pleased to flesh out the story while adding his own spin. On the day after the arrest, he fielded at least thirty long-distance calls from Chicago reporters and passed along tidbits and observations that cast Leo in the worst possible light. Leo was trying to put up "a brave front" in jail, the prosecutor told one paper, "constantly acting a part, just as he acted a part during the days of his affluence and success in Chicago." But he was cracking under the strain and begging for news of his wife, children, and mother. Jail officials, Sbarbaro said, had mounted a suicide watch, in case he had "a secret plan for the defeat of justice."

Rumors swirled; none was too outlandish for the newspapers to repeat. He had made nighttime forays into the woods at Pinehurst, and millions of dollars might be buried on the grounds, "a modern version of Capt. Kidd's treasure." Two armed bodyguards had accompanied him wherever he went in Nova Scotia—which was news to Thomas Raddall and the many others who had befriended the fun-loving Lou Keyte. Leo, it was said, had carried a gun himself, and the ever-exuberant *Herald and Examiner* claimed a revolver had been found in his hip pocket when he was captured. Sbarbaro chuckled when he tried to picture Leo brandishing a pistol. "Koretz is not a gunman," he assured Halifax newspaper readers. "He does not carry a gun—he wouldn't shoot anyone." Leo wouldn't even shoot a moose.

The subject of all this gossip and speculation settled into life in the Halifax County Jail. A guard claimed he changed his clothes twice a day, producing a new suit—complete with matching spats—from one of the three suitcases that had accompanied him to jail. He spent much of his time in the privacy of the janitor's quarters, nicknamed the jail's "guest room," and ordered his meals from the Carleton, the hotel where Sbarbaro and William McSwiggin were staying.

Concerns that he was suicidal evaporated. He seemed at ease when he mixed with the other prisoners, including a convicted murderer and a couple of rumrunners. He chatted, cracked jokes, and rolled up his silk sleeves to demonstrate his prowess at cards.

"Course I want to know him," one of the rumrunners told a reporter. "Why, he got away with real dough; lots more than a bootlegger gets."

A half-dozen times a day, one paper reported, a jail official answered the telephone to hear a woman's voice on the line. "How is Mr. Koretz today?" began a typical exchange.

"Fine; who's speaking?"

"Oh just a friend." Leo clearly had many women friends; the jailor swore he never heard the same voice twice.

Leo's love of flashy, expensive clothes was fodder for one more story. Not long before his arrest, he had supposedly ordered three pairs of fur-trimmed silk pajamas from Hiltz's tailor shop, at an outlandish cost of $150. The *Evening Mail* gave the story credence in a bold headline: FUR-TRIMMED SILK PAJAMAS FOR "LOU KEYTES."

Within hours the anecdote was being reported in several Chicago papers, reinforcing Leo's reputation as a free spender with an eclectic taste in clothes.

THE RETURN

THE TRAIN CARRYING reporters for the Chicago papers reached Halifax three days after the arrest. The group took rooms at the Carleton, the hotel Sbarbaro was using as his headquarters, then headed for the county jail. The sheriff refused to let them interview his prisoner, but the newsmen, who were accustomed to roaming through police stations and cell blocks back home, were not about to let that stop them.

Austin O'Malley of the *Herald and Examiner* scored the first interview. He was one of the stars of the Hearst papers, perhaps the most aggressive and resourceful reporter in a city filled with resourceful, aggressive reporters. He was "brilliant, literate, scholarly, with the instincts of a Sherlock Holmes," one colleague recalled. He also cut a flamboyant figure, dressing in black, carrying a cane, and shielding his eyes under the wide brim of a fedora, also black. He had solved more crimes than many policemen, perhaps because one of his favorite ploys was to flash a silver star and impersonate one. Talking his way into the Halifax County Jail must have been easy.

In O'Malley's interview, published on November 28, an unrepentant and defiant Leo emerged. Yes, he had received "several million dollars" from people who had begged to invest in his ventures. But they were victims of a risky investment gone sour, he claimed, not fraud. "I had lost most of the money that was intrusted to my care. I knew the crash was inevitable and I could not face the music. The sum and substance of the proposition is that I used bad judgment."

Leo made similar claims to Donald Ewing, a *Daily Tribune* correspondent. "There was no swindle," he insisted. "A lot of people insisted that I handle their money—they just forced it on me—and then when things went wrong they blamed it on me. . . . I never asked any one to invest with me. I refused hundreds of thousands of dollars." To Gregory Dillon of the *Daily News*, he expressed regret for the losses smaller investors had suffered, but he added, "The others can stand it."

Leo seemed to think—or at least wanted everyone in Chicago to think—that he could beat the charges. The smooth-talking purveyor of fake mortgages and worthless oil stock was trying to sell something almost as far fetched: his innocence. He was heading home to try to convince a jury that "he never swindled any one out of a penny," Ewing wrote in the *Daily Tribune*. "He will not confess anything, will not plead guilty and will not admit that he has ever done anything wrong."

LEO'S DEPICTION OF THE Bayano swindle as nothing more than a failed business venture—and himself as the innocent victim of his investors' greed and inflated expectations—did not wash in Chicago. Leo had been clever—he had tried to cover his tracks by issuing receipts for payment, rather than stock certificates, to many investors—but not clever enough. Robert Crowe shrugged off the notion that Leo could beat the charges. There were no Panamanian oil fields and there never had been. And while Leo's suckers had lined up for the fleecing, this made no difference in the eyes of the law. The fake dividends paid to investors to keep the scheme afloat "consummated a fraud on Koretz's part," Crowe explained to reporters, "and makes a confidence game case stand up beautifully."

But Crowe was taking no chances. He had sent his best prosecutors to Halifax to plug any legal loopholes. And as Leo pleaded his case to a succession of Chicago reporters, the state's attorney suspended his war on gangsters long enough to appear before a grand jury seeking more indictments. By coincidence, Leo's brother Ferdinand was serving on the jury. Excused from the session, he waited on a bench outside the jury room, smoking and declining reporters' requests for an interview.

Crowe emerged with three fresh indictments for theft, fraud, and operating a confidence game. Leo was accused of taking $11,500 from Francis Matthews and $4,000 each from two investors, Stella Gumbiner—the mother-in-law of Ludwig Koretz—and Percy Simon. The third indictment was one of the weaker ones: Simon had received Bayano stock certificates, but Leo had convinced him to hand them back, leaving nothing on paper to prove he had ever invested.

No paper trail. Money offered and tendered without solicitation. Crowe was diving into murky legal waters. Leo may have been counting on his victims to be too embarrassed to file a criminal complaint and face him in court. "Koretz's victims," noted the *Daily News,* "are not likely to display in their offices a placard saying, 'One Was Swindled Here.'" Crowe responded by ordering his investigators to fan out in search of more victims willing to testify.

Sidney Kahnweiler, another Bayano victim, was onboard. "Tell a jury what I know about him?" he exclaimed when contacted by a reporter. "I should say I will. He isn't a safe man to have about." If Crowe needed help, chimed in Leon Weil, who was nursing a grudge as well as losses approaching $7,000, "I'll be right there to help in the grand unmasking." Alfred Decker, who had thirty-five thousand reasons to want him behind bars, vowed to do "all in my power to aid his conviction." Simon Westerfeld, whose cousin had married one of Leo's brothers, was out $31,000 and eager "to help get for Koretz what he deserves."

Crowe needed all the ammunition he could muster. He was under pressure to stand down and allow the federal government to prosecute Leo first, on charges of using the mail to defraud. Federal investigators had amassed enough evidence for additional indictments, and while it was not an extraditable offense, it was a serious one. If convicted, he faced five years in prison and a $5,000 fine on each count. A conviction on the state charges carried a heavier penalty—a term of one to ten years behind bars—but that had to be weighed against the growing concerns over whether those charges would stick. Did Leo see a technicality that Crowe and his assistants had missed? Did he have a hidden stash to grease the wheels of justice or to hire a top-notch lawyer to plead his case? One pundit cautioned Crowe not to brag too loudly about having a solid case, since his nemesis, Clarence Darrow, "may take that as a challenge."

Ben Hecht, for one, viewed Chicago's justice system through the cynical eyes of a newsman who had watched too many defense lawyers "pull 'innocent' verdicts like rabbits out of a hat." The poor and unpopular were usually convicted, while the rich and powerful bought their way out of legal jams. "Money was in itself a guarantee of special treatment," Hecht recalled. "Big Business was in that day as sacred as religion, and a millionaire was as rare in a defendant's chair as an archbishop." It was anyone's guess what a jury would think of a man sharp enough to make his millions at the expense of people who should have known better. "It is to be hoped," the *Daily News* warned, "that the prosecuting mechanisms of this county will be proof against Leo Koretz's exquisite self-salesmanship."

There was another consideration: How long would it take to put him on trial? The state courts of Cook County were notorious, as one Chicago newspaper warned, for "slow, technical, antiquated procedure," while their federal counterparts had streamlined their rules to speed up trials. US District Attorney Edwin Olson, who was openly accusing the state courts of corruption, threatened a showdown; in his opinion, the feds had the stronger case, and a trial in the federal courts would ensure that Leo was convicted. One legal point was clear: if federal charges took precedence, Crowe could still prosecute, and for that, Leo had Charles Ponzi to thank. The United States Supreme Court had ruled in 1922, in a case Ponzi had fought and lost, that a defendant convicted of federal charges could be tried on state charges based on the same criminal acts.

The new indictments strengthened Crowe's hand; if Leo was acquitted of the main charge of defrauding Samuel Richman, he would be prosecuted on the others. The additional counts also made it unlikely that Leo would have enough money to get out of jail while he awaited trial. Bail on the four indictments was set at $100,000.

As gangland slayings escalated and critics questioned the state's attorney's resolve to fight crime, Crowe was determined not to allow his high-profile, headline-grabbing prize to slip away. "Leo Koretz is my prisoner," he told reporters, "and I propose to try him without interference from any one." He was confident he could secure as many as forty indictments, if need be, and had enough evidence for a conviction on every one of them.

"If he were indicted and tried separately for all his frauds we should be able to sentence him to a thousand years in jail," Crowe predicted. "It will be time enough for the federal men to come forward when we are through with Koretz. They are welcome to him then."

THE CHICAGO PAPERS OFFERED fresh reports out of Halifax linking Leo with a succession of women, most of them young. A little digging revealed Topsy's identity. Tracked down in Caledonia, Mabelle Banks denied she had been engaged to a man she now knew was not only married, but an accused con artist to boot. "There really was nothing between Lou Keyte . . . and myself," she insisted. "I knew him well, frequently saw him at his estate, and frequently went to chaperoned parties he gave." She also tried to defuse the scandal of being found in Leo's hotel room when he was arrested, claiming her father had been with them and had just stepped out when the officers knocked on the door.

George Banks defended his friend—and, by association, his beleaguered daughter—in the pages of the *Gold Hunter*. The "daily press teem with inaccuracies and very highly colored write ups, entirely misleading," he wrote, though he made no effort to separate fact from fiction. Lou Keyte—Banks still could not bring himself to use Leo's real name—"was at all times courteous, genial and acted the part of a gentleman in every respect."

On November 26, Nova Scotia's attorney general completed his review of Leo's activities since his arrival in the province. There were "no grounds whatever," Walter O'Hearn announced, "to suspect that the man had committed any crime while under Canadian jurisdiction." John Sbarbaro was free to take his prisoner home. Another of Crowe's assistants, Thomas Marshall, arrived on the night of November 27 after a roundabout trek from Chicago to Springfield, the Illinois capital, then on to Washington and Ottawa, to assemble the papers needed for extradition. Crowe was taking no chances; Marshall had drafted the charges against Leopold and Loeb and was considered the in-house expert on legal paperwork.

Leo would leave Saturday morning by train, accompanied by Sbarbaro, McSwiggin, and Marshall. Connolly and Scriven would join them, and the prisoner would remain in Scriven's custody until he was handed over to the authorities in Chicago. Private compartments were booked on the Ocean Limited, the Canadian National Railway's run to Montreal, where Leo and company would make a connection to Chicago. The black-hatted O'Malley and the other Chicago newsmen bought tickets and looked forward to two days of interviews with Leo and plenty of sensational revelations. A *Daily Tribune* cartoonist envisioned a warm welcome at the train station, with disgruntled creditors and hopeful criminal lawyers lining up for a crack at the swindler and a chorus of Bayano investors singing "Hail to the Cheat!"

AN AUTOMOBILE TURNED OFF Spring Garden Road and approached the gate to the Halifax County Jail on the evening of Friday, November 28. The driver turned off the headlights and, when the gate opened, backed into the yard. Deputy Sheriff Rainard Scriven and another man climbed in. The car swung onto the street and disappeared into the darkness.

A few blocks away, a reporter for the *Acadian Recorder* buttonholed Joseph Connolly on the sidewalk. Would his client make a statement before boarding the train in the morning? No, Connolly said, the reporter would be wasting his time if he showed up at the station— Leo would have nothing to say. As for the Chicago newspapermen, they were in for "a surprise in the morning." Connolly jumped into a car, the same one that had stopped at the jail. It drove away.

The car headed for the waterfront and pulled up to a gangway on Pier 2, where John Sbarbaro and Thomas Marshall stood in front of the towering hull of the *Caronia,* a Cunard liner bound for New York from England. *Caronia* was in port just long enough to land 132 passengers, five tons of cargo, and seven hundred sacks of mail. Connolly, Scriven, and the third man emerged from the car, and all five boarded the vessel. They sailed at midnight. Not even officials with Cunard's Halifax office knew about the last-minute additions to the passenger list, let alone the name of the fifth man.

Leo Koretz left Nova Scotia the way he had arrived in March—with his true identity a closely guarded secret.

THE CHICAGO NEWSMEN, MEANWHILE, were celebrating their final night in Halifax. William McSwiggin was with them, to ensure no one suspected there was a plan afoot to spirit the swindler out of the city. The group gathered at Leo's old stomping grounds, the Royal Nova Scotia Yacht Squadron, which afforded a close-up view of the lights of the departing *Caronia* as it slipped past. It was several hours before they heard rumblings of the clandestine departure.

Frantic efforts were made to find out where Leo was and where he was headed. Phones rang all over the city, rousing people from their sleep. One reporter placed a long-distance call to Crowe's home. "I give you my solemn word," Crowe said, still groggy from being jarred awake, "that so far as I know Koretz leaves with Sbarbaro and Marshall by train Saturday morning." Leo had been dreading the prospect of being at the mercy of the newsmen on the long ride back to Chicago. Connolly, it turned out, had masterminded the plot to outfox them.

More calls were made to Chicago newsrooms. When the reporters discovered that Leo was on the *Caronia,* a wireless message was flashed to the vessel; Sbarbaro did not respond. Thought was given to hiring an airplane to intercept the liner at sea or chartering a special train to New York. But there was nothing the reporters could do.

They boarded the train to Montreal the following morning, wading through a crowd that had assembled at the station in hopes of catching a glimpse of Leo before he left.

The 19,000-ton *Caronia* could carry more than fifteen hundred and offered a dance hall, a gymnasium, and a plant-filled conservatory as diversions. With no way to escape, Leo was allowed to roam the vessel and took his meals in the dining room. It was a rough, thirty-four-hour voyage; the *Caronia* pitched and rolled in heavy seas whipped up by a blizzard that paralyzed New England that weekend. He found the trip more enjoyable than Sbarbaro, Marshall, and Scriven, all of whom were seasick.

The liner docked at the Cunard piers on the Hudson River, opposite West Fourteenth Street, late on a clear and chilly Sunday morning. The train to Chicago did not leave Pennsylvania Station until 2:55. Leo, it was said, suggested lunch at the Commodore, next door to Grand Central Terminal. It was not clear whether he knew the ritzy hotel from his days of masquerading as Lou Keyte—it was a short walk from his old East Forty-Eighth Street apartment—or as the millionaire promoter of oil stocks. The maître d' recognized him and ushered the group to Leo's favorite table by a window. Leo ordered sirloin steak smothered in hearts of guinea hens and, when not eating, puffed on cigars. All Scriven remembered of the meal was how fastidious Leo was, wiping each piece of cutlery with his napkin before he used it.

A crowd gathered outside the hotel entrance as word spread about the identity of the man enjoying steak and cigars. Leo was hustled through the kitchen and out a back door. At the station the group posed for photographers before boarding the Broadway Limited for the overnight ride to Chicago. Leo stood glumly, the brim of a cap almost covering his eyes.

Ducking inside a Pullman sleeper car, Leo settled into the comfort of a private compartment with its own drawing room and individual sleeping berths. He spent much of the trip gazing out the window as snow-covered towns and farmers' fields whizzed past. He played solitaire. He smoked cigars.

He had taken a liking to Scriven and began introducing him as "my guardian angel." At some point on the journey, he confided to the sheriff's deputy why he had lived such a fast-paced lifestyle in Nova Scotia. "Every fugitive from justice lives in dread of the arm of the law," he explained, "and they have to keep their minds occupied or they would go crazy. Some lead the gay life, others take to drink. I preferred the gay life."

Reporters along for the final leg of the journey were desperate to get Leo to speak with such headline-worthy candor. Only Harry Reutlinger of the *Evening American* managed to get him to open up. Described as an "ingratiating chap," Reutlinger had convinced Oscar Felsch, one of the Chicago White Sox players paid to throw the 1919 World Series, to tell his story to the *American*. He tried to work his magic on the architect of Chicago's latest scandal.

"I knew you before," Leo said when Reutlinger approached, "but I can't think where we met." He probably remembered the World Series scandal scoop.

"Probably tried to sell me some stock," the reporter wisecracked.

"Nope, guess not," he replied, as playfully as the Leo of old, "for had I tried I would have succeeded." But he looked tired and nervous. Reutlinger asked about his health. Leo would only say that his condition was "very grave" and getting worse. Diabetes, Reutlinger predicted when his story appeared, "may cheat the state courts." If he was convicted and sent to prison, "he will never come out alive."

They played cards. Leo lost. "Can't even have any luck in cards," he said. He went back to smoking and contemplating the scenery. The combative Leo of the past few days, the man in the Halifax County Jail who denied swindling anyone, was gone.

They were somewhere in Indiana when he turned to Reutlinger. "I'm going back to Chicago," he said at last, "and try and rectify matters."

State's Attorney Robert Crowe and his prosecutors pose with Leo.
Behind them are John Sbarbaro, left, and William McSwiggin, second from right,
who had raced to Halifax to oversee Leo's arrest.

30

THE CONFESSION

"SAY," ASKED THE slim woman wrapped in fur, tapping a policeman on the arm, "who's coming in?"

"Oh, a hypnotist, lady," was the straight-faced reply. "He used to make people think they got what they didn't."

"You're kidding me. Honest, who's coming in?"

"Why, lady, he's a kind of banker. People gave him lots of money."

As many as two thousand people jammed the platform of Union Station for a glimpse of the banker-hypnotist, "the money magician," as one paper put it, "who made millions disappear." Not even a blast of winter weather over the weekend could keep them away. It was the kind of welcome "usually accorded a President or foreign potentate," the *Evening Post* noted, "so dense was the crowd of curiosity seekers in all ranks of life."

The focus of all the attention, clad in a suit the unseasonable color of summer grass, arrived at half past ten. Leo had been awake since seven and looked tired, even though he had slept well. He pocketed his last box of cigars.

He emerged from the Pullman and hesitated for a moment, taken aback at the size of the crowd. His face broke into a crooked smile. He looked "half-bitter, half-glad, half-amused," in the opinion of a re-porter who was better at description than math, "and wholly cynical." He walked head-down and with a slight limp, his shoulders stooped beneath his brown overcoat, his cap again pulled down almost over his eyes. An explosion of flash powder confirmed the magician's arrival.

"There he is," someone cried.

"He got away with $7,000,000," another voice confirmed.

Twenty policemen in blue uniforms and a squad of detectives elbowed their way into the crowd, some threatening to use their clubs as they struggled to clear a path. Reporters followed, shouting questions no one answered. A line of cars was waiting at the Canal Street entrance to ferry Leo and his entourage to the state's attorney's office.

WHEN THEY WERE FIRST introduced, both were fresh out of law school and trying to make their mark. Two decades later, they were meeting again as accused and prosecutor. They greeted each other by their first names, as if they had never lost touch. Leo called the state's attorney Bob.

A reporter asked Crowe about their shared past. "Didn't buy any Bayano stock, did you?"

"No, I didn't. But I didn't know about it," he joked, "or I might have."

It was about noon when Leo arrived at Crowe's offices in the Criminal Court Building on West Hubbard Street, an imposing, Romanesque-style tower just north of the Loop where Cook County had been dispensing justice since the 1890s. The Leopold and Loeb trial had played out within its white granite walls; Ben Hecht and Charlie MacArthur used its fourth-floor press room as the setting for the antics portrayed in their play *The Front Page*.

A platoon of reporters and photographers had trailed Leo across town and was waiting in an outer office. They were ushered in and given ten minutes to snap photographs and ask questions. Leo shook hands with the reporters he recognized and posed for photos without complaint. His face would be plastered over the next edition of every Chicago paper. Crowe posed with him as well, to make sure everyone knew it was the state's attorney, not the feds, who was determined to put America's most notorious swindler behind bars.

When the photographers were done, Leo stood to one side of the office. He did not look the part of a man ready to put up a fight in court. His green suit was baggy and wrinkled. A grease stain was visible on the front of his jacket, and a soiled handkerchief drooped from the breast pocket. His blue polka-dot bow tie was askew; his thinning hair needed to be reunited with a comb. A man known for flaunting expensive rings and cuff links was down to his last piece of jewelry, a gold wristwatch.

He twirled his eyeglasses on the forefinger of his right hand as he was machine-gunned with questions.

"How did you keep out of the clutches of the law?"

"What are your plans for defense?"

Leo ignored some questions and deflected others.

"Have you noticed any of your investors in the crowds here?" None appeared to have shown up at Union Station to witness his return.

He smiled. The question broke the ice. "You are kind to me and them to refer to them as investors."

"Well, is there anything you do want to talk about?" one of the reporters asked.

He produced a cigarette and asked for a light. "Oh, I might say that matches are rather expensive in Halifax," he said, as playful for a moment as he had been when he joked about having no Bayanoes. "Two boxes for 5 cents."

The newsmen were banished to the outer office, and Crowe, Sbarbaro, and Marshall began questioning Leo. Half an hour later, Crowe asked Leo's lawyer, Connolly, to join them. Midway through the afternoon, a stenographer was summoned.

Crowe emerged with an update. "Koretz," he announced, "is talking freely." There would be no courtroom battle, no defense claim that Leo was the hapless victim of greedy investors who had forced him to take their money. The creator of the Bayano Syndicate was dictating his confession.

Deadlines loomed for the evening editions. Crowe ducked out

now and then with the highlights, to ensure his name was attached to the revelations when they appeared in print. Leo admitted he had netted at least $2 million over the course of almost two decades. He was fuzzy on the details but acknowledged he had used money from new investors to pay dividends to those who already held shares.

"The losses had become so heavy that I saw there wasn't a chance for me ever to get straight again," he told Crowe.

Now, with no way out, he mustered the courage he had lacked a year earlier, when he fled. "I have done wrong. I want to be punished. I am going to plead guilty and take my punishment." He said he wanted to set an example for Mentor. "I want my son . . . to know, absolutely, that wrongdoing is wrong; that it means punishment as well as unhappiness. By pleading guilty and going to the penitentiary, I hope to be able to teach my son, beyond a doubt, that he must never do wrong."

Adolph and Emil Koretz had warmed a waiting-room bench for much of the afternoon, hoping for a chance to see their brother. Crowe allowed them in. They shook hands with Leo and huddled in a corner, speaking in whispers.

"Forget that I have ever lived," Leo said. "The crime is mine and I will not share my penalty with you. I don't want to see you; I don't want to see anybody."

He asked about his mother, how she was taking the news. Not well, he learned. She had been told of his capture and was confined to bed, refusing to eat or speak. He asked them to relay a message: The only women who had lived with him at Pinehurst, he lied, were the housekeeper and servants. Tell her, he pleaded, that his friendships with women during his sojourn in Nova Scotia "were only platonic."

Crowe held a final press briefing. While Leo insisted he had handed over every cent that was left, Crowe was not so sure. "I believe he is holding something back. He spent a lot of money in recent years, but he had an enormous amount."

A reporter wondered what had most surprised the state's attorney as he listened to the confession. It was the fact "that people seemed to throw their money at him," he replied. "Koretz is not what one might call a brilliant man. . . . He is not fascinating or particularly impressive. But people threw their money at him! That's what astounds me."

MAE DROPPED OUT OF sight, leaving her Winnetka home early on the day of Leo's return to avoid the press. After everything he had done, after all the women he had chased and charmed, should she swallow her pride? Should she go to him? "She is pathetically eager for news of her husband," admitted a relative. "But she does not know what to do, whether she should seek to see him or not."

She would have to make the first move. "I've hurt her enough," Leo said when asked if he hoped to see her again. "No matter how much I want to see her, I will not ask her to come to me. She knows where I am."

"I don't think I've got the right to inquire about her," he added, "or the children."

Leola Allard, a *Herald and Examiner* reporter, turned up at Mentor's hospital room, where he was still recovering from hernia surgery. He was sitting in a rocking chair and smoking a cigarette.

"Your father says he is very sorry he has hurt your mother so much," Allard told him. Leo hoped his guilty plea would teach his son a lesson. Mentor did not seem to care what his father thought.

"Is that so? Well, I don't think mother will be interested," he replied. "She wants to be let alone."

LEO SPENT HIS FIRST night back in Chicago in a room at Briggs House, a Loop hotel rebuilt after the Great Fire. Three detectives stood guard. The hotel doctor was called in to lance a painful boil on his leg, an ailment that commonly plagued diabetics. Leo, the doctor noticed, did not wince as the needle was inserted; perhaps he was too worn out to feel the pain.

The next afternoon, the second of December, he was escorted back to the Criminal Court Building to testify before Harry Parkin, the referee overseeing Leo's bankrupt estate. Lawyers for Chicago

Title and Trust wanted to question him under oath as they pursued the money trail. The figures were not adding up: Leo claimed to have collected some $2 million from investors, but an audit showed he had taken in that much—$2,164,975.73, to be exact—selling Bayano stock and rice farm mortgages from the first day of January 1922 until he fled to New York. Over that period he had paid out a little more than $233,000 in dividends, leaving more than $1.9 million in his pockets. And that was for just shy of two years. He had been up to his neck in some form of swindle or fraud for close to two decades. Where was the rest of his loot?

The lawyers for Chicago Title and Trust, Maurice Berkson and Joseph Fleming, were convinced more money, perhaps another $500,000, was stashed somewhere. Crowe agreed to make Leo available for questioning, even though it was hard to argue with the *Evening Post*'s contention that it was "probably constitutionally impossible for the gentleman to tell the truth." There was one condition: he would have to stay on the state's attorney's turf, and in his custody, in case federal agents were tempted to scoop him up on the mail-fraud charges.

Harry Parkin set up temporary shop in the grand jury room of the Criminal Court Building. The *Daily Tribune* sent one of its best reporters, Genevieve Forbes Herrick, to cover the closing acts of the Bayano saga. Herrick's tenacity and flair for description had earned her plum assignments such as this. She had once posed as an Irish immigrant and crossed the Atlantic in steerage to expose the mistreatment of newcomers at Ellis Island. And not only had she covered the blockbuster Leopold and Loeb trial, but she had altered the timing of its outcome: she had convinced the judge to delay his ruling on whether to impose the death sentence so that it would not interfere with her wedding to her colleague John Herrick.

The hearing, Herrick informed *Tribune* readers, ranked as "one of the strangest bankruptcy proceedings ever held." For the rest of the afternoon and much of the evening, Leo sat in the witness box and explained how he had teased millions of dollars from the pocketbooks of hundreds of people—his extended family, his closest friends, and some of Chicago's leading businessmen and professionals. He spoke almost in a monotone as he described the inner workings of the great Bayano swindle. Herrick began to think she was back in the classroom. "He might have been a wise old professor of economics, explaining a short cut to a difficult problem," she later wrote, only this professor was describing "how he paid dividends with capital and made capital of dividends." It was like the introductory lecture of a course in Swindling 101.

After making a career out of lying, Leo discovered, the truth came easily. The Arkansas rice farms had started out as legitimate investments, he said, then ballooned into a labyrinth of worthless paper. "The majority of the mortgages did not exist." Bayano, he admitted, was a sham from the start. "There never was any such syndicate. There never was any land as I described. There is no Panama Trust company."

"Was there any oil on your property?" Joseph Fleming asked.

No, he said.

He was asked to describe his operations in detail.

"How far back do you want me to go?"

"About nineteen or twenty years," said Crowe, who was monitoring the proceedings and knew, after having heard Leo's confession the evening before, how the story began.

He talked about how, as a newly married and struggling lawyer, he had sold fake mortgages. The fraud snowballed as he stole more money to cover his earlier crimes. The Arkansas farmland followed the same pattern.

He told how David Nieto had swindled him and inspired him to create his Bayano masterpiece. He told how people had clamored to invest as word spread of his lucrative timber holdings in Panama. Then, he said, his mouth twisting into a wry smile, "I mentioned to a friend that oil had been discovered on the land. Yes, the news spread rapidly. They began to besiege me with money for certificates."

There were bursts of laughter as he described how easy it had been to dupe his victims. He began to tell of a prominent Chicago businessman who had hounded him for stock, then stopped. "I won't give you his name, or any name if you are going to use them," he said. Leo did not mind taking people's money, it seemed, but drew the line at holding them up to ridicule.

Fleming asked him to continue, saying, "Well, we're only interested in the assets."

It was the businessman, outraged to discover that Leo had sold more shares to his partner than to him, who had demanded more.

"And that is not an isolated case, is it?" asked Joseph Connolly, Leo's lawyer, to underscore how much money poured in without solicitation.

"That is certainly not an isolated case."

At times, Leo struggled to remember the details. Did he start out claiming to own one million acres in Panama, or five million? He could not recall the year he met Nieto, or when he first journeyed to Panama. He was not even sure how old he was. "Forty-five or 46," he said. "I think I am 45." He had turned forty-five the previous summer, when he was still Lou Keyte, master of Pinehurst Lodge.

Leo had no idea how many bogus mortgages he had sold or how much investors had sunk into the imaginary timber and oil of distant Bayano. He had destroyed most of his records, including the book with the black cover that he had used to keep track of money coming in and dividends paid out. He reminded his listeners that he had tried to dissuade many people from investing, as if this somehow lessened the magnitude of his crimes. In fact, negative salesmanship had been one of his most effective marketing tools.

He was asked why he had sent Henry Klein and his companions to Panama, when he knew they would find nothing.

"I was disgusted at myself and disgusted at the people who had wealth and demanded something for nothing," he replied. "And I was indifferent as to how the matter ended."

Then Leo paused for a moment, long enough for a smile to form on his lips and a puzzled look to take over his face.

"It is rather hard for me to explain just how I began to believe in the thing myself," he said, blinking as he stared into space, "but I did."

He had spun so many lies about Bayano riches to so many people for so many years that it had all begun to seem real.

Not a single investor was in the room to hear this remarkable admission—or to challenge his claim that he was mostly guilty of being too accommodating to greedy people who demanded "something for nothing."

Maurice Berkson took over the questioning and zeroed in on Leo's lack of remorse for his victims. Not all Bayano investors were wealthy, Berkson pointed out. Had he forgotten the widow and the clergyman, people of modest means, who had suffered heavy losses?

"No, I haven't forgotten them," replied Leo, who seemed to have expected the question. "But they were two of the most insistent persons who besieged me with requests for stock. They wouldn't let me alone."

He was asked about the tens of thousands of dollars he had distributed to his family and in-laws before skipping town. It was money his relatives had invested, he insisted, and each of them had received less than they had paid in. "On this point," Herrick noted, "he is making a desperate fight." The man notorious for swindling his own family was doing everything he could to relieve them of the taint of receiving stolen money. There was another reason for the payments: he had hoped members of his family would use some of the money to help Mae and the children. The expensive jewelry he had collected had been another attempt to leave her something to live on.

"I didn't dare leave my wife any money because I know her principles and I am positive"—he stressed these words, for emphasis—"that she would not accept a penny of that kind of money. But I knew if the family were well provided for, they would take care of her."

Where, he was asked, was the rest of the money?

There was nothing left and nothing hidden, he swore, not in Canada or the United States or anywhere else. Leo was adamant: he had accounted for every cent he had obtained by theft, fraud, or swindle. The rest of the money had been spent to support his extravagant lifestyle or returned as dividends. If the lawyers for Chicago Title and

Trust were right, if there had to be more money stashed somewhere, he was not about to let them in on the secret.

The hearing dragged on into the evening. Leo became so drowsy he could barely keep his eyes open. In the glare of the room's harsh electric lights, he looked worn out and near collapse. Parkin finally called an adjournment, ending the ordeal. Leo was slated to appear the next afternoon before Jacob Hopkins, the chief justice of the superior court's criminal division, to follow through on his pledge to plead guilty.

"I am indifferent to what may happen now," Leo muttered, to no one in particular, before he was taken back to the hotel for the night.

31

THE RECKONING

"LEO KORETZ, IN an indictment returned by the grand jury of November, 1923, you are charged with the crime of larceny as bailee," the court clerk announced, reciting a much-practiced script. "How do you plead—guilty or not guilty?"

Leo stood directly in front of the judge's bench, in the midst of a crush of lawyers, licking his lips nervously. The wrinkled green suit he had been wearing for three days looked as worn and tired as he did, his bow tie was still askew, and his complexion was as white as chalk. Robert Crowe—chin thrust out, face expressionless—was stationed close enough to ensure he would be in photographs recording this moment.

"Guilty," Leo replied. His voice was surprisingly strong and clear, almost a bark. It was ten minutes past two on Wednesday, December 3.

The sixth-floor courtroom of the Criminal Court Building could accommodate three hundred, and a crowd "reminiscent of the Loeb-Leopold affair," which it had hosted that summer, was on hand. Photographers' flash powder generated so much smoke that some of the windows had to be opened to clear the air. The judge had ordered bailiffs to close the courtroom so that Leo could be brought in. Henry Klein made it inside, along with Stella Gumbiner. Somewhere in the sea of faces were Adolph and Emil Koretz and their sister Louise.

In all, Leo pleaded guilty to charges of larceny, larceny as bailee (theft of property held for safekeeping), and operating a confidence game that related to four of his victims—Gumbiner, Samuel Richman,

Leo and Crowe stand before the judge's bench in Chief Justice Jacob Hopkins's courtroom. Leo pleaded guilty on December 3, 1924, to charges of theft and operating a confidence game.

Francis Matthews, and Percy Simon. Chief Justice Hopkins adjourned the sentencing until the following day. Leo would spend the night next door in the Cook County Jail.

As Gumbiner left the courtroom, she paused and patted him on the arm. "It's all right, Leo," she whispered, "everything's all right. Let's forget it."

He was taken to Crowe's office for more questioning and a brief visit with his siblings. It was the first time he had seen Louise since his return, and she greeted him with a kiss, tears streaming down her cheeks. As they left, Adolph stopped to make a statement to the press. "Just say for us that we think as much of our brother as we ever did," he said. "We are going to stick by him. It is the only thing to do. Of course it is all a great tragedy."

LEO AWOKE IN CELL 13 to a hearty breakfast of ham and eggs with toast, cupcakes, and coffee. His family had it sent in from a nearby restaurant that catered to higher-class prisoners, and the owner, Joe Stein, tossed in a carton of cigarettes and a couple of fifteen-cent cigars. At noon, he was taken under guard to Stein's to have lunch with Ferdinand, Emil, Ludwig, and Adolph. One paper described it as "a veritable family farewell banquet."

He was back in Hopkins's courtroom at two o'clock and looked ill at ease as he repeatedly cleaned his glasses with a handkerchief. The weather outside was cold and drizzly, extending a rude welcome to Calvin Coolidge on his first visit to the city as president. Coolidge had just delivered a luncheon speech to business leaders at the Drake, which had been "transformed into a temporary White House for the day." Had Leo found a legitimate outlet for his talents as a salesman, he might have been among those in the audience.

The hearing opened with a surprise motion: Leo was allowed to withdraw his plea of guilty to the charges involving Stella Gumbiner. A flaw had been found in the wording of the allegations, Crowe explained. The indictment was stayed, but the state reserved the right to refile the allegations. Matthews, Richman, and Simon were called to testify.

"Koretz urged me to invest in his oil lands," Richman said, proving that Leo had persuaded at least one of his victims to buy shares. Matthews said Leo had told him in 1921 that oil had been discovered on his Bayano holdings. He had held off buying shares until shortly before the crash.

"Do you realize now that his enterprises were pure out and out swindles?" asked George Gorman, Crowe's chief assistant.

"I do."

Joseph Connolly established that some investors had recouped money as dividends and stood to reclaim more through the bankruptcy proceedings. After the confession was read into the record, the state rested its case.

The defense called two doctors to confirm Leo's poor health. Dr. Leland Light had attended to Leo at Briggs House and declared him "a very, very sick man." His pulse rate was high and he was running a fever. "He has a severe case of diabetes. Unless his condition improves he will die soon."

Milton Mandel testified that he had begun treating Leo for diabetes in 1919.

"Do you think a prison term would shorten his life?" Connolly asked.

"That is hard to answer. . . . It might if he were given hard manual labor."

Gorman saw an opening.

"If this man had done a little light labor instead of swindling all these people, his health would be in better condition." It was as much a comment as a question.

"Emphatically, yes," Mandel agreed.

Hopkins looked down from the bench, his face stern and his double chin spilling over his collar. Confronted with the pale, weary figure before him and the medical evidence confirming the seriousness of his illness, Hopkins opted for mercy. The minimum sentence on each of the three counts was one to ten years in prison. If Hopkins ordered the sentences to run consecutively, Leo faced a term of from three to thirty years. In this case, he said, "the ends of justice will be met" if the sentences were served concurrently, telescoping them into a single term of one to ten years.

"This defendant freely admits his guilt," he said, "and in view of his poor health I believe the minimum sentence is proper." Leo would be eligible to apply for parole after serving a mere eleven months. At worst, if every application for early release was turned down, he would be out in a little more than six years.

Reporters studied his face to gauge his reaction. He heaved a sigh, and a smile slowly took shape on his lips. It was not clear whether he was pleased or simply resigned to his fate.

"That means death," he said. "I'll never come out alive."

THE PRESS WAS OUTRAGED at the sentence. "Koretz, who has never shown even the faintest glimmer of sympathy for relatives and friends who were his victims," the *Herald and Examiner* complained, "found sympathy in the most unexpected place of all—the court-room." One of the paper's readers was upset enough to fire off a letter to the editor. "Steal two million dollars, more or less, and get wide world publicity and a year punishment," Joseph Delehanty wrote. "But if you steal a dollar or less to save yourself or someone else from starvation you get ten to twenty years—that's what you call law!"

The *Daily Tribune* held its tongue but republished—and appeared to endorse—a scathing editorial from a paper in Wisconsin that condemned the sentence as a "farce" and a miscarriage of justice. "We frequently hear it said that the courts are for the rich, and when we see a criminal like Leo Koretz, one of the most notorious swindlers of our time, get off with the lightest punishment possible, we are forced to admit that there are some grounds for the statement that courts show favors," complained the editor of the *Sheboygan Press-Telegram*. Leopold and Loeb had callously murdered a child and escaped the death penalty, "and now a brazen faced swindler, who cleaned up millions through fraud, gains sympathy at the hands of the court." In Nova Scotia, where the case remained big news, one editor found it hard to believe that Leo could be back on the street in less than a year. "The criminal of today, particularly in Uncle Sam's country, if he has money or influence behind him, fares not so badly."

Crowe was determined that Leo would serve the full six years and two months. The state's attorney had stood before the public as the man who would bring Leo to justice, and it now appeared as if the Bayano wizard had managed to swindle the entire Chicago justice system. Crowe's office dispatched a letter to the state board responsible for pardons and parole, asking it to reject any application for early release. The judge, who was taking the brunt of the criticism, sent a letter of his own. "I have shown the defendant every consideration he is humanely entitled to," wrote Hopkins. "He should be required to serve the maximum penalty and I sincerely trust he will be required to do so."

Leo might have had another ticket to freedom. As the judge and state's attorney were drafting their letters, the *Evening Post* was reporting that some of his victims might petition the governor to grant a pardon. "All these investors were his friends and still are," one of them, a man identified only as Lou, told the paper. Crowe had watched too many crooks go free to ignore such talk. He knew better than anyone that the doors to the state's prisons were revolving ones. The governor, Lennington Small, was making a mockery of justice in Illinois by pardoning or commuting the sentences of hundreds of prisoners. There were allegations that influence and money could buy pardons, and convicts were being put back on the streets without warning or official explanation. Many had been sent there by Crowe, and for all he knew, the governor could be one of the Bayano investors who had swallowed their losses in silence.

But the state's attorney had an ace to play. There had been no flaw in the indictment withdrawn just before Hopkins imposed the minimum sentence. Crowe had held it back on purpose, in case Leo or those still loyal to their onetime benefactor applied for and won a pardon or early release. The charges of swindling Stella Gumbiner could be reinstated until the last month of 1927, to put him on trial—and back in prison.

PAVEMENT SLICK WITH DRIZZLE glistened beneath bug-eyed headlights as the car carrying Leo, his guards, and his lawyer, Joseph Connolly, made the forty-mile journey from downtown Chicago to Joliet. Leo stared out the window, the tip of a cigar glowing beneath the brim of his newsboy's cap, his bow tie stuck at two o'clock. The cars that followed carried the reporters who would document the last moments before he was locked away inside the Illinois state prison.

They were almost there when he began to speak. "This seems to be my last chance to get a word before the public," Leo said. He had a statement to make, and he wanted his companions to pass it along to the reporters once he was behind bars.

"If I get out alive I will devote the rest of my days to restore the money of those who lost," he said. "I'm going to start making a clean living the first day I'm out and make thorough restitution."

The walls and watchtowers of the prison emerged from the fog, a nightmarish mass of sand-yellow limestone. The car jerked to a stop in front of the main administration building, a castle keep of a structure with pencil-thin turrets pointing into the black sky. It was a quarter past nine.

"Well," he said to the man seated next to him, "this is the end of the rainbow—it's up to me to pay for chasing it now."

Leo and his guards got out and headed to the iron-plated main door.

"So long, Leo," someone, Connolly perhaps, called from inside the car. "You'll be out in eleven months, unless you get foolish and try to jump the prison wall."

The thought made Leo laugh.

"Stranger things than that have happened," he replied.

THE FINAL SWINDLE

"BARS, GUARDS, SOBER faces, hard labor, coarse food, no pleasure, no liberty, few comforts."

This was the *Daily Tribune*'s grim description of life in Joliet in 1924. The prison had been built before the Civil War, in an era when penitentiaries were designed to punish, not to reform. "The cells are small and dark," the newspaper noted, "relics of the old prison days." Two men shared a space four and a half feet wide, eight feet deep, and seven feet high, sleeping on iron bunks bolted to the wall, one above the other. Eleven hundred men convicted of the most serious crimes on the books—murderers, armed robbers, rapists, burglars, and gangsters, along with the occasional con man—were paying their debt to society within Joliet's fortress walls.

Leo's rumpled green suit was finally retired from service, and he was issued a prison uniform: a coat and a pair of baggy trousers made of dark blue denim, with a matching cap; wool shirt and socks; flannel underwear; a pair of heavy, blunt-toed shoes. The days of tailored suits and silk pajamas—let alone fur-trimmed ones—were over. He was taken to the prison barbershop and emerged with his head shaved. He was fingerprinted, mug shots were taken, and his measurements and educational and work history were recorded. Leopold Koretz was now convict no. 9463.

Leo had asked to be punished, and the State of Illinois was pleased to oblige. There were no toilets in the cells; he relieved himself in a bucket and dumped the contents at a trough in the prison yard each morning before breakfast. The cell blocks reeked of urine and excrement. He took a three-minute shower once a week, and the lights were turned out every night at nine o'clock. Every man was counting the days until he was sent to a new prison, Stateville, just opened nearby, where each cell had a toilet, hot and cold running water, a radiator, and a window that allowed sunlight to flood in. Inmates were being transferred at a rate of about a hundred a month, but it could be a year or more before Leo, the thrill killers Leopold and Loeb—who were serving their life sentences in Joliet—and other wealthy or famous prisoners enjoyed such comforts. They would be among the last to be moved, to ensure the staff was not accused of favoritism.

The prison doctor, W. R. Fletcher, examined no. 9463 on his second full day in Joliet. The register of prisoners, the only surviving record of his medical condition upon arrival, listed his heart and lungs as being in good shape. "He is very ill from diabetes," Fletcher announced to the press, "but he is not more so than other men who are performing regular duties." His poor health earned him two concessions: he was given a cell to himself and one of the cushiest jobs in the prison. Richard Loeb was in the furniture factory, assembling chairs; Nathan Leopold was spending his days winding rattan to make lamps and rockers. But such entry-level tasks were considered too strenuous for Leo, who was handed a stick with a nail protruding from one end and sent into the prison yard. He would spend his days collecting litter—fitting punishment for a man who had spent much of his life creating worthless scraps of paper.

How well he would hold up in prison, and for how long, was an open question. Con men were among the lowest of the low in Joliet's hierarchy, shunned and almost as detested as sexual offenders. They tended to be older and better educated than the men locked up with them, and had betrayed the only things that mattered inside—loyalty and trust. Leo would be trapped in this hellish world for at least a year, and if Crowe and the chief justice had their way, he would be behind bars until 1931. Even if he managed to win early parole, or Governor Small was feeling generous with his pardons, his legal troubles were far from over. Crowe could reinstate the withdrawn indictment and send him back to prison, and the next judge might not be as lenient. The state's attorney was also sitting on a complaint that Leo had embezzled $90,000 as trustee of the estate of the publisher Daniel Stern. And there was the prospect of a federal prosecution after his release. In reality, US District Attorney Edwin Olson had concluded that no judge in Chicago would send Leo back to prison for using the mail to defraud, not after he had been convicted under Illinois law for what amounted to the same offense. Federal charges were quietly dropped. Leo, it appears, was never informed of the district attorney's decision. But it would have made little difference as he faced the bleak years ahead.

No one suspected it yet, but Leo had an escape plan.

A FEW DAYS BEFORE 1924 made way for a new year, Leo was relieved of his work duties. He was so ill he no longer had the strength to wander the prison yard with his pointed stick. He had lost twenty pounds in less than a month, dropping his weight to below 150. His voice was a hoarse whisper and his pale skin had taken on a sickly copper hue. On December 26 he was admitted to the prison hospital, a grim stone building with steel-barred windows. Leo was put on a restricted diet, and Fletcher administered insulin shots to try to reverse the ravages of diabetes. The new drug, doctors had found, prevented some patients from lapsing into a coma, the final stage of the disease. He was unable to sleep and, by one account, begged for narcotics to ease his pain.

"Koretz's condition is serious," Fletcher told the press. "He is steadily growing worse despite our treatments . . . it is a question if his vitality will respond." The press offered conflicting reports. The *Daily Tribune* described him as on his deathbed; the *Daily News* countered that death did not appear imminent.

About noon on January 7, Leo slipped into a coma. Prison officials did not contact his family until the following day. Emil, Adolph, and Mentor rushed to Joliet. Leo's brothers stood vigil beside his cot for several hours, but he never regained consciousness. Mentor could not bear to see his father, not even to say good-bye, and waited in the warden's office.

Mae was notified but received the message late in the day. Despite all the heartache and disgrace she had endured, despite her resolve to never see him again, she boarded a train for Joliet.

At 8:40 in the evening of January 8, Leo took a last deep breath. His brothers had retreated to the warden's office to join Mentor. A guard, Michael Leonard, was the only witness to his final moments. Leo Koretz—the man hailed in the Chicago press as the "king of con men" and "the greatest swindler of all time," the flamboyant entertainer and lavish spender—was dead at age forty-five. He had served thirty-four days of his sentence.

The news was relayed to Mae when her train arrived at the Joliet station about an hour later. "If I had only known that Leo was in such a critical condition I would have been down before," she said. "I would have liked to have told him goodbye."

The body was released to his family the following morning. Mae asked to see him at the funeral home of O'Neil and Barry in Joliet and emerged from the viewing room in tears, leaning on Mentor for support. She returned to Chicago to finalize the arrangements for burial that afternoon. Mentor and Adolph stayed behind to accompany the body to Waldheim Cemetery in the western suburb of Forest Park. Adolph was handed $44.32; it was all the money Leo had left when he died.

THE FUNERAL WAS SIMPLE and swift. "No crowds; no elaborate funeral cortege; no pallbearers; no heaped up flowers; still fewer heaped up eulogies," noted the *Daily Tribune*'s Genevieve Forbes Herrick. "Nothing but the minimum for the man who always loved the maximum."

A hearse pulled into the cemetery about half past three, with a car carrying Adolph and Mentor close behind. The vehicles stopped about fifty feet from the gate, where a mound of wet clay glistened on the snow-covered ground. A shovel had been discarded in haste and lay on top of the pile. A knot of relatives and friends, no more than fifty in all, gathered at the graveside. A gray granite headstone bearing the letter K in Gothic script and KORETZ in capitals marked the family plot and bore the name of Leo's father, Henry. Leo would be laid to rest alongside his long-dead oldest brother, Max. The coffin, as gray as the headstone, emerged from the hearse. A spray of pink roses on the lid and a wreath of roses and narcissi served as the only floral tributes. The sky was clear and a bright winter blue; the sun was low in the sky and struggling to keep the temperature above freezing.

Mae stood at the foot of the grave, encased in black. The collar of her coat, pulled up to hide her face from photographers, muffled her sobs. Julius, Ferdinand, Adolph, and Emil, accompanied by their wives, looked on. If Ludwig was there, none of the reporters hovering on the sidelines recognized him. A sister-in-law clung to Mae's arm, and Mentor stood with them, wiping tears from his eyes. Mari was thought to be too young to see her father buried; Leo's mother, who had barely survived his exposure as a fraud, was too weak and too ill to attend. The mood was somber and restrained. Few of the other mourners shed tears for the man who had disgraced his entire family.

Rabbi Felix Levy of Emanuel Congregation conducted the service. "In the grave all sins are forgotten," he said, perhaps thinking for a moment of the money he had sunk into worthless Bayano stock. He recited the Kaddish, a traditional funeral prayer, in Hebrew. "He was joined to us not only in bonds of blood but in bonds of love," the rabbi continued, in English. "The link in the family chain that has been broken will be reunited soon in another world."

The pink roses shivered in the breeze as the coffin was lowered. "The pain of life, which he had already begun to know," Levy intoned, "has been changed for the peace of death."

Herrick, the *Trib* reporter, overheard the whispered comment of one of the cemetery employees. "Most people who had done a thing like this couldn't be buried in consecrated ground," the man said, gesturing. "They'd have been put 'way back there."

Mourners at Leo's graveside on January 9, 1925. A Chicago Daily Tribune *reporter described the swindler's modest funeral as "the minimum for the man who always loved the maximum."*

Levy lifted a lump of clay. "Earth to earth," he recited as he tossed it onto the coffin. At two minutes past four, the service was over. The mourners dispersed, and the men who would have buried Leo in less hallowed ground retrieved their shovels and closed the grave.

Herrick searched for the right words to capture the moment, to close the final chapter of the Bayano oil swindle. They appeared in the next day's *Tribune*.

"Leo Koretz," she wrote, "the man who loved superlatives, the man who bought things by the dozens, the score, the gross; Leo, the lavish host who had a hospitality complex, is left alone."

THEN, TWO DAYS AFTER the funeral, a front-page headline in the *Herald and Examiner* reported Leo's death as a suicide: RE-VEAL KORETZ KILLED SELF WITH SWEETS: LURED DEATH BY SCORNING SUGAR TABOO.

The paper's source was Fletcher, the prison doctor, who revealed that Leo had smuggled a three-pound box of chocolates into Joliet. How he had managed to slip the contraband past guards and prison staff—on his own or through an accomplice on visitors' day—Fletcher did not say. Leo had finished off the box before it could be confiscated.

"Candy was poison to Koretz," the paper explained. "No more so than to any other incurable diabetic. But it was poison," making suicide "a reasonable conclusion." Syrup often accompanied prison meals, giving him easy access to more sugar. Guards monitoring the mess hall had watched Leo swap the food on his plate for extra serv-ings of syrup and reckoned he consumed twice as much as the other inmates.

Whether chocolates and syrup had killed Leo, let alone whether he had eaten them in a bizarre bid to commit suicide, Fletcher could not say. Diabetics craved sugar-rich foods to replace the glucose their bodies were unable to process, which was why one of the treatments employed in severe cases, in preinsulin days, was a starvation diet and the gradual reintroduction of calories, in hopes of restoring normal digestion. Leo may have been unable to control his cravings or he may have known exactly what he was doing. While it was "uncommon" for diabetics to deliberately overeat to commit suicide, an American authority on the disease had noted a few years earlier, it was not un-heard of. And a diabetic "could kill himself by eating sugar," Fletcher conceded.

Leo had returned to Chicago, Fletcher believed, convinced he did not have long to live. And he had cheated justice as brazenly as he had cheated Bayano investors. All his talk about atoning for his crimes and paying back the money he had stolen was just that—talk. Leo had predicted his prison term would be a death sentence, and he had been right.

"Leo Koretz gave up," Fletcher told the *Herald and Examiner*. "His death, in my opinion, was due to the letdown in the manner of his living. Believing himself to be afflicted with an incurable ailment, he abandoned all caution and restraint and indulged in dissipations that at least aggravated, if they did not cause, the condition in which we found him when he entered the penitentiary."

"He didn't care what happened. He became a fatalist. He thought he was going to die. He thought he would live recklessly while he lived. He did. And he died."

OR DID HE?

Two months after the hasty funeral, Bayano investors began to hear rumors that Leo was alive and had been seen in Halifax.

Someone had died on January 8, 1925, in the hospital in the Joliet prison, someone had been buried in Waldheim Cemetery the following day—but was it Leo? Was it possible the man who had fooled his relatives and closest friends for so long had faked his own death? Leo had escaped from the United States and evaded police for almost a year; could he have feigned illness as part of a plot to escape?

A rabbi, who was not identified in the press—it may have been Felix Levy—notified the authorities, and the story soon hit the newspapers. "I have heard," the rabbi told federal prosecutors in Chicago, "that another body—the remains of some poor unfortunate who had died of tuberculosis—was buried in the coffin marked with the name of Koretz. Leo has gone back to Canada, where he has friends who will protect him indefinitely. My authority for this story is excellent. Koretz has been seen by men who know him and they are positive."

The office of the state's attorney was notified. Crowe was prepared to have the body exhumed to find out who was buried in the Koretz family plot. "This is certainly worth an investigation," he told the press. "Go ahead and dig him up."

An investigator was assigned to find out whether Leo had pulled one last swindle. The rumor gained some traction when it was pointed out that a single guard had been with him when he died and that since the funeral service had been conducted at the graveside, the casket had been closed.

Joliet's warden, John Whitman, assured the state's attorney that prison officials had been aware "that rumors of suicide or fraud might be expected" if Leo died, and had taken precautions. Medical specialists had been called in to confirm the seriousness of his diabetes. After he died, Whitman said, dozens of people who had seen him since his arrival at Joliet had viewed the body, and all of them confirmed it was Leo. The dead man's fingerprints had been taken, and they matched the set recorded when Leo was admitted in December. Further confirmation came from reporters who had accompanied him on the drive to the prison and had seen his body at the funeral home. And, of course, Mae, Mentor, and two of his brothers had viewed the body before the casket was closed. The investigation concluded there was no need for an exhumation.

"It is obvious that Koretz is dead," conceded an official of the state's attorney's office. But given Leo's track record of deception, he added, "there seems to be no reason to apologize for having made an inquiry."

Fletcher, the prison doctor who was being cast in the role of Leo's latest dupe, went public to squelch the rumors and defend his reputation. "The man who died January 8," he told the press, "was the man who gave his name as Leo Koretz when he was received at the prison a month before his death."

It was "preposterous," prison officials said, to suggest that Leo had somehow managed to cheat death and fool his captors with one grand, final swindle. "Koretz is dead," Joliet's assistant warden insisted, "and the rumor is absurd."

As absurd and as preposterous, perhaps, as the notion that somewhere, deep in the jungles of Panama, there flowed a river of black gold.

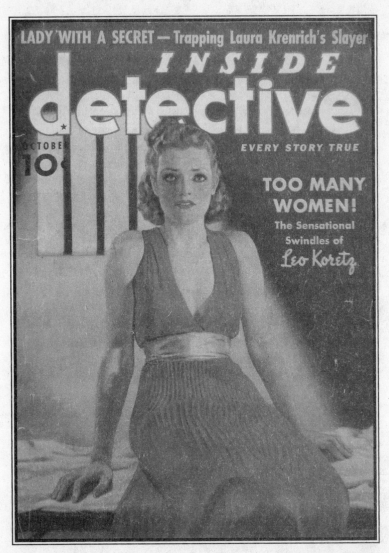

LADY WITH A SECRET — Trapping Laura Krenrich's Slayer

INSIDE

detective

OCTOBER

10¢

EVERY STORY TRUE

TOO MANY WOMEN!

The Sensational
Swindles of
Leo Koretz

*Leo's swindle—and his many love affairs—became fodder for crime magazines,
and his story made the cover of the October 1938 issue of* Inside Detective.

EPILOGUE

ROW UPON ROW of headstones and vaults fan out from Des Plaines Avenue in Forest Park, about ten miles west of the Loop. Just inside gate 46 of Waldheim Cemetery, on lot 102 of section 4, a monument squats beside a graveled access lane.

The stone bears the names of Leo's parents. Marie died in 1927, in her eightieth year, her passing deemed worthy of a brief news item—thanks to her son—in at least one Chicago paper. Two smaller stones face it, one for Max, the brother who died young, and the other for Louise, a sister who passed away in 1933. A fourth, only a few feet from the access lane, is square and plain and looks more like a thick slab of patio stone than a grave marker. Grass almost obscures the single word chiseled into one edge: SON.

This modest memorial—toppled and left facedown, hiding the full inscription—marks the final resting place of Leo Koretz.

Leo seemed destined to be remembered as one of history's most proficient fraud artists. His bizarre death-by-chocolate demise alone should have earned him a lasting place in the popular imagination. The *Herald and Examiner* proclaimed him—no doubt to the chagrin of the Yellow Kid—the "greatest confidence man Chicago ever produced." The *New York Times* stood in awe of his audacity and formidable powers of persuasion. "Leo Koretz bears witness against that ancient fallacy that business men lack imagination," an editorial writer noted. "Perhaps it is as well for us that the prosaic minions of the law intervened before he went down to Wall Street, there to cast his poet's eye, in fine frenzy rolling, from this sordid, exiguous earth to the blue sky of heaven."

And for many years after his death, Leo's name was almost as synonymous with rob-Peter-to-pay-Paul swindles as Ponzi's would become. A lawyer who fled Chicago in 1929 with money he was supposed to have invested for his friends was a "second Leo Koretz." The Bayano fraud was still notorious enough in the 1940s that the authors of a criminology textbook referenced Leo, only by his surname, as a member of the "swindling brigade who made their reputations at the expense of unwary investors."

Leo's exploits—and in particular his many love affairs—proved irresistible to the editors of the true-crime and detective magazines he had loved so much to read. His story was first featured in a 1938 edition of *Inside Detective* under the breathless cover headline TOO MANY WOMEN! THE SENSATIONAL SWINDLES OF LEO KORETZ. Embellished accounts followed in the pulp magazines of the fifties, from *Master Detective* to *For Men Only,* often illustrated with photos of women in provocative poses. "With oil he was master of them all," one article began, "but he learned too late never to trust a blonde." Leo picked up more mistresses, a raft of new aliases, a sixty-foot yacht for cruising Lake Michigan, and a yellow Rolls-Royce, just like the Great Gatsby's, for his trips from Pinehurst to Halifax. But the best-researched article, in *True: The Man's Magazine,* written in 1952 by future Pulitzer Prize winner W. A. Swanberg, was dead-on in its description of Leo as "the swindler of the century" and "probably the most skillful propagandist of the pre-Goebbels era." Ben Hecht, the Chicago journalist-turned-playwright who had a ringside seat to the collapse of the Bayano bubble, added a further twist. He recalled the "prince of thieves" in his 1954 memoir, *A Child of the Century,* and claimed that one of Leo's girlfriends smuggled in the box of chocolates that killed him in Joliet, a tantalizing but invented detail often repeated when brief accounts of

Leo's fraud surfaced in magazine articles or in anthologies of famous crimes and swindles.

But Charles Ponzi and his postal-coupon scheme have eclipsed Leo's fake Panamanian oil wells in the popular imagination. Ponzi continued to make headlines long after Leo's death, pulling a land fraud in Florida and ending up back in prison in 1927 to serve an additional seven-year term for his postal-coupon fraud. He was released from prison in 1934 and deported to Italy and died penniless in South America in 1949. His name was invoked so often when dividends-from-capital swindles were exposed that the *Encyclopaedia Britannica* recognized the term *Ponzi scheme* in 1957 and the *Oxford English Dictionary* soon followed suit. Leo had devised his more elaborate and more brazen schemes more than a decade before Ponzi came along; he was a marathoner who was running long after Ponzi's hundred-yard dash ended in a prison cell. Fame and notoriety, however, went to the fraudster who stumbled first and died last. It is fitting, perhaps, that a man who spent much of his life cheating others was cheated out of his rightful place in the history of financial scams.

The swindle that 520 Percent Miller pioneered, Leo Koretz perfected, and Charles Ponzi made famous became the template for countless scams that followed. In today's world of complex investment vehicles and shareholders obsessed, as always, with maximizing returns, the "Koretz scheme"—to give Leo his due at last—thrives. People are still searching for a financial savior to lead them to the promised land of riches, just as scores of wealthy Chicagoans once looked to a trusted friend to make them even wealthier. Almost eight decades after the Bayano swindle, the Texas financier Allen Stanford was convicted and imprisoned on charges of using his Caribbean-based bank to finance a lavish lifestyle; investors were bilked out of more than $7 billion.

The most reviled swindler of our time, of course, is Bernie Madoff, who ran his gigantic fraud for at least sixteen years and probably longer. When Madoff's scheme collapsed in 2008, a casualty of that year's stock market meltdown, an estimated $18 billion in investors' money vanished. Sentenced to a 150-year prison term as inflated as his promises of easy wealth, he reigns as perpetrator of the most costly and far-reaching stock fraud in history.

Both Leo and Madoff preyed, for the most part, on people who were already rich. "The average person thinks I robbed widows and orphans," Madoff has complained from his prison cell. "I made wealthy people wealthier." Leo trotted out a similar rationale when he was exposed, expressing disdain for victims "who had wealth and demanded something for nothing." Each took money from relatives and close friends and exploited ties to the Jewish community, making them both perpetrators of an "affinity fraud"—a crime in which someone in a close-knit group takes advantage of the friendship and trust of fellow members. Leo and Madoff were obsessed with secrecy and made their victims feel as if they were part of a select group that was set for life. Madoff, his biographer Diana Henriques has noted, "expected his lucky clients to keep quiet about being in his elite club," and he turned down many others eager to invest, just as Leo did. In terms of the scale of their frauds, staying power, and sheer audacity, Leo Koretz and Bernie Madoff stand apart in the pantheon of pyramid-building swindlers.

Swindlers sell dreams of easy wealth, and that's a commodity as much in demand today as it was when Leo was inviting Chicagoans to join his Bayano club. John Kenneth Galbraith described the twenties as "a time of madness," a decade-long frenzy of stock market gambling that raged until the Wall Street collapse of 1929 brought the party to an abrupt end. It was money madness, driven by "an inordinate desire," as Galbraith put it, "to get rich quickly with a minimum of physical effort." The dot-com bubble, the stock market meltdown, and Madoff's spectacular fraud are sobering reminders that the money-mad 1920s was an era not so different from our own. Then, as now, an economic boom, reckless investors, and lax oversight of the financial system led to an inevitable crash. And greed can still trump common sense. Investors and shareholders want the highest possible returns, regardless of whether the product is a blue-chip stock or the risky, mortgage-backed securities that brought the global financial system crashing down in 2008. Plenty of people are as desperate as ever to claw their way into the stratosphere the One Percent inhabit. Con men who promise to get them there can attract followers as eager and devout as the would-be oil executives who went on a wild-goose chase to Panama.

Today, the Bayano River valley remains almost as remote and little known as it was when Leo made it the talk of Chicago. In the mid-1970s an American travel writer described a trip up the river as "a safari into Panama's most untamed green hell." The builders of the Pan-American Highway gave up trying to hack their way through the swamps and jungles about one hundred miles to the southeast, leaving a fifty-mile break, known as the Darién Gap, in a route that stretches from Alaska to the tip of South America. The upper section of the river was dammed in the 1970s to provide hydroelectric power to Panama City, creating an artificial lake that attracts anglers hoping to hook the tarpon and other species found in its waters. The region is still a good place to find alligators and, for some, a good place to turn an illegal buck—it is close enough to the Colombian border to earn a reputation as "a perfect gateway for drug trafficking." So far, though, no one has found oil there.

IT WAS AN HOUR past sunset when three men emerged from the Pony Inn saloon in Cicero, just west of the Chicago city limits, on an April evening in 1926. Machine guns erupted from a line of cars rolling past on Roosevelt Road. The cars sped off, leaving the white brick facade of the saloon peppered with bullet holes and three men dead. Two of the victims, Jim Doherty and Tom Duffy, were gunmen for the O'Donnells, a West Side gang of beer runners. The third, shot twenty times in the back and neck as he tried to escape, was William McSwiggin, one of State's Attorney Robert Crowe's most skilled and loyal prosecutors.

One question—who killed McSwiggin?—transfixed the city for months. McSwiggin had been a rising star on Crowe's staff, a police officer's son hired fresh out of law school in 1924. One of his first assignments had been to travel to Nova Scotia with John Sbarbaro to fetch Leo Koretz. McSwiggin, Doherty, and Duffy had grown up together and had worked on Crowe's election campaigns; on the day of the killing, McSwiggin's companions had overseen a recount of primary ballots on behalf of the Crowe-Barrett Republicans. If the state's attorney's critics needed proof of the ties between politicians and organized crime, this was it.

Crowe tried to pin McSwiggin's murder on Chicago's leading mob boss and the O'Donnell gang's chief rival, Al Capone. Not only had Capone ordered the hit, Crowe claimed, but he had led the attack and wielded one of the machine guns. Capone went into hiding but surrendered three months later, proclaiming his innocence. "I didn't kill him. Why should I?" he told newsmen. "I liked the kid." Capone was released for lack of evidence, and no one was ever charged with the murders.

The allegations swirling after McSwiggin's death made it impossible for Crowe to run for mayor in 1927—Big Bill Thompson returned from the political wilderness to reclaim that prize. There were 120 underworld killings in 1926 and 1927, but Cook County prosecutors failed to secure a single conviction. Crowe was accused of protecting gangsters, and the Genna crime family, it was said, had hosted a dinner in his honor. He sought a third term as state's attorney in 1928 but was defeated in the primaries, dashing his dreams of higher office.

Crowe had craved power as much as Leo Koretz had coveted other people's money. They lived in a world of corruption and excess, where lawmen consorted with the criminals they were supposed to put behind bars, where reaping sky-high returns on a friend's stock tip seemed as natural as asking a stranger for directions to the nearest illegal bar. They knew how to get what they wanted, whether it was teasing money from the pockets of the gullible or using threats and intimidation to win elections. Leo, who claimed he had never sought a dollar from a single investor, was the slick operator who stole millions and betrayed everyone who trusted or befriended him. Crowe, the prosecutor who brought the Bayano swindler to justice, was the politician who allowed organized crime to thrive in Chicago. Their success was artificial and temporary; their downfall, inevitable.

Crowe had cashed in on Leo's arrest and imprisonment only to see his political ambitions die, along with his young assistant, in a hail of bullets. He returned to public life in the 1940s, as a judge of the Illinois Superior Court. When challenged on his record as state's attorney during his campaign for the judgeship, Crowe chose his words carefully: "no one ever by proof," he said, had "substantiated any charge of dishonest or corrupt official act" on his part. He died in Chicago in 1958, a few days shy of his seventy-ninth birthday. The allegations of corruption and collusion stirred up by the murder of William McSwiggin, his obituary in the *Daily Tribune* noted, were "a smashing blow" from which Crowe "never rallied."

In Leo's Canadian refuge, the exploits of the charming American millionaire with the scandalous lifestyle gradually faded from memory.

Mementos of his summer in Nova Scotia probably found their way into more homes in the province than he ever did. Hundreds of people jammed a showroom in downtown Halifax in January 1925 when the contents of Pinehurst—everything from furniture and firearms to linen and towels—went on the auction block. The deed to Pinehurst itself was folded into Leo's bankrupt estate, and the lodge was sold in 1926 to Henry Klein for the knocked-down price of $7,600. Klein resold it within a couple of months, helping to offset his massive losses. N. F. Douglas and Company, merchants and lumber dealers in Caledonia, bought the lodge in the 1960s, and it remained in the Douglas family for more than thirty years. After the Douglas family sold the property in 1997, the unoccupied lodge became a magnet for vandals and was torn down.

Rainard Scriven, Leo's "guardian angel," returned from Chicago as something of a celebrity, his arrival afforded front-page treatment in the Halifax press. The sheriff's deputy applied for the $10,000 reward for Leo's capture, on behalf of himself and Malcolm Mitchell, the keeper of the Halifax County Jail. Others had played bigger roles in unmasking Lou Keyte, among them the tailor Francis Hiltz and the Bank of Nova Scotia officials Horace Flemming and William Davies, and it was widely reported that Hiltz and Flemming would split the money. But Scriven and Mitchell, as the arresting officers, cited the wording of the wanted poster, which sought Leo's "apprehension and return." Davies, the bank's top official in Chicago, was the only other person to file a claim. The receivers referred the dispute to a judge, but the bankruptcy file contains no record of who received the reward.

Joseph Connolly, the defense attorney, made a splash upon his return from Chicago as well, showing off a platinum watch he received from Leo's brothers to thank him for his efforts. Connolly began to dabble in theater and was tapped during the Second World War to mount a musical-comedy show, *Meet the Navy*, to entertain Canadian servicemen. After the war he wound up in Hollywood for a short time, as an assistant producer when *Meet the Navy* was made into a movie. He made a brief turn on the political stage, mounting an unsuccessful bid for election to Canada's House of Commons in 1949, and died in 1955 at age fifty-nine.

Leo's friend and sometime chauffeur George Banks continued to publish the *Gold Hunter* in Caledonia until shortly before his death in 1944. Mabelle, the woman Leo called Topsy, left Caledonia and married a doctor in Reno in 1929. The couple settled in Oregon and died together in a house fire in 1958. Laurie Mitchell found a new patron after his falling-out with Leo. He served as Zane Grey's guide and skipper on several excursions to the South Pacific in the late 1920s, in search of marlin and other big fish off New Zealand and Tahiti. The two parted ways in 1931, and Mitchell died of heart disease in California a few months later; he was sixty-one.

Thomas Raddall, who went on to become one of Canada's most successful and best-known authors of historical novels and popular history, published his memoirs in 1976 and recalled the dinner-dances and parties hosted by the "jolly millionaire" from the States. When researchers compiled an oral history of the Caledonia area in the late 1970s, one of the old-timers they interviewed was Maurice Scott, the barber who spent many afternoons shooting pool with Leo. "It was quite a big blow up—quite a story," he told them. "Things never were the same after he left."

IN MARCH 1925, AFTER months of negotiations between the receiver and Internal Revenue Service officials, the US government withdrew its claim against Leo's estate for more than $753,000 in unpaid income tax. The underlying legal question—was stolen money taxable as income?—would not be resolved until 1927. That year the US Supreme Court ruled that money earned from bootlegging and other criminal activities must be reported and taxed, giving federal agents the green light to prosecute and imprison Al Capone for tax evasion in 1931.

The truce in the Koretz tax battle cleared the way for a final distribution of $535,000 in cash and assets salvaged from the ruins of the swindle. Members of Leo's immediate family had returned every cent they received before he fled. Mae's mother and her sister Etta Speyer held out for a better deal and managed to keep half the $75,000 he left to them. Other relatives and friends Leo had compensated accepted modest settlements from the bankruptcy receiver. The claims of 147 creditors—the losses of those investors who came forward, plus money owed to everyone from tailors and jewelers to the phone company—added up to more than $2.1 million. After lawyers' fees and other expenses, investors recovered sixteen cents on the dollar. Isaac Wilbraham, the dining car steward who invested $20,000, recovered a paltry $3,190. Alfred Lundborg, the tailor who stitched the Henry Heppner and Company label inside a suit jacket and unwittingly sealed Leo's fate, got back just $280 of the $1,750 he invested. Charles Cohn, who had been among the seventeen investors who feted their "Ponzi" at the Drake Hotel in 1922, saw his $55,125 investment shrink to $8,800. Leo ruined Anna Auerbach's reputation and added insult to injury by leaving her—and her theater owner husband—almost $21,500 poorer. Harry Parkin, the referee, filed his final report in June 1927, closing the book on proceedings that had dragged on for three and a half years.

Henry Klein's claim of $459,645.82, a figure approaching $6 million today, was the largest. He recovered $73,000 and change, plus any profit he made when he sold Pinehurst. He went back into the liquor business after Prohibition ended, and amassed a $1 million fortune before he died in 1947 at seventy-three. He left half of it to charity.

The Bayano swindle added a refinement to the law—ironically, not to the law of fraud. Lewy Brothers, the Loop jewelers who allowed Leo to walk away with diamond bracelets worth almost $15,000 shortly before he disappeared, sued to recover the pieces from Chicago Title and Trust. The bracelets had been not sold but supplied on approval, lawyers argued, and the receiver could not sell them to compensate creditors. Lewy Brothers fought the case to the circuit court of appeals, which ordered the gems returned in June 1925. Leo had never intended to ask Mae to pick out the one he would buy, the court ruled, voiding the sale. Decades later, the case was still being used as a precedent when allegations arose that individuals or companies had improperly obtained goods before declaring bankruptcy.

FERDINAND AND JULIUS KORETZ each lost about $37,000 in the swindle, a figure approaching $500,000 today. Emil was out $31,000, while Ludwig took an $11,500 hit. Adolph and his wife, Rachel, claimed a combined loss of more than $16,000. Leo's mother, Marie, saw $32,000 vanish. In all, his crimes cost members of his immediate family almost $170,000; these days that would be in excess of $2 million. The financial losses, staggering as they were, paled against the emotional toll the swindle took on every member of the Koretz family. Someone they loved and admired had betrayed their trust.

Julius's family had barely recovered financially when the Depression dealt a second blow. "What a devastating thing this must have been to the family," says his grandson Andrew Goodman, a lawyer who practices in Minneapolis. Leo "did this to people he knew, people

who loved him—and ripped them off." Andrew's twin brother, Bill
Goodman, who also lives in Minnesota, once asked his grandfather
about Leo. It was in the 1970s, almost a half century after the Koretz
family's world came crashing down. He instantly regretted having
broached the subject. Julius "had this look on his face that I'd never
seen before, and he just said, 'We don't talk about that,'" Bill recalls.
"It still pained him."

Mae continued to sell coal, and eventually fuel oil, to make ends
meet. "It was a terrible thing for her," recalls a grandniece, Jane Siegel
of Chicago, who was born the year Leo was captured and remembers
visits with her aunt Mae. "She had everything and then suddenly she
had nothing." The disgrace, Siegel adds, "was probably worse than
anything." Mae never remarried and died in November 1941 at age
fifty-eight. She left a modest estate: an estimated $4,700 in stocks,
bonds, and mortgages; deeds to three vacant suburban lots; and $79.46
in cash. Her daughter, Mari, trained as a stenographer, married a salesman, and raised two children. She died in 1975.

Mentor Koretz had learned to play the piano as a child, and performing at nightclubs became his ticket out of Chicago and away from
the stigma of being the son of Leo Koretz. He took the stage name
Red Kearns (his trademark was an oversize red handlebar mustache),
played speakeasies and nightclubs, and proved to be as much of an
entertainer as his father. "He was a personality," recalls Andrew Goodman. "You wouldn't forget him if you met him." In the 1960s, Red
Kearns and His Rinky Tink Piano was a featured act at Dixieland clubs
in the United States and Canada. A promotional photograph from
those years shows a round-faced, balding man wearing a smile as broad
as his mustache and a derby like the ones his father favored.

Mentor married a nightclub singer and dancer, raised four children, and was known to flash a business card claiming he had launched
his career playing in Al Capone's speakeasies. He also made no secret of the fact that he had gotten to know another former Chica-
goan who wound up in Texas: Jack Ruby, the Dallas nightclub owner
who gunned down Lee Harvey Oswald, President John F. Kennedy's

assassin. Mentor died in Texas in 1971 and appears to have legally changed his name to escape his past; the death certificate identified him as Mentor Henry Kearns.

When Julius died in 1973, a few weeks before his ninety-second birthday, he was the last of Leo's surviving siblings. Like Julius, members of his generation—the ones who bore the brunt of the embarrassment and financial ruin—spoke rarely, if at all, about the man many descendants knew only as their mysterious uncle Leo. Henry Beck, a nephew, was barely in his teens when Leo went to prison and knew few details of his crimes, says his daughter, Carol Stelzer, who lives in the Chicago suburb of Arlington Heights. She first heard about Leo in the 1960s, when her father mentioned in passing that her great-uncle had been sent to prison for selling bogus stocks. Almost forty years later, while researching her family tree, she recalls, "I discovered the whole story of Leo's scam and the impact it had on all of my family members."

The Goodman twins were in their teens when their parents told them a bare-bones version of the swindle, how Leo had sent investors to Panama and had been tracked down in Canada through an item of clothing. Chats with relatives and a little research over the years filled in some of the blanks, and the passage of time has made Leo more of a black sheep than a pariah. "I'm not ashamed," says Bill. "Everyone has a degree of fame, so I can brag that my great-uncle was this great shyster." His only worry is that the story is almost too unbelievable to be true. "Most of the time," he adds, "people think I'm just making it up."

Andrew often regales acquaintances with what he knows of the tale, using Leo's chocolate-induced death as the punch line. It is, he says, "a great story to tell."

ACKNOWLEDGMENTS

LEO KORETZ WORKED alone when he pulled off one of the longest, most elaborate, and most audacious confidence games in history. Telling his story was another matter, and would have been impossible without the assistance and generosity of many people.

I am grateful to family members who shared stories about Leo—Andrew Goodman, Bill and Mary Goodman, Carol Stelzer, Ellen Cooler, Jane Siegel, and Mari Kaye Kearns Bayes—and to Alan Steinfeld for providing his genealogical work on the Koretz family.

Archivists and librarians in the United States and Canada joined my search for information about Leo, and I cannot thank them enough for their patience and assistance. In Chicago, Scott Forsythe and Ray Johnson identified records at the National Archives and Records Administration (NARA), Great Lakes Region, while Phil Costello and Julius Machnikowski located court files in the archives of the Clerk of the Circuit Court of Cook County. Karen Siciliano at Lake View High School and Julie Lynch and Chris Scanlon at Chicago's Sulzer Regional Library made it possible to re-create Leo's high school days, while librarian Jona Whipple at the Chicago-Kent College of Law was as determined as I was to confirm the year of Leo's graduation. Staff at the Illinois State Archives in Springfield, the library of the University of Illinois at Urbana-Champaigne, the Chicago History Museum, and Chicago's Newberry library provided archival material and access to newspapers on microfilm. Thanks as well to Mary Beth Perros of the Will County Clerk's Office, Beatriz Ulloa-Mireles of the Will County Coroner's Office, and Januari Smith and Stacey Solano of the Illinois Department of Corrections for their help in searching for records of Leo's death in Joliet prison.

In New York, Eric Robinson of the New-York Historical Society library helped trace Leo's movements in the city. Olivia Wall took me on a tour of the St. Regis Hotel, which remains as grand as it was when Leo stayed there in the 1920s. Jennifer Lee of the Rare Book and Manuscript Library at Columbia University provided W. A. Swanberg's invaluable research notes.

Linda Aylward of Peoria's Bradley University Library, Deb Bier at the Peoria Public Library, and Robert Killion of the Peoria Historical Society uncovered details of Robert Crowe's early life. NARA archivists William Creech in Washington and Tab Lewis in College Park, Maryland, tracked down investigative files on the Koretz case. Thanks as well to Salesa Richards of the Ohio Historical Society in Columbus for access to Zane Grey's diaries.

In Halifax, John MacLeod, Garry Shutlak, Gail Judge, Philip Hartling, and many others at Nova Scotia Archives and Records Management provided advice and located records. Karen Smith and Tina Usmiani of Dalhousie University's Archives and Special Collections guided me through Thomas Raddall's papers. Patricia Chalmers, Tasya Tymczyszyn, and Elaine MacInnis of the University of King's College Library fielded what must have seemed like an endless stream of interlibrary loan requests.

Others were instrumental in tracking down records in Nova Scotia. Rebecca Foley, curator of the North Queens Heritage House Museum and Archives in Caledonia, answered my queries about people and places. Linda Rafuse and Kathy Stitt helped me navigate the collections of the Queens County Museum in Liverpool. Cathy LeBlanc of Kejimkujik National Park and community volunteer Norm Green located a recording of Maurice Scott's recollections of Leo's time in Nova Scotia. I would never have found it, though, without the help of

Dr. James Morrison of the Department of History at Saint Mary's University in Halifax, who conducted the interview in 1977. Staff of the Queens County Land Registration office in Liverpool located deeds to Pinehurst and other properties. In Bridgewater, Linda Bedford, Barb Thompson, and Kendra Power of the DesBrisay Museum also fielded requests for information.

Martin Lanthier of the National Archives of Canada in Ottawa and Anne Dondertman of the Thomas Fisher Rare Book Library in Toronto helped me identify archival records. Genealogist Sarka Kocarikova combed archives in the Czech Republic for details of Leo's family background and early life.

Jaclyn Greenberg, one of my journalism students, researched archival and court records in Chicago, and another former student, J. Matthew Gillis, tracked down references to Leo's alter ego, Lou Keyte, in the Nova Scotia press. I am grateful to Chicago researcher Mark Mandle for compiling the *Daily Journal*'s coverage of the Bayano swindle on short notice. The staff of Waldheim Cemetery kindly kept the gates open a few minutes past closing time one summer's day to ensure that a visitor from Canada was able to locate Leo's final resting place, and Waldheim's Stephen Ginsberg fielded follow-up questions.

Halifax-based legal historian Barry Cahill shared information about Leo's lawyer, Joseph Connolly. Thomas Raddall's son, Dr. Thomas Raddall of Liverpool, and former Liverpool mayor John Leefe shared stories they were told about Leo's time in Nova Scotia. Toronto journalist Matthew McClearn helped me track down information on his great-grandfather, who was one of the guests Leo entertained at Pinehurst. In a strange coincidence, Matt is a former student and newsroom colleague, and a good friend.

Blair Douglas of Caledonia, whose family used Pinehurst as a summer retreat for many years, showed me around the lodge back in 1992 and shared the local lore about Leo. Renowned photographer Sherman Hines offered a tour of his Museum of Photography in Liverpool, located in the former town hall where Leo catered dances and charmed the community. Claudine LeBlanc and David White, who teach at

Liverpool Regional High School, directed me to information on tuna fishing in the area and Zane Grey's 1924 visit.

Evanston resident Tom Clancy helped me locate the former site of Leo's lakeside mansion. Eminent Canadian historian Michael Bliss shared his knowledge of the early insulin treatment of diabetics, while Bill Zimmerman of Wolfville, who once owned the site of Laurie Mitchell's Tuna Inn, offered insights into the man who brought Leo to Nova Scotia.

Hilary McMahon of Westwood Creative Artists in Toronto shared my passion for Leo's story and made sure this book became a reality. I would like to express my gratitude to Linda McKnight of Westwood for her early support of my work and to Naomi Wittes Reichstein for believing in this project. A writer could not ask for a better or more insightful editor than Amy Gash at Algonquin, who sharpened the book's focus and recognized the parallels between Leo's story and the rise and fall of his nemesis, Cook County State's Attorney Robert Crowe. Thanks, too, to Rachel Careau for her thorough copyediting.

To say that Kerry Oliver has heard a lot about Leo's exploits over the years is an understatement. She has listened, encouraged, suggested, and advised for so long that I cannot begin to list the many ways she has contributed to this book. It is to her that I am the most grateful, for her love and support.

A NOTE ON SOURCES

NOTHING WAS AS it seemed in Leo Koretz's make-believe world of mysterious syndicates and Panamanian oil fields. The handful of accounts written long after he was caught added fresh layers of myth and distortion, fooling readers as expertly as Leo had hoodwinked investors. But the real story of the man who pioneered and mastered the Ponzi scheme is so gripping—and, at times, so incredible—that it needs no embellishment.

I discovered Leo and his swindle by chance. I was thumbing through a drawer of index cards at Nova Scotia's public archives in the late 1980s when an entry caught my eye. Typewritten and yellowed with age, it directed researchers to Halifax newspaper coverage of an intriguing incident in 1924.

> Leo Koretz (alias Lou Keytes), from Chicago, swindled $2 million in phony oil scheme. Hid out in Nova Scotia. Arrested and taken back to the U.S. where he died in prison.

Here was a story begging to be told. I did some digging and published a magazine article on the Bayano swindle and Leo's life on the lam in Canada. But I had only scratched the surface, and over the years, I picked away at the research for this book. Uncovering Leo's past and piecing together how he had worked his swindle became part hobby, part obsession. I compiled the detailed coverage of the case that had appeared in the Chicago and Halifax newspapers. I made contact with Leo's descendants. I tracked down court records of his crimes and eyewitness accounts of his activities. I visited Leo's Canadian hideaway while Pinehurst Lodge was still standing, walked the streets of the North Side neighborhood where he grew up, checked out his haunts in New York City.

I was determined to learn the truth about a larger-than-life figure who rarely, if ever, told the truth himself. And Leo's story, I discovered, is woven into the fabric of the corrupt politics and gang warfare that plagued Chicago in the 1920s. His life and his swindle parallel the rise to power of Cook County State's Attorney Robert Crowe, one of the most controversial figures of the time; the Bayano fraud and its spectacular collapse is Crowe's story, too.

This book separates fact from fiction. Every word in quotation marks, every headline, comes from a newspaper account or interview, a court document, or a diary or letter tucked away in an archive. (Spelling variations of the time, such as *clew* for *clue* and *through* abbreviated to *thru*, have been retained.) Dialogue is presented as it was recorded; scenes and events are portrayed as they were described in contemporary accounts and documents. Thanks to Chicago's sharp-eyed reporters, we know that Leo was chauffeured around the city in a maroon Rolls-Royce limousine and that the polka-dot bow tie he wore the day he dictated his confession was blue. The smoke from camera flash powder was so thick the day he pleaded guilty that courtroom windows were opened to clear the air—we know this, because Halifax deputy sheriff Rainard Scriven was there and recalled this detail in a press interview. We know that the billiard table in Leo's Evanston home was so big it would have cost a small fortune to remove it because this was the conclusion of the bankruptcy officials who liquidated his assets.

Much of the material presented here has been drawn from the extensive newspaper coverage of Leo's schemes and his life as a fugitive and of Crowe's efforts to find and prosecute him. While the journalists of 1920s Chicago thrived on one-upmanship and sometimes played loose with the facts, their reports remain the most reliable source of information on the Bayano swindle and Crowe's manhunt. With the best reporters on six dailies chasing down the story, few details were overlooked, and almost everyone Leo befriended, fooled, or swindled was tracked down and interviewed. Court records and archival research in the United States and Canada added new details and insights and often confirmed what was reported in the press. The transcript of Leo's confession has disappeared from court files, but his testimony at a bankruptcy hearing was recorded almost verbatim in the newspapers, making it possible for the master swindler to explain, in his own words, how he devised and operated his audacious scam.

The sources of quotations can be found in the endnotes that follow. Archival records are also identified, but information drawn from books and other published works is cited only when the source is obscure or facts may be in dispute. Genealogical resources such as census returns, city directories, professional guides, and steamships' passenger lists provided background information on people and were used to trace their movements. Names were checked against these and other official records, since spellings sometimes varied in press accounts. The amounts individual investors sank into Leo's schemes were compiled from creditors' claims filed with the bankruptcy court.

All dollar figures are those used at the time. Where figures have been converted to their value today, this has been done using an online conversion tool developed by the Economic History Association and accessible at www.measuringworth.com/uscompare. Conversion rates for the early 1920s fluctuate, and unless otherwise noted, 1923—the pivotal year in this story—has been used as the benchmark. In terms of purchasing power, $1 in 1923 is equivalent to about $13 today. A $1,000 share in the Bayano Syndicate, of course, remains as worthless now as it was when Leo was selling the shares in the Roaring Twenties.

NOTES

CHAPTER 1

3 to honor a financial wizard Details of the Drake banquet, who attended, and what was said are drawn from "'Ponzi' Koretz Once Feted at De Luxe Feast," *Chicago Daily Tribune*, December 14, 1923; and "Koretz Feted by Friends in 'Gratitude,'" *Chicago Evening American*, December 14, 1923.

3 most spacious hotel *The Blackstone and the Drake 1924: Shopping List and Points of Interest Information Book* (Chicago: Drake Hotel Company, 1924), 34.

4 Standard Oil had offered Grand jury indictment, dated February 1924, in United States v. Leo Koretz, p. 2. RG 21, U.S. District Court, Northern District of Illinois, Eastern Division, Chicago. Criminal Case Files, 1873–1978, case no. 12242, National Archives and Records Administration (NARA), Great Lakes Region, Chicago. The offer was reported in "Oil Swindle Nets Millions," *Chicago Daily Tribune*, December 13, 1923.

5 wealthiest Jew in Chicago "Locate Koretz, Expect Arrest in a Few Days," *Chicago Daily Tribune*, December 20, 1923.

5 an outstanding example "Cashed 40 Checks for $400,000," *Chicago Evening American*, December 15, 1923.

6 one of those kinds of places "Rolls-Royces in Koretz Garage," *Chicago Evening American*, December 14, 1923.

6 in the $20 million range Affidavit of Basil Curran, dated June 16, 1924, filed in In the Matter of Leo Koretz, Bankrupt, case no. 32520. RG 21, Bankruptcy Records, 1898 to 1979, Records of the U.S. District Court, Northern District of Illinois, Eastern Division, Chicago. NARA, Great Lakes Region, Chicago.

6 a rating of 100 per cent "Koretz Dupes Get $400,000," *Chicago Daily Tribune,* December 14, 1923.

6 a personal magnetism W. A. Swanberg, "The Fabulous Boom of Bayano," in *The Double Dealers: Adventures in Grand Deception,* ed. Alexander Klein (Philadelphia: J. B. Lippincott, 1958), 17.

6 a genius with the ladies "Koretz Liked the Ladies, but Liked 'Em Safely Married," *Chicago Evening American,* December 15, 1923.

6 His manners were wonderful Ibid.

8 He has always been good "'Fox' Seen in Loop Monday; Plane, Pilot Hunted," *Chicago Evening American,* December 15, 1923.

8 the era of wonderful nonsense Hugh Rawson and Margaret Miner, *The Oxford Dictionary of American Quotations,* 2nd ed. (New York: Oxford University Press, 2006), 292; also quoted in John J. McPhaul, *Deadlines and Monkeyshines: The Fabled World of Chicago Journalism* (Englewood Cliffs, NJ: Prentice-Hall, 1962), 223.

8 More people were comfortably well-off John Kenneth Galbraith, *The Great Crash, 1929* (New York: Time, 1961), 8.

8 I want a great deal of money F. Scott Fitzgerald, *This Side of Paradise* (New York: Collier Books, 1986), 268.

8 the only great city Quoted in Donald L. Miller, *City of the Century: The Epic of Chicago and the Making of America* (New York: Simon and Schuster, 1996), 17.

8 No other place butchers William Joseph Showalter, "Chicago Today and Tomorrow," *National Geographic* 35, no. 1 (January 1919): 3.

10 Do as the lady wishes! Wayne Andrews, *Battle for Chicago* (New York: Harcourt, Brace, 1946), 121.

11 Koretz would not take "Here's Story of Koretz, Business Hypnotist," *Chicago Evening American,* December 14, 1923.

11 I tried to dissuade people "Koretz Tells How the 'Suckers' Bit," *New York Times,* December 3, 1924.

11 a sort of negative salesmanship Edwin Baird, "Too Many Women!" *Inside Detective,* October 1938, 31.

12 I mentioned to a friend "Koretz Tells How the 'Suckers' Bit," *New York Times,* December 3, 1924.

12 In his former existence The slides were reproduced in the *Chicago Evening American,* December 18, 1923.

13 Everybody had confidence in him "How He Did It Told by Friend Who Took His Word," *Chicago Evening American*, December 14, 1923.

13 the very soul of honor "Koretz's Rise to Wealth Reads like Dime Novel," *Chicago Evening Post*, December 13, 1923.

13 His followers were devout "More Participators Tell Experiences with Koretz," *Chicago Evening American*, December 15, 1923.

CHAPTER 2

14 tempted to buy some shares The comment was reported in "Curious Crowds at Union Station to Get Peep at Leo Koretz," *Chicago Evening American*, December 1, 1924.

15 a system of wholesale robbery George J. Svejda, *Castle Garden as an Immigrant Depot, 1855–1890* (US Department of the Interior, National Parks Service, 1968), 128–30, available online at http://www.nps.gov/history/history/online_books/elis/castle_garden.pdf. Conditions inside Castle Garden are described in Milton Meltzer, *Taking Root: Jewish Immigrants in America* (New York: Dell, 1976), 52; and "Just from the Steerage," *New York Times*, March 9, 1888.

16 Leopold Koretz had been born Information on the Koretz family in Bohemia is based on the Jewish Register Rokycany, births/marriages/deaths 1874, 1875, microfilm HBMa 1782, p. 4, National Archives, Prague, and the following records in the State District Archives, Rokycany: Jewish Register Rokycany, births 1791–1872; marriages/deaths 1802–1932, pp. 6, 7, 10–11, 51, 110; Register of Rokycany Citizens, book 61, p. 95; List of Applications for Passport, book 78, record nos. 53, 59, 65, 68; Domicile Register of Rokycany, book 129A, house no. 10, p. 14; Domicile Register of Rokycany—Index, book 129 I, pp. 141, 951; Book of Issued Home Certificates 1870–1931, book 79, record nos. 946, 1149, 1150, 1349, 1380; Book of Issued Home Certificates 1853–1957, book 77, record nos. 78, 81, 184.

16 rife with ethnic tension This overview of Bohemia in the 1880s and its Jewish population is based on Elizabeth Wiskemann, *Czechs and Germans: A Study of the Struggle in the Historic Provinces of Bohemia and Moravia*, 2nd ed. (New York: St. Martin's, 1967), 1; Hillel J. Kieval, *The Making of Czech Jewry: National Conflict and Jewish Society in Bohemia, 1870–1918* (New York: Oxford University Press, 1988), 13; and Wilma Abeles Iggers, ed., *The Jews of Bohemia and Moravia: A Historical Reader* (Detroit: Wayne State University Press, 1992), 13, 20, 25, 94, 213–14.

18 the delightfulest ship *Wikipedia* entry for "Rivers Class Ocean Liner." *Werra* is described in Clas Broder Hansen, *Passenger Liners from Germany, 1816–1990* (West Chester, PA: Schiffer Books, 1991), 34. The cargo of gold and silver is noted in "Gold Rolling In," *Sacramento Daily Record-Union*, September 7, 1887.

18   settle in a black mass   Charles Dudley Warner, *Studies in the South and West with Comments on Canada* (New York: Harper and Brothers, 1889), 185.

18   No city in the world   Miller, *City of the Century*, 178 (see chap. 1 notes).

19   Chicago is the boss city   Emmett Dedmon, *Fabulous Chicago: A Great City's History and People* (New York: Atheneum, 1983), iv.

19   City of the Big Shoulders   Carl Sandburg, "Chicago," in *Chicago Poems* (New York: Dover, 1994), 1.

19   a macabre must-see for visitors   The celebrated actress Sarah Bernhardt, who was among the visitors, struggled "to get rid of the horrible vision of the stockyards" when she performed in the city in the early 1880s. Dedmon, *Fabulous Chicago*, 169; Miller, *City of the Century*, 199 (see chap. 1 notes).

19   unbelievable depravity   Herbert Asbury, *The Gangs of Chicago: An Informal History of the Chicago Underworld* (New York: Thunder's Mouth, 2002), 246. The judge's comment is noted on p. 123.

19   inhabited by savages   Quoted in Erik Larson, *The Devil in the White City: Murder, Magic, and Madness at the Fair That Changed America* (New York: Crown, 2003), 52.

19   police were too overwhelmed   See Richard C. Lindberg, *To Serve and Collect: Chicago Politics and Police Corruption from the Lager Beer Riot to the Summerdale Scandal, 1855–1960* (Carbondale: Southern Illinois University Press, 1998), chapter 6; and Asbury, *The Gangs of Chicago*, chapter 5. At any given time in the 1890s, Asbury estimated, there was only one patrolman on duty for every twenty thousand residents (93–94).

19   astonishing Chicago   Mark Twain, *Life on the Mississippi* (New York: Harper and Brothers, 1901), 433–34.

20   first and only veritable Babel   George W. Stevens, *The Land of the Dollar* (New York: Dodd, Mead, 1897), 144.

20   an accepted part of American life   Thomas Sowell, *Ethnic America: A History* (New York: Basic Books, 1981), 77–78.

20   a German enclave   Descriptions of North Town (now known as Old Town) and its history are drawn from the author's July 2009 visit and street-side plaques that record the neighborhood's past.

21   an immense epitome   "The Opening of the Fair," *Chicago Daily Tribune*, May 2, 1893, reprinted in *A Century of Tribune Editorials* (Freeport, NY: Books for Libraries Press, 1970), 64.

22 *Ad astra per aspera* Descriptions of Lake View High are drawn from *Fifteenth Annual Report of the Lake View High School for the Year Ending June 20, 1889* (Chicago: Stromberg, Allen, 1889).

22 **the great money-raiser** James Weber Linn, Lights and Darks, *Chicago Herald and Examiner,* December 3, 1924.

22 **could get blood** Ibid.

22 **idealistic** "'As Your Personal Friend,'" *Chicago Daily Tribune,* December 18, 1923.

22 **scrupulous character** Ibid.

22 **teamed up** "High Schools in the Finals," *Chicago Daily Tribune,* March 5, 1898.

23 **For Conquest or for Humanity** Descriptions of the commencement exercises are drawn from "Many Get Diplomas," *Chicago Daily Tribune,* June 24, 1898; and "Programs: Commencement and Rhetorical Exercises, 1876–1926," Lake View High School Collection, box 1, folder 20, Sulzer Regional Library, Chicago.

23 **century of usefulness** "The Passing of the Century," *Chicago Daily Tribune,* January 1, 1901, reprinted in *A Century of Tribune Editorials,* 71.

23 **a man of small stature** "The Peoria Infernal Machines," *New York Times,* August 3, 1881. For Crowe's Fenian ties, see Niall Whelehan, *The Dynamiters: Irish Nationalism and Political Violence in the Wider World, 1867–1900* (New York: Cambridge University Press, 2012), 77–78.

24 **to momentarily terrorize and paralyze** Newspaper article dated August 28, 1898, in the Peoriana Collection, vol. 15, p. 21, Peoria Public Library, Peoria, IL.

25 **I never had any liking** Quoted in Alvin V. Sellers, *The Loeb-Leopold Case with Excerpts from the Evidence of the Alienists and Including the Arguments to the Court by Counsel for the People and the Defense* (Brunswick, GA: Classic, 1926), 241.

25 **a fan of pulp-fiction novels** Ibid., 265.

25 **fluent talker** "Crowe or Igoe? Both Are Young and Ambitious," *Chicago Daily Tribune,* September 17, 1920.

CHAPTER 3

26 **As the country grows older** "Degrees Given Young Lawyers," *Chicago Daily Tribune,* June 9, 1901. Leo's graduation year is confirmed in Chicago-Kent College of Law *Alumni Directory, 1907,* p. 25, preserved in Chicago-Kent College of Law—Miscellanea folder, Chicago Historical Society.

26   without distinction as to sex   John Moses and Joseph Kirkland, eds., *History of Chicago, Illinois*, vol. 2 (Chicago: Munsell, 1895), 112.

27   In the practice of law   "Degrees Given Young Lawyers," *Chicago Daily Tribune*, June 9, 1901.

27   a local school with pretensions   Robert Stevens, "History of the Yale Law School: Provenance and Perspective," in *History of the Yale Law School: The Tercentennial Lectures*, ed. Anthony T. Kronman (New Haven: Yale University Press, 2004), 12.

27   the principles and rules   Quoted from the Yale Law School catalogue in Laura Kalman, *Legal Realism at Yale, 1927–1960* (Chapel Hill: University of North Carolina Press, 1986), 98.

27   docile enough and lazy enough   Arthur L. Corbin, "Sixty-Eight Years at Law," *Yale Law Report* 11 (1965): 21.

27   I paid more attention to Raffles   Quoted in Sellers, *The Loeb-Leopold Case*, 265 (see chap. 2 notes).

27   spoke feelingly of the bonds   "Winston Churchill at Yale," *New York Times*, December 14, 1900.

27   the capable man   "Bourke Cockran at Yale," *New York Times*, June 26, 1900.

28   marched in company formation   "A Yale Republican Club," *New York Times*, October 6, 1900.

28   squared off over the sale   The story is told in Edgar Lee Masters, *Levy Mayer and the New Industrial Era* (New Haven: Yale University Press, 1927), 40–42. The firm is now known as Mayer Brown, with an international roster of 1,600 lawyers, and has ranked in the top twenty of *American Lawyer* magazine's list of the world's highest-grossing law firms.

28   a martyr to his work   "Levy Mayer's Burial to Wait Return of Wife," *Chicago Daily Tribune*, August 15, 1922.

29   The so-called trust   "Corporations in Illinois," *New York Times*, January 5, 1902.

CHAPTER 4

30   Here Lies Sleeping Beauty   "Orders Her Epitaph in Gold," *Chicago Daily Tribune*, January 17, 1908.

30   Leo took the dog home   "How Koretz Got His Start—Took Money Bequeathed to a Dog," *Chicago Evening American*, December 15, 1923.

31   in partnership with Daniel Belasco   Leo described being "associated" with Belasco in his "Answer," dated December 28, 1920, filed in Maurice K. Over v. Leo

Koretz, case no. 356959 (1920), Superior Court—Divorce, Law, Chancery files, Archives of the Clerk of the Circuit Court, Cook County, IL, room 1113, Richard J. Daley Center, Chicago. Leo was described as Belasco's law partner in "Belasco's $100,000 Estate Lost in Koretz Swindle," *Chicago Daily Journal,* December 14, 1923.

31 He always had ambitions "Reviews 20 Years He Has Known Koretz, Beginning in School," *Chicago Evening American,* December 14, 1923.

31 I was a very poor Leo outlined how his fake mortgage scheme worked in his confession to prosecutors and at his bankruptcy hearing. See, for example, "Koretz Confesses Life of Swindling," *New York Times,* December 2, 1924; and "Koretz Tells Detailed Story of How He Worked Swindle," *Chicago Herald and Examiner,* December 3, 1923.

32 radiated warmth "Mrs. Koretz Is Heroic as Her World Crashes," *Chicago Daily Tribune,* December 14, 1923.

32 Golden Ghetto Irving Cutler, *The Jews of Chicago: From Shtetl to Suburb* (Urbana: University of Illinois Press, 2009), 85; Edward Mazur, "Jewish Chicago: From Diversity to Community," in *Ethnic Chicago,* ed. Melvin G. Holli and Peter d'A. Jones (Grand Rapids, MI: William B. Eerdmans, 1984), 50.

33 one of the last agricultural frontiers Henry C. Dethloff, "Rice Revolution in the Southwest, 1880–1910," *Arkansas Historical Quarterly* 29, no. 1 (Spring 1970): 66.

33 we had a good rice country W. H. Fuller, "Early Rice Farming on Grand Prairie," *Arkansas Historical Quarterly* 14, no. 1 (Spring 1955): 72.

33 prejudiced against it as a food G. T. Surface, "Rice in the United States," *Bulletin of the American Geographical Society* 43, no. 7 (1911): 505.

33 many tillers of the soil "Koretz's Rise to Wealth Reads Like Dime Novel," *Chicago Evening Post,* December 13, 1923.

34 one of the first to realize Robert W. Chowning, *The History of St. Francis County, Arkansas, 1954* (Forrest City, AR: Times-Herald, 1954), 118–19.

34 taught me farm values "Koretz Tells His Life Story," *Chicago Daily News,* December 2, 1924.

34 did not exist Ibid.

36 a "tangle" of land titles "Koretz's Rise to Wealth Reads Like Dime Novel," *Chicago Evening Post,* December 13, 1923.

36 in some cases many times over "Koretz N.Y. Victims Found," *Chicago Daily Tribune,* December 17, 1923.

CHAPTER 5

37 one of the wildest David McCullough, *The Path between the Seas: The Creation of the Panama Canal, 1870–1914* (New York: Touchstone/Simon and Schuster, 1977), 22.

37 far-away, mysterious place David Fairchild, "The Jungles of Panama," *National Geographic* 41, no. 2 (February 1922): 131.

38 Whenever we see Lester D. Langley and Thomas Schoonover, *The Banana Men: American Mercenaries and Entrepreneurs in Central America, 1880–1930* (Lexington: University Press of Kentucky, 1995), 35–36.

39 I fell—fell hard Leo recounted his dealings with Nieto and Belasco in December 1924, in court testimony widely reported in the press.

40 a hatred for all strangers Henry Pittier, "Little-Known Parts of Panama," *National Geographic* 23, no. 7 (July 1912): 648.

40 huge and numerous Image and text of stereographic photograph entitled "On the Bayano River, Interior Panama—Indians Supplying Panama Soldiers at a Frontier Pass." *Underwood and Underwood Glass Stereograph Collection 1895–1921,* Smithsonian Institution Collections, RSN 21266, viewable online at http://collections.si.edu. The photo is not dated but was taken sometime between 1904 and 1910.

41 the big idea "Koretz Confesses Life of Swindling," *New York Times,* December 2, 1924.

CHAPTER 6

42 It was a hard blow "'Wizard' Koretz Once Victimized in Deals Similar to His Own,'" *Chicago Evening American,* December 14, 1923.

42 "wild-cat" schemes "Koretz's Climb Dates to Death of 'Rich' Dog," *Chicago Herald and Examiner,* December 16, 1923.

42 It was a posh resort Descriptions of the Hotel Del Monte are drawn from Julie Cain, *Monterey's Hotel Del Monte,* Images of America Series (Charleston, SC: Arcadia, 2005).

42 Mae had quit her teaching "Koretz Panama Explorers Tell of Alligators," *Chicago Daily Tribune,* December 19, 1923; and "Canada Moves to Give Koretz Back to U.S.," *Evanston News-Index,* November 24, 1924.

43 I got deeper "The Making of a Criminal as Told by Koretz Himself," *Chicago Evening American,* December 2, 1924.

43 made the whole country seem safe David Howarth, *The Golden Isthmus* (London: Collins, 1966), 252.

43   vast supplies of timber   "Big Plantation Bought in Panama," *Los Angeles Sunday Herald,* February 20, 1910. See also "Californians Purchase Vast Tract in Panama," *San Francisco Call,* March 20, 1910; and "Big Panama Land Deal," *New York Times,* March 20, 1910.

43   stuck with me   Leo described how he devised his Bayano swindle in "Koretz Confesses Life of Swindling," *New York Times,* December 2, 1924; and "The Making of a Criminal as Told by Koretz Himself," *Chicago Evening American,* December 2, 1924.

44   vast timber interests   Mae described the 1911 Panama trip in court testimony. See "Arrest Mrs. Auerbach, Is Police Order," *Chicago Daily News,* December 17, 1923; and "He Left Me Broke, Mrs. Koretz Says," *Chicago Evening American,* December 18, 1923.

44   local color   "'Wizard' Koretz Once Victimized in Deals Similar to His Own,'" *Chicago Evening American,* December 14, 1923.

44   a report extolling the resources   The extracts and details of the report that follow are drawn from "Koretz Painted Bayano Lands as Paradise of Timber and Sugar Cane," *Chicago Herald and Examiner,* December 14, 1923. The report was produced as evidence at Leo's bankruptcy hearing: see "Koretz Tells His Life Story," *Chicago Daily News,* December 2, 1924.

CHAPTER 7

47   met all obligations promptly   Klein described his early dealings with Leo in court testimony. See, for instance, "Koretz Reported to Be within Day's Train Ride of City," *Chicago Evening Post,* December 19, 1923.

48   I always made money   "Koretz Found, Belief of U.S. Authorities," *Chicago Daily News,* December 19, 1923.

49   I'll consult Mr. Fischer   Ibid.

49   travelled quite a bit   Descriptions of the syndicate's principals are drawn from "Launch World-Wide Hunt for Koretz, Who Swindled Chicago Business Men Out of Millions," *Chicago Evening Post,* December 13, 1923; and "Koretz Kept No Books in Office, Says Secretary," *Chicago Evening Post,* December 18, 1923.

50   a hint here   "Reveal Plan of Wizard to Buy Yacht 'Speejacks,'" *Chicago Evening American,* December 18, 1923.

50   He never discussed his affairs   "How He Did It Told by Friend Who Took His Word," *Chicago Evening American,* December 14, 1923.

50   he utilized to a weirdly   "Koretz N.Y. Victims Found," *Chicago Daily Tribune,* December 17, 1923.

51   I tried my best to buy   "Here's Story of Koretz, Business Hypnotist," *Chicago Evening American,* December 14, 1923.

51   I have been trying to figure   "How Koretz Made Them Eager to Buy," *Chicago Herald and Examiner,* December 14, 1923.

51   I didn't go out after prospects   "Koretz Arrest Halts $1,000,000 Scheme," *Chicago Daily News,* November 28, 1924.

51   I'm only letting my real friends   "Hunt Rich Lawyer and $1,000,000," *Chicago Herald and Examiner,* December 13, 1923.

51   Koretz was a brilliant student   "One Victim Says Koretz Gave Loot to Poor," *Chicago Evening American,* December 18, 1923.

52   would not lend you $5   "Here's Story of Koretz, Business Hypnotist," *Chicago Evening American,* December 14, 1923.

52   I never suspected him   "More Participators Tell Experiences with Koretz," *Chicago Evening American,* December 15, 1923.

52   I thought he was doing   Ibid.

52   That is the whole secret   "Koretz Secret—He Sold Shares Only to 'Those He Loved,'" *Chicago Evening American,* December 14, 1923.

52   Every time I would get   "Woman Gives New Clew to Leo Koretz," *Chicago Daily News,* December 20, 1923.

53   My money was Leo's   "Koretz' Brother Tells of $175,000 for Family," *Chicago Daily News,* December 19, 1923.

53   I turned over every cent   Koretz Found, Belief of U.S. Authorities," *Chicago Daily News,* December 19, 1923; and "Koretz Reported to Be Within Day's Train Ride of City," *Chicago Evening Post,* December 19, 1923.

53   I never wanted members   "Koretz Arrest Halts $1,000,000 Scheme," *Chicago Daily News,* November 28, 1924.

53   The man had his own relatives   Richman's comments were widely reported in the Chicago press, including "Hunt Two More Women, Both in Society, in Koretz Triangle," *Chicago Evening American,* December 19, 1923.

54   the bedroom of Chicago   Michael H. Ebner, *Creating Chicago's North Shore: A Suburban History* (Chicago: University of Chicago Press, 1988), 210, 241.

54   one of the show places   "Rolls-Royces in Koretz Garage," *Chicago Evening American,* December 14, 1923. Descriptions of the mansion that follow are based on press reports and bankruptcy court records.

55   Mr. Koretz was most sensitive   "Koretz Book Lover, Conrad His Idol," *Chicago Evening American,* December 19, 1923.

55   probably the most exalted position   *Time Capsule, 1923: A History of the Year Condensed from the Pages of Time* (New York: Time, 1967), 213.

55 the hub of business activity *Chicago Central Business and Office Building Directory, 1908* (Chicago: Winters, 1908).

55 I always have had a beautiful "Koretz Arrest Halts $1,000,000 Scheme," *Chicago Daily News,* November 28, 1924. Other press reports described the layout and furnishings.

56 a striking specimen of skyscraper Leslie A. Hudson, *Chicago Skyscrapers in Vintage Postcards* (Charleston, SC: Arcadia, 2004), 53.

57 Leo sent over money His generosity was noted in an article published in the *Chicago Daily News* on October 26, 1917, which is referenced in research notes labeled "*True*: Koretz, Leo," p. 9, Ms. Coll/Swanberg, W. A., box 58, Rare Book and Manuscript Library, Columbia University, New York (Swanberg Papers). The money was used to buy ice cream for the wounded soldiers.

57 also engaged in rice growing World War I Draft Registration Cards, 1917–1918, Cook County, IL, card no. 3070 (serial no. 3637) for Leo Koretz, available online at ancestry.com.

57 the most wonderful woman "Mrs. Koretz to Go to Work," *Chicago Evening American,* December 18, 1923.

57 The women were crazy "Koretz Liked the Ladies, but Liked 'Em Safely Married," *Chicago Evening American,* December 15, 1923.

57 played flappers and unmarried women "2 True Bills in $7,000,000 Fraud, Report," *Chicago Herald and Examiner,* December 15, 1923.

58 He was so sympathetic "Koretz Liked the Ladies, but Liked 'Em Safely Married," *Chicago Evening American,* December 15, 1923.

58 The poor woman "Love-Making Role Not in Leo Koretz' Swindling Scheme," *Chicago Evening American,* December 18, 1923.

58 never liked or trusted "Reviews 20 Years He Has Known Koretz, Beginning in School," *Chicago Evening American,* December 14, 1923.

58 Now and then the thought "Friends Sorrow for Plight of Wife of Swindler; Aid Her," *Chicago Evening American,* December 14, 1923.

59 became indignant at their lack "More Participators Tell Experiences with Koretz," *Chicago Evening American,* December 15, 1923.

59 It was like a hot tip "3 True Bills Today to Raise Koretz Bail," *Chicago Evening American,* November 28, 1924.

59 you could have told me "Koretz Secret—He Sold Shares Only to 'Those He Loved,'" *Chicago Evening American,* December 14, 1923.

59 The few investors who sought "Koretz Vendor of False Mortgages, Is New Charge," *Chicago Evening Post,* December 15, 1923.

59 Sure thing "Koretz N.Y. Victims Found," *Chicago Daily Tribune,* December 17, 1923.

60 I have never received "'Close Friend' of Koretz Tells How Family 'Lost All,'" *Chicago Evening American,* December 19, 1923.

60 There was no turning back "The Making of a Criminal as Told by Koretz Himself," *Chicago Evening American,* December 2, 1924.

60 business . . . was dull "Koretz Tells His Life Story," *Chicago Daily News,* December 2, 1924.

CHAPTER 8

62 ALL CHICAGO SEEKS SOLUTION *Chicago Daily News,* July 26, 1919, quoted in Gary Krist, *City of Scoundrels: The Twelve Days of Disaster That Gave Birth to Modern Chicago* (New York: Crown, 2012), 152.

62 I grabbed her Quoted in Krist, *City of Scoundrels,* 164.

63 Seldom has the populace "Watchman Confesses Murder of Child," *New York Times,* July 28, 1919.

63 morons Krist, *City of Scoundrels,* 139.

63 There will be a general *Chicago Daily Tribune,* July 29, 1919, reproduced in Simon Baatz, *For the Thrill of It: Leopold, Loeb, and the Murder That Shocked Chicago* (New York: HarperCollins, 2008), 200.

63 If the evidence shows Quoted in Baatz, *For the Thrill of It,* 200; and Krist, *City of Scoundrels,* 247.

63 subnormal Krist, *City of Scoundrels,* 140–41.

63 knowing his weakness Ibid.

63 a dastardly crime Sellers, *The Loeb-Leopold Case,* 239–40 (see chap. 2 notes).

64 I'm sorry Quoted in Baatz, *For the Thrill of It,* 201; and Krist, *City of Scoundrels,* 248.

64 exact and just Press response to the Fitzgerald sentence was compiled in a campaign pamphlet, "Judge Robert E. Crowe: His Platform and Record of Achievements," dated September 15, 1920, 6–7, in Hal Higdon Research Papers on Leopold and Loeb case, ca. 1920–1980, series 3, box 2, Chicago History Museum.

65 vigorous and quick-tongued Lloyd Lewis and Henry Justin Smith, *Chicago: The History of Its Reputation* (New York: Blue Ribbon Books, 1929), 441, 461.

66 a professional occupation Editorial published March 30, 1926, quoted in Carroll Hill Wooddy, *The Chicago Primary of 1926: A Study in Election Methods* (Chicago: University of Chicago Press, 1926), 13.

66 the wild doings Paul Michael Green, "Irish Chicago: The Multiethnic Road to Machine Success," in *Ethnic Chicago*, ed. Holli and Jones, 417 (see chap. 4 notes).

66 dictator-like office Lewis and Smith, *Chicago*, 441.

67 Fallen is Babylon! Quoted in Karen Abbott, *Sin in the Second City: Madams, Ministers, Playboys, and the Battle for America's Soul* (New York: Random House, 2007), 283.

67 aggressive, but with more education Wooddy, *The Chicago Primary of 1926*, 18.

67 brilliant record Quoted in "Judge Robert E. Crowe: His Platform and Record of Achievements," 3–4.

67 Once upon a time Lloyd Wendt and Herman Kogan, *Big Bill of Chicago* (Indianapolis: Bobbs-Merrill, 1953), 11.

68 became as safe as the flivver Quoted in Sellers, *The Loeb-Leopold Case*, 241 (see chap. 2 notes). *Flivver* was slang for any car that was old, small, and cheap.

68 swift, uncompromising and stern Quoted from *Chicago Evening American*, March 12, 1918, in "Judge Robert E. Crowe: His Platform and Record of Achievements," 4

68 anarchy "Indict 17 Negro Rioters," *New York Times*, August 5, 1919.

69 the most fair-minded man The *Chicago Defender*, quoted in "Judge Robert E. Crowe: His Platform and Record of Achievements," 5.

69 presided over a special grand jury "Haywood Surrenders; Bail Fixed at $10,000," *New York Times*, January 6, 1920; "Indict Leaders of Communists," *New York Times*, January 22, 1920; "Rose Pastor Stokes Indicted in Chicago," *New York Times*, January 24, 1920.

69 the sixth largest German city Douglas Bukowski, *Big Bill Thompson, Chicago, and the Politics of Image* (Urbana: University of Illinois Press, 1998), 62.

CHAPTER 9

70 the same glow of pride Swanberg, "The Fabulous Boom of Bayano," 20 (see chap. 1 notes). Descriptions of suite 629 are based on press reports.

70 MADE FROM THE FIRST LOG Ibid.

71 YES, WE HAVE NO BAYANO "Koretz Dupes Get $400,000," *Chicago Daily Tribune,* December 14, 1923.

71 **Each step you take in The Drake** Quotations and descriptions of the Drake are drawn from Robert V. Allegrini, *Chicago's Grand Hotels: The Palmer House, Hilton, the Drake, and the Hilton Chicago* (Charleston, SC: Arcadia, 2005), 57–67; and *The Blackstone and The Drake 1924,* 34, 69, 134 (see chap. 1 notes).

71 **Real millionaires** "'Love-Making' Role Not in Leo Koretz' Swindling Scheme," *Chicago Evening American,* December 18, 1923.

71 **I casually mentioned that oil** "Koretz Tells Detailed Story of How He Worked Swindle," *Chicago Herald and Examiner,* December 2, 1924.

72 **They began to besiege me** "10 Year Prison Term Confronts Koretz," *Chicago Daily Tribune,* December 3, 1924.

72 **They thrust it on me** "Koretz Admits 18 Years of Swindling," *Chicago Herald and Examiner,* December 2, 1924.

72 **this amount would be doubled** "Launch World-Wide Hunt for Koretz, Who Swindled Chicago Business Men Out of Millions," *Chicago Evening Post,* December 13, 1923.

73 **Hooray! Look what I just got** "Koretz N.Y. Victims Found," *Chicago Daily Tribune,* December 17, 1923; and "Say Koretz Planned Christmas 'Clean-up,'" *New York Times,* December 17, 1923.

73 **much persuasion** "More Participators Tell Experiences with Koretz," *Chicago Evening American,* December 15, 1923.

73 **Now, look here, Leo** "Koretz N.Y. Victims Found," *Chicago Daily Tribune,* December 17, 1923.

74 **Questions were asked of me** "Koretz on Stand Tells How He Worked Swindle," *Chicago Evening American,* December 2, 1924.

74 **prosperity band-wagon rolled along** Frederick Lewis Allen, *Only Yesterday: An Informal History of the Nineteen-Twenties* (New York: Harper and Brothers, 1931), 181.

74 **There is radio music** Quoted in ibid., 78.

74 **new age of locomotion** "Life in Chicago Streets," *Chicago Daily Tribune,* December 29, 1923.

75 YOU SHOULD HAVE $10,000 William E. Leuchtenburg, *The Perils of Prosperity, 1914–32* (Chicago: University of Chicago Press, 1958), 9.

75   **It's a racket**   Quoted in Roger M. Olien and Diana Davids Olien, *Easy Money: Oil Promoters and Investors in the Jazz Age* (Chapel Hill: University of North Carolina Press, 1990), 11.

76   **America is running through**   Christopher Tugendhat and Adrian Hamilton, *Oil: The Biggest Business,* rev. ed. (London: Eyre Methuen, 1975), 74–75, 77–78.

76   **stark, staring, oil mad**   Quoted in Jules Tygiel, *The Great Los Angeles Swindle: Oil, Stocks, and Scandal during the Roaring Twenties* (New York: Oxford University Press, 1994), 14.

77   **for more concentrated robbery**   Allen, *Only Yesterday,* 154. Harding's creation of the word *normalcy* for *normality* is noted on p. 126.

CHAPTER 10

78   **They must, first of all**   Edwin H. Sutherland, *The Professional Thief: By a Professional Thief* (Chicago: University of Chicago Press, 1937), 56, n. 13.

78   **live a chameleon existence**   Frank W. Abagnale, *The Art of the Steal: How to Protect Yourself and Your Business from Fraud, America's #1 Crime* (New York: Broadway Books, 2001), 5, 14, 20.

79   **must be able to make anyone**   David W. Maurer, *The Big Con: The Story of the Confidence Man* (New York: Anchor Books, 1999), 143.

79   **must have something loveable**   Sutherland, *The Professional Thief,* vii.

79   **would have propelled them**   Introduction to Maurer, *The Big Con,* ix–x.

79   **an enterprising New Yorker**   The *New York Herald* coined the term in its coverage of Thompson's fraud. See Gary Lindberg, *The Confidence Man in American Literature* (New York: Oxford University Press, 1982), 6; and Richard Rayner, *Drake's Fortune: The Fabulous True Story of the World's Greatest Confidence Artist* (New York: Doubleday, 2002), 47–48.

79   **is a covert cultural hero**   Lindberg, *The Confidence Man in American Literature,* 3.

79   **It is a good thing**   Ibid., 6 (emphasis in original).

80   **They wanted something for nothing**   Quoted in the afterword to J. R. Weil and W. T. Brannon, *Con Man: A Master Swindler's Own Story* (New York: Broadway Books, 2004), 329.

80   **Nobody . . . would ever be eager**   Ben Hecht, *Gaily, Gaily* (Garden City, NY: Doubleday, 1963), 196–97.

81 We all crave easy money   Quoted in Mitchell Zuckoff, *Ponzi's Scheme: The True Story of a Financial Legend* (New York: Random House, 2005), 108.

81 PONZI HAD NOTHING ON LEO   *Halifax Herald,* November 25, 1924, republished in the *Halifax Evening Mail,* November 25, 1924.

82 the whole thing falls down   Sutherland, *The Professional Thief,* 62, n. 22.

82 There is never enough money   Charles P. Kindleberger, *Manias, Panics and Crashes: A History of Financial Crises* (New York: Basic Books, 1978), 35.

CHAPTER 11

83 Four Reasons Why   "What Is the Duty of the State's Attorney? . . . Who Is the Man Judge Robert E. Crowe?" (1920). Campaign pamphlet preserved in the Wisconsin Historical Society Library Pamphlet Collection, Madison, WI, pp. 12–13.

84 I was just tired of her   Quoted in Michael Lesy, *Murder City: The Bloody History of Chicago in the Twenties* (New York: W.W. Norton, 2007), 14.

84 regrettable error   Quoted in Baatz, *For the Thrill of It,* 213–14 (see chap. 8 notes).

84 an asinine finding   Ibid.

84 entirely unbefitting   Ibid.

84 Justice has been done   "Decree Noose for Wanderer, 'Boob's' Killer," *Chicago Daily Tribune,* March 19, 1921.

84 It is the finality   Robert E. Crowe, "Capital Punishment Protects Society," *Forum,* February 1925, reproduced in *The Death Penalty: Opposing Viewpoints,* 2nd ed., ed. Carol Wekesser (San Diego: Greenhaven, 1991), 41–46.

85 Cook County is extremely fortunate   Quoted in Lesy, *Murder City,* 73.

85 referring to him as Judge Crowe   For instance, see Clarence Darrow's references to him at the Leopold and Loeb sentencing hearing, reproduced in Clarence Darrow, *Attorney for the Damned* (New York: Simon and Schuster, 1957), 30, 67. See also "Robert E. Crowe, Prosecutor, Dead," *New York Times,* January 20, 1958.

85 Fighting Bob   "Robert Crowe Services Set for Tomorrow," *Chicago Daily Tribune,* January 20, 1958.

86 the most remarkable attempt   "The Conspiracy That Failed," *Chicago Daily Tribune,* April 20, 1923, reproduced in *A Century of Tribune Editorials,* 94 (see chap. 2 notes).

86 The end of the Lundin-Thompson   Quoted in Bukowski, *Big Bill Thompson,* 133 (see chap. 8 notes).

86 Reports and rumors reaching me Quoted in Lindberg, *To Serve and Collect*, 169 (see chap. 2 notes).

86 my efforts to close hell-holes Wooddy, *The Chicago Primary of 1926*, 29 (see chap. 8 notes).

86 refer to Crowe as "Bobby" Ibid.

87 suspicion and cobwebs Bukowski, *Big Bill Thompson*, 140 (see chap. 8 notes).

87 difficult to refuse a favor Wooddy, *The Chicago Primary of 1926*, 12 (see chap. 8 notes).

87 as corrupt as the Thompson-Lundin Ibid., 98–101. Wooddy sets out allegations of corruption and patronage leveled against the Crowe-Barrett faction in detail.

87 call a halt to killing Quoted in Lesy, *Murder City*, 106.

88 caught fast trains "Raid Chicago Bucket Shops," *New York Times*, June 3, 1923.

CHAPTER 12

89 touted his latest project The mocked-up page was reproduced in *Chicago Daily Tribune*'s December 17, 1923, edition under the headline "Koretz's Wife to Tell Her Story to Referee Today."

89 We were told that the big five "Launch World-Wide Hunt for Koretz, Who Swindled Chicago Business Men Out of Millions," *Chicago Evening Post*, December 13, 1923.

90 When you wish the Bayano Leo Koretz to Alex Fitzhugh, June 7, 1923, reproduced on p. 6 of the grand jury indictment, dated February 1924, in United States v. Leo Koretz (see chap. 1 notes).

90 That is simply astounding Alex Fitzhugh to Leo Koretz, September 11, 1923, quoted in "Order 'Koretz Plane' Stopped," *Chicago Daily Journal*, December 13, 1923.

90 All our boats are in "Claims Koretz Gave Wife Cash," *Chicago Herald and Examiner*, December 28, 1923.

90 was interested in oil enterprises Affidavit of Basil Curran, dated June 16, 1924, filed in In the Matter of Leo Koretz, Bankrupt (Chicago) (see chap. 1 notes).

91 who were rich Robert A. M. Stern, Gregory Gilmartin, and John Massengale, *New York 1900: Metropolitan Architecture and Urbanism, 1890–1915* (New York: Rizzoli, 1983), 261, 267.

91   neither the Grand Dukes   Christopher Gray, "A Grand Hotel Recalls Its Roots," *New York Times,* May 29, 2005.

92   He talked perpetually   "N.Y. Victims of Koretz Say He Is There," *Chicago Evening American,* December 17, 1923.

92   the wives of wealthy husbands   "Arrest Mrs. Auerbach, Is Police Order," *Chicago Daily News,* December 17, 1923; and "N.Y. Woman Tells of Tip on Flight of Promoter," *Chicago Evening American,* December 17, 1923.

93   I thought he was just kind   "Order 'Koretz Plane' Stopped," *Chicago Daily Journal,* December 13, 1923.

93   He was a very kind man   "More Participators Tell Experiences with Koretz," *Chicago Evening American,* December 15, 1923.

93   of the rosy outlook   "Launch World-Wide Hunt for Koretz, Who Swindled Chicago Business Men Out of Millions," *Chicago Evening Post,* December 13, 1923.

93   an official of Standard Oil   Investigators found Loomis's June 9, 1923, letter to Matthews in Leo's office in the Majestic Building in December 1923. It was reproduced in the *Chicago Evening American*'s December 14, 1923, edition, under the headline "Koretz Fled with Million in Boat; Hunt Woman Accomplice."

94   By the way, judge   Accounts of Leo's conversations with Fisher are based on the following press interviews with the judge: "Wife's Advice Keeps Judge from Quitting Bench for Koretz Job," *Chicago Evening American,* December 15, 1923; "Judge Exposes Koretz Plot," *Chicago Daily Tribune,* December 16, 1923; "Koretz N.Y. Victims Found," *Chicago Daily Tribune,* December 17, 1923; "Lambs Sought Out Koretz and Begged for a Shearing; Got It," *Chicago Daily Journal,* December 13, 1923.

95   the fundamental right   *Time Capsule/1923,* 198 (see chap. 7 notes).

96   I want men   "Oil Swindle Nets Millions," *Chicago Daily Tribune,* December 13, 1923.

96   I knew when they got there   "Koretz Tells Detailed Story of How He Worked Swindle," *Chicago Herald and Examiner,* December 2, 1924.

96   It doesn't seem possible   Ibid.

97   I talked Bayano   "'Guilty': To Be Koretz Plea," *Chicago Daily Tribune,* December 2, 1924.

97   I knew the bubble would burst   "10 Year Prison Term Confronts Koretz," *Chicago Daily Tribune,* December 3, 1924.

97   The losses had become so heavy   "Koretz Admits 18 Years of Swindling," *Chicago Herald and Examiner,* December 2, 1924.

97 I was disgusted "10 Year Prison Term Confronts Koretz," *Chicago Daily Tribune,* December 3, 1924.

98 we do not want to lose "Koretz Fled with Million in Boat; Hunt Woman Accomplice," *Chicago Evening American,* December 14, 1923.

98 asked the State Bank The transactions that follow were reported in "Koretz Loot May Be $7,000,000," *Chicago Herald and Examiner,* December 14, 1923; "Koretz Dupes Get $400,000," *Chicago Daily Tribune,* December 14, 1923; "Koretz Fled with Million in Boat; Hunt Woman Accomplice," *Chicago Evening American,* December 14, 1923; and "Bootlegging Trail Leads Up to Koretz," *Chicago Daily News,* December 18, 1923.

98 I knew it was all over "Koretz Tells Detailed Story of How He Worked Swindle," *Chicago Herald and Examiner,* December 2, 1924.

CHAPTER 13

99 an attractive brunette This episode was widely reported. See, for instance, "Girl Offers Koretz Clue," *Chicago Evening Post,* December 14, 1923.

100 Three of the six men Biographical information on members of the Bayano inspection group is drawn from the following press reports: "Oil Swindle Nets Millions," *Chicago Daily Tribune,* December 13, 1923; "Launch World-Wide Hunt for Koretz, Who Swindled Chicago Business Men Out of Millions," *Chicago Evening Post,* December 13, 1923; "Here's Story of Koretz, Business Hypnotist," *Chicago Evening American,* December 14, 1923; "Cashed 40 Checks for $400,000," *Chicago Evening American,* December 15, 1923; "Panama Never Heard of Wily Mr. Leo Koretz," *Chicago Daily Tribune,* December 16, 1923; "Back from Bayanoland," *Chicago Daily News,* December 18, 1923; and "Order 'Koretz Plane' Stopped," *Chicago Daily Journal,* December 13, 1923.

100 I didn't know just what "Chicagoans Sent to Big Paying Jobs, Borrow Carfare," *Chicago Evening American,* December 18, 1923.

101 live like kings "Koretz Dupes Found a River," *Chicago Herald and Examiner,* December 18, 1923.

101 He told us he wanted "Koretz Found, Belief of U.S. Authorities," *Chicago Daily News,* December 19, 1923.

101 BON VOYAGE "Reveal Plan of Wizard to Buy Yacht 'Speejacks,'" *Chicago Evening American,* December 18, 1923.

101 fully confident that everything "Back from Bayanoland," *Chicago Daily News,* December 18, 1923.

101   some oil play in Panama   William D. McCain, *The United States and the Republic of Panama* (New York: Russell and Russell, 1965), 102–3. Gulf and another big player, Sinclair Oil, had ceased their exploration efforts by 1929, McCain notes, "without apparent success."

102   The chief articles of export   James Langland, ed., *Chicago Daily News Almanac and Year-Book for 1924* (Chicago: Chicago Daily News Company, 1923), 649.

102   SHOOT   "Chicagoans Sent to Big Paying Jobs, Borrow Carfare," *Chicago Evening American,* December 18, 1923.

102   Leo Kahnweiler, a diamond salesman   Kahnweiler and Agatstein described the events that follow in Transcript of Record, December 10, 1924, pp. 2–3, 7–10, filed in Lewy Brothers Co. v. The Chicago Title and Trust Company. RG 276: Records of the U.S. Court of Appeals, Seventh Circuit Court—Chicago, Records and Briefs, case no. 3523, NARA, Chicago.

103   a small fortune in jewels   "Koretz Relatives to Give Up $300,000," *Chicago Daily News,* December 13, 1923; and "Doris Keane Sought as Key in Koretz Hunt," *Chicago Daily News,* December 22, 1923.

103   turned up at his brother's   Emil described his meeting with Leo in press interviews and court testimony. See, for instance, "Koretz Dupes Get $400,000," *Chicago Daily Tribune,* December 14, 1923.

103   dinner at a South Side hotel   "Koretz Tells His Life Story," *Chicago Daily News,* December 2, 1924; and "Koretz Tells How the 'Suckers' Bit," *New York Times,* December 3, 1924.

104   Sarah Mandel was at home   She described her meeting with Leo in several press accounts, including "Teacher, Her Brother Surrender $25,000 Koretz 'Oil Dividend,'" *Chicago Evening American,* December 14, 1923.

105   Leo bid us good-by   "Koretz in Texas, Is Latest Clue," *Chicago Evening American,* December 22, 1923.

105   Leo accepted their invitation   The job offer and the dinner with the Schoeners were widely reported in the Chicago papers and in "Say Koretz Planned Christmas 'Clean-up,'" *New York Times,* December 17, 1923.

106   Julius Koretz was in New York   Julius's testimony describing his last night with Leo appeared in the following press accounts: "Woman Gives New Clew to Leo Koretz," *Chicago Daily News,* December 20, 1923; "Charge Koretz Took Half of $200,000 Estate," *Chicago Evening Post,* December 20, 1923; "Crowe on Hot Koretz Trail," *Chicago Daily Journal,* December 20, 1923; "Koretz In-Laws under Quiz," *Chicago Evening American,* December 21, 1923; and "Hunt Koretz 'Conscience' Fund," *Chicago Evening American,* December 22, 1923.

107   We are in sight of land   "Launch World-Wide Hunt for Koretz, Who Swindled Chicago Business Men Out of Millions," *Chicago Evening Post,* December 13, 1923.

107   promoters and would be experts   C. D. Mell, "A Report on the Timber Tract of the Bayano River Lumber Company in the Province of Panama, R.P." (unpublished typescript, no date), New York Botanical Garden, LuEsther T. Mertz Library, Bronx, NY. While Mell's report states the month but not the year of his inspection tour, Ellis Island passenger lists confirm he visited Panama in 1923 and returned to New York on December 27 aboard SS *Cristobol.*

108   we began to worry a bit   "Koretz Panama Explorers Tell of Alligators," *Chicago Daily Tribune,* December 19, 1923.

108   We were staggered   "Chicagoans Sent to Big Paying Jobs, Borrow Carfare," *Chicago Evening American,* December 18, 1923.

108   The blueprint is a big fake   Research notes labeled "*True:* Koretz, Leo," p. 9 (Swanberg Papers) (see chap. 7 notes).

109   "Why," they were told   "Koretz Panama Explorers Tell of Alligators," *Chicago Daily Tribune,* December 19, 1923.

109   NO TRACE OF THE LAND   The telegrams are quoted in "Launch World-Wide Hunt for Koretz, Who Swindled Chicago Business Men out of Millions," *Chicago Evening Post,* December 13, 1923; "Oil Swindle Nets Millions," *Chicago Daily Tribune,* December 13, 1923; and "Cashed 40 Checks for $400,000," *Chicago Evening American,* December 15, 1923.

109   we were convinced   "Chicagoans Sent to Big Paying Jobs, Borrow Carfare," *Chicago Evening American,* December 18, 1923. Klein described some of the events in Panama in his Affidavit in Aid of Extradition, sworn November 20, 1924, pp. 2–3. RG 59, State Department records, Central Decimal File, 1910–1929, file 242.11 K84: Leo Koretz—As Tabbed, Box 3383, NARA, College Park, MD.

110   nothing of importance   "Torn Letter Clew to 'Other' Koretz Loves," *Chicago Daily News,* December 15, 1923.

110   greatly upset   "Koretz Writes Son to Be Honest Man," *Chicago Daily News,* December 27, 1923.

CHAPTER 14

111   hurtled westward   Details of the wreck of the Twentieth Century Limited, unless otherwise noted, are drawn from "9 Die, 39 Injured in Wreck," *Chicago Daily Tribune,* December 10, 1923, republished in *13 Bell-Ringers of 1923: News Stories Selected for Exceptional Merit from the Thousands Written by Chicago Tribune Reporters* *during the Past Year* (Chicago: Chicago Tribune, 1923), 59–64; "15 Die in Century Wreck," *Chicago Daily Tribune*, December 9, 1923; "Engineer Admits He Speeded Past Caution Signals," *Chicago Daily Tribune*, December 12, 1923; and "No Century Wreck Inquest," *Chicago Daily News*, December 12, 1923.

112 We thought he had been killed Emil's quotations appeared in "Koretz Dupes Get $400,000," *Chicago Daily Tribune*, December 14, 1923; and "Woman in Koretz Case," *Chicago Daily Journal*, December 14, 1923.

112 desperate to confront Leo George Murray, a former Hearst reporter in Chicago, told of Polachek's trip to the station in search of Leo in his memoirs. Polachek, he wrote, invested $80,000 "in a Zionist scheme floated by the Ponzi of the time" and decided "to meet the man at the train and get his money back before the swindler got wind of the danger and tried to flee." While Murray did not name the promoter, Polachek is listed in court documents as one of Leo's creditors and filed a claim for $22,000. George Murray, *The Madhouse on Madison Street* (Chicago: Follett, 1965), 218–19, 222; List of claims filed and allowed . . . third and final dividend, October 30, 1926, p. 10, filed in In the Matter of Leo Koretz, Bankrupt (Chicago) (see chap. 1 notes).

112 Arrangements were made "Woman in Koretz Case," *Chicago Daily Journal*, December 14, 1923.

113 a letter arrived for Milton Simon Descriptions of the arrival of Leo's letter and the contents of the suitcase are based on the testimony of Simon and Klarkowski. Transcript of Record, December 10, 1924, pp. 8–9, 11–12, filed in Lewy Brothers Co. v. The Chicago Title and Trust Company (see chap. 13 notes).

113 she would never keep his tainted money Leo explained his motives at his bankruptcy hearing. See "10 Year Prison Term Confronts Koretz," *Chicago Daily Tribune*, December 3, 1924.

113 If you think my son "Koretz Writes Son to Be Honest Man," *Chicago Daily News*, December 27, 1923.

113 Dear Son Mandel recited the letter, as he remembered it, at Leo's bankruptcy hearing. This version appeared in "Don't Follow My Example, Koretz Writes His Son," *Chicago Evening Post*, December 27, 1923.

114 might put bad thoughts "Claims Koretz Gave Wife Cash," *Chicago Herald and Examiner*, December 28, 1923.

114 I can't touch that money Details of the family conference and the legal advice given the family are drawn from "Woman Gives New Clew to Leo Koretz," *Chicago Daily News*, December 20, 1923.

115 personally led the raid Details of the searches of the Majestic Building office and the Drake suite are based on the following press reports: "Koretz Relatives to Give Up $300,000," *Chicago Daily News,* December 13, 1923; "Oil Swindle Nets Millions," *Chicago Daily Tribune,* December 13, 1923; "Meteoric Rise to Wealth of 'Self-Made' Koretz," *Chicago Evening American,* December 14, 1923; "Koretz Loot May Be $7,000,000," *Chicago Herald and Examiner,* December 14, 1923; and "Koretz Dupes Get $400,000," *Chicago Daily Tribune,* December 14, 1923.

116   It looks like a serious case   "See Million Oil Swindle," *Chicago Daily News,* December 12, 1923.

116   There are a hundred other   "Oil Swindle Nets Millions," *Chicago Daily Tribune,* December 13, 1923.

CHAPTER 15

119   OIL SWINDLE NETS MILLIONS   The headlines appeared in the December 12 edition of the *Chicago Daily Journal* and the December 13 editions of the *Chicago Daily Tribune* and the *Chicago Evening Post.*

119   Koretz worked almost exactly opposite   "Koretz Dupes Get $400,000," *Chicago Daily Tribune,* December 14, 1923.

119   LAMBS SOUGHT OUT KORETZ   *Chicago Daily Journal,* December 13, 1923.

119   DUPED BY SON   *Chicago Evening American,* December 14, 1923.

120   World's Greatest Newspaper   The motto, first used in advertisements in 1909, was registered as a trademark and began appearing on page 1 in 1911. John Tebbel, *An American Dynasty: The Story of the McCormicks, Medills and Pattersons* (Garden City, NY: Doubleday, 1947), 82. Circulations of Chicago's dailies are based on figures that appear in Lloyd Wendt, *Chicago Tribune: The Rise of a Great American Newspaper* (Chicago: Rand McNally, 1979), 458, 486, 491.

121   wily, bold and imaginative   McPhaul, *Deadlines and Monkeyshines,* 113 (see chap. 1 notes).

121   *coarseness* and *slang* and a *low tone*   Robert W. Jones, *Journalism in the United States* (New York: E. P. Dutton, 1947), 431, 450–53 (emphasis in original).

121   "plugged" crime and scandal   W. A. Swanberg, *Citizen Hearst: A Biography of William Randolph Hearst* (New York: Charles Scribner's Sons, 1961), 351.

121   A GOOD Newspaper   *Chicago Evening American,* December 14, 1923.

121   A Paper for the Family   *Chicago Evening American,* December 21, 1923.

121   KILLS MOTHER IN ROW   *Chicago Evening American,* December 14, 1923.

121   Fist was her dentist   *Chicago Evening American,* December 21, 1923.

121   a screaming woman running   Swanberg, *Citizen Hearst*, 35; Ben Hecht, *A Child of the Century* (New York: Simon and Schuster, 1954), 144.

121   cheap, trashy and senseless stuff   H. L. Mencken. "Reflections on Journalism: From the *Baltimore Evening Sun*, Dec. 29, 1924," in *The American Journalism History Reader*, ed. Bonnie Brennen and Hanno Hardt (New York: Routledge, 2011), 147.

121   to unearth, snatch or wangle   Descriptions of newsgathering practices are drawn from the memoirs of McPhaul and Hecht. See McPhaul, *Deadlines and Monkeyshines*, 8, 12–13, 91–92, 123–24, 176–81 (see chap. 1 notes); and Hecht, *A Child of the Century*, 113, 123–24, 126.

122   critics dismissed the central characters   Ben Hecht, Charles MacArthur, and George W. Hilton, *The Front Page: From Theater to Reality* (Hanover, NH: Smith and Kraus, 2002), 19, 40–41.

123   so that the family would get   "Reveals Woman Spy in Koretz Swindle," *Chicago Daily News*, December 14, 1923.

123   unusually honest   "Koretz Dupes Get $400,000," *Chicago Daily Tribune*, December 14, 1923.

123   KORETZ KIN WHO SCORNED   *Chicago Evening American*, December 15, 1923.

123   I thought I was rich   "Koretz Reported to Be within Day's Train Ride of City," *Chicago Evening Post*, December 19, 1923.

123   Leo . . . is still our brother   "'Fox' Seen in Loop Monday; Plane, Pilot Hunted," *Chicago Evening American*, December 15, 1923.

123   This—this isn't our shame   "Old Mother of Koretz Collapses," *Chicago Evening American*, December 14, 1923.

123   I was never so disappointed   "Koretz's Rise to Wealth Reads Like Dime Novel," *Chicago Evening Post*, December 13, 1923.

124   I cannot understand   "'Ponzi' Koretz Once Feted at De Luxe Feast," *Chicago Daily Tribune*, December 14, 1923.

124   That . . . tells the story   "More Participators Tell Experiences with Koretz," *Chicago Evening American*, December 15, 1923.

124   It is amazing   "Woman in Koretz Case," *Chicago Daily Journal*, December 14, 1923.

124   undoubtedly the cleverest   "Koretz N.Y. Victims Found," *Chicago Daily Tribune*, December 17, 1923.

124 suffered from a sort "Friends Sorrow for Plight of Wife of Swindler; Aid Her," *Chicago Evening American*, December 14, 1923.

124 I am having the will changed "More Participators Tell Experiences with Koretz," *Chicago Evening American*, December 15, 1923.

124 It is like a nightmare "Koretz's Rise to Wealth Reads Like Dime Novel," *Chicago Evening Post*, December 13, 1923.

124 It seems astounding "Crowe on Hot Koretz Trail," *Chicago Daily Journal*, December 20, 1923.

124 There are so many inexplicable "Girl Offers Koretz Clue," *Chicago Evening Post*, December 14, 1923.

125 I am still unable "Wife's Advice Keeps Judge from Quitting Bench for Koretz Job," *Chicago Evening American*, December 15, 1923.

125 Everything is fine, just fine "Mrs. Koretz Is Heroic as Her World Crashes," *Chicago Daily Tribune*, December 14, 1923.

125 WIFE SUFFERS, TOO *Chicago Evening American*, December 15, 1923. **125 LEFT DESTITUTE BY KORETZ** *Chicago Herald and Examiner*, December 14, 1923.

125 Why are they talking about "Mrs. Koretz Will Work," *Chicago Daily News*, December 17, 1923.

125 She is a very sick "Wife of Koretz Seriously Ill in Collapse," *Chicago Evening American*, December 15, 1923.

126 greatest rogue of modern times "Psychology of Leo Koretz," *Chicago Literary Times* 1, no. 21 (January 1, 1924): 1–2. There is no byline on the piece, but Hecht described himself as the paper's "chief and sometimes sole contributor" and noted that his friend and associate editor, Maxwell Bodenheim, "fitfully helped me fill the pages." Hecht, *A Child of the Century*, 319–20, 338–39. Hecht parlayed his success as a playwright into a career as a Hollywood screenwriter. When he wrote the screenplay for 1939's *It's a Wonderful World*, starring James Stewart and Claudette Colbert, he offered a tip of the hat to Leo by giving one of the supporting characters, a policeman, the name Sergeant Koretz.

126 There was no other woman "Launch World-Wide Hunt for Koretz, Who Swindled Chicago Business Men out of Millions," *Chicago Evening Post*, December 13, 1923.

CHAPTER 16

127 Koretz? Where do they get Davidson's comments and his description of Bronson have been compiled from reports in the Chicago papers.

128 a tremendous shock Auerbach's comments were reported in "Koretz Liked the Ladies, but Liked 'Em Safely Married," *Chicago Evening American,* December 15, 1923; and "2 True Bills in $7,000,000 Fraud, Report," *Chicago Herald and Examiner,* December 15, 1923.

129 He was a Don Juan "Seek 2 Chicago Women Friends of Oil Juggler," *Chicago Daily Tribune,* December 16, 1923.

129 You can do well McPhaul, *Deadlines and Monkeyshines,* 172 (see chap. 1 notes).

129 She lives in a fashionable "Police Guard Hotel Room of Mrs. Auerbach to Serve Subpoena in Koretz case," *Chicago Evening Post,* December 15, 1923.

129 I don't want to cast odium *Chicago Daily Tribune,* December 15, 1923.

130 BARE KORETZ'S DOUBLE LIFE Ibid.

130 Here . . . he passed his afternoons "Torn Letter Clew to 'Other' Koretz Loves," *Chicago Daily News,* December 15, 1923.

130 She was not the woman "Police Guard Hotel Room of Mrs. Auerbach to Serve Subpoena in Koretz Case," *Chicago Evening Post,* December 15, 1923.

130 I wasn't the only woman "Torn Letter Clew to 'Other' Koretz Loves," *Chicago Daily News,* December 15, 1923.

130 I have absolute faith "Cite Wife of Auerbach in Koretz Case," *Chicago Herald and Examiner,* December 16, 1923.

132 TORN LETTER CLEW *Chicago Daily News,* December 15, 1923. The contents of the letter and Leo's links to Fraser and Schoener were the subject of numerous reports in the Chicago press and the *New York Times.*

132 not unattractive little woman "Koretz Mystery Woman Found," *Chicago Herald and Examiner,* December 17, 1923.

132 I shudder now to think "Arrest Mrs. Auerbach, Is Police Order," *Chicago Daily News,* December 17, 1923.

132 Koretz' complicated affairs "Torn Letter Clew to 'Other' Koretz Loves," *Chicago Daily News,* December 15, 1923.

132 I drove a great part "N.Y. Woman Tells of Tip on Flight of Promoter," *Chicago Evening American,* December 17, 1923; and "Arrest Mrs. Auerbach—Order," *Chicago Daily Journal,* December 17, 1923.

133 series of "love nests" "Koretz Knew Women in Many Cities," *Chicago*

Herald and Examiner, December 17, 1923; and "Say Koretz Planned Christmas 'Clean-up,'" *New York Times,* December 17, 1923.

133 For four days "Seek 2 Chicago Women Friends of Oil Juggler," *Chicago Daily Tribune,* December 16, 1923.

133 the ancient triumvirate Ibid.

133 real cause of the swindler's flight "Bare Koretz's Double Life," *Chicago Daily Tribune,* December 15, 1923.

133 several times against her will "Order 'Koretz Plane' Stopped," *Chicago Daily Journal,* December 13, 1923.

133 I want action "Question Mrs. Auerbach on Flight of Koretz," *Chicago Daily Tribune,* December 18, 1923.

134 My only acquaintance with him Auerbach's statement and Sbarbaro's comments are drawn from two press reports: "Question Mrs. Auerbach on Flight of Koretz," *Chicago Daily Tribune,* December 18, 1923; and "Koretz Indicted; U.S. Warrant for Arrest Issued," *Chicago Evening Post,* December 18, 1923.

134 I knew and know nothing "Call Kin before Grand Jury," *Chicago Evening American,* December 17, 1923.

134 We have no desire "Question Mrs. Auerbach on Flight of Koretz," *Chicago Daily Tribune,* December 18, 1923.

134 concerned itself as much with inquiring "Koretz Reported to Be within Day's Train Ride of City," *Chicago Evening Post,* December 19, 1923.

134 We find that a grave injustice These quotations appeared in "Locate Koretz, Expect Arrest in a Few Days," *Chicago Daily Tribune,* December 20, 1923; and "Woman Gives New Clew to Leo Koretz," *Chicago Daily News,* December 20, 1923.

CHAPTER 17

137 Yes, it was a terrible surprise Klein was quoted in "Mrs. Koretz Will Work," *Chicago Daily News,* December 17, 1923; "Mrs. Koretz Left Penniless," *Chicago Daily Journal,* December 17, 1923; and "Mrs. Koretz to Go to Work," *Chicago Evening American,* December 18, 1923.

137 dressed as a widow "Find Koretz Trail in S. America, U.S. Hears," *Chicago Evening Post,* December 17, 1923.

138 whether he is real Mae's testimony was widely reported in the Chicago press.

139 My one regret "Arrest Mrs. Auerbach, Is Police Order," *Chicago Daily News,*

December 17, 1923.

139 Yes madam "Son of Wizard Goes to Work Selling Shirts in Evanston Store," *Chicago Evening American,* December 19, 1923.

139 We had heard about oil "Koretz Dupes Found a River," *Chicago Herald and Examiner,* December 18, 1923.

139 We talked to everybody "Chicagoans Sent to Big Paying Jobs, Borrow Car-fare," *Chicago Evening American,* December 18, 1923.

140 KORETZ DUPES FOUND A RIVER *Chicago Herald and Examiner,* December 18, 1923.

140 ARGONAUTS OF OIL RETURN *Chicago Daily News,* December 18, 1923.

140 Haven't you fellows had enough? "Bayano River Sextet Back, Sad and Mum," *Chicago Evening Post,* December 18, 1923.

140 I have a lot of good Ibid.

140 Our offices are under our hats "Four of Koretz Panama Party Sadly Come Home," *Chicago Herald and Examiner,* December 19, 1923.

140 that Koretz' promotion was a fraud "Bayano River Sextet Back, Sad and Mum," *Chicago Evening Post,* December 18, 1923.

140 You'd think that legal experience Kaufman's Comment, *Chicago Evening American,* December 14, 1923.

141 Just one small conversation "Oil Swindle Nets Millions," *Chicago Daily Tribune,* December 13, 1923.

141 One of the richest oil fields *Chicago Daily News,* December 14, 1923.

141 BUBBLE, BUBBLE, TOIL AND TROUBLE *Chicago Evening American,* December 15, 1923.

141 leading financial laxative From Pillar to Post, *Chicago Evening Post,* December 19, 1923.

141 I did not think it strange "Koretz Kept No Books in Office, Says Secretary," *Chicago Evening Post,* December 18, 1923.

141 I loaned a little money "Koretz Found, Belief of U.S. Authorities." *Chicago Daily News,* December 19, 1923.

142 We will never give up "Blackmail Koretz for Million?" *Chicago Herald and Examiner,* December 19, 1923.

142 It was every cent "Court Must Make Us Return $75,000," *Chicago Evening*

American, December 19, 1923.

142 he had felt "intimidated" "Call Man to Quiz on Offer to Find Him," *Chicago Evening American,* December 22, 1923.

142 nothing criminal "Ask $25,000 to Reveal Hiding Place of Koretz," *Chicago Daily Tribune,* December 22, 1923.

143 Knowing Leo Koretz "Claims Koretz Gave Wife Cash," *Chicago Herald and Examiner,* December 28, 1923; and "Seek Koretz in the West," *Chicago Daily News,* December 28, 1923.

144 swallowed their losses "Koretz Is Caught at Halifax Hotel," *New York Times,* November 24, 1924.

144 sucker list "Locate Koretz, Expect Arrest in a Few Days," *Chicago Daily Tribune,* December 20, 1923.

144 You can name your own Ibid.

144 revelation would "ruin" him "N.Y. Victims of Koretz Say He Is There," *Chicago Evening American,* December 17, 1923; and "Find Koretz Trail in S. America, U.S. Hears," *Chicago Evening Post,* December 17, 1923.

144 in an uproar "Meteoric Rise to Wealth of 'Self-Made' Koretz," *Chicago Evening American,* December 14, 1923.

145 heaviest investors Hecht, *A Child of the Century,* 154 (see chap. 15 notes). Information on Brisbane and his fortune is drawn from Oliver Carlson, *Brisbane: A Candid Biography* (New York: Stackpole Sons, 1937), 16, 254, 266, 278.

CHAPTER 18

147 these birds would now be The Key West incident was recounted in the December 23, 1923, letter of US Marshal B. E. Dyson to Attorney General Harlan F. Stone. RG 60, Department of Justice records, Classified Subject Files, file 36-18-3 (Leo Koretz), box 9131, NARA, College Park, MD.

148 One who has faith "Anonymous Letters Made Public by Crowe," *Chicago Evening Post,* December 18, 1923.

148 This case is too big "Koretz Here in Skirts, Report," *Chicago Herald and Examiner,* December 21, 1923.

148 I intend to keep my staff "Crime in County Cut in Half by Crowe and Aids," *Chicago Daily Tribune,* January 31, 1924.

148 Something's rotten in official Denmark Kaufman's Comment, *Chicago*

Evening American, December 14, 1923.

148 Who was asleep *Chicago Evening Post,* December 19, 1923.

149 huge returns "Koretz Indicted; U.S. Warrant for Arrest Issued," *Chicago Evening Post,* December 18, 1923.

149 The main thing now "Koretz Reported to Be within Day's Train Ride of City," *Chicago Evening Post,* December 19, 1923.

149 scope and dignity "Bootlegging Trail Leads Up to Koretz," *Chicago Daily News,* December 18, 1923.

149 We hope that the federal officials "Locate Koretz, Expect Arrest in a Few Days," *Chicago Daily Tribune,* December 20, 1923.

150 Dresses expensively The wording of the bulletin is included in Swanberg's research notes. See *"True:* Koretz, Leo," 23 (Swanberg Papers) (see chap. 7 notes).

150 to supply several humorous magazines "Koretz Is Soviet Finance Minister, 'Hot Tip' to U.S.," *Chicago Evening American,* December 22, 1923.

150 I never heard the name "Koretz One Swindler She Missed, Says Doris Keane," *Chicago Herald and Examiner,* December 22, 1923.

150 the super-Ponzi "'Locate' Koretz in Many Climes; Now Seek Aids," *Chicago Daily Tribune,* December 25, 1923.

150 the Panama Ponzi "Bare Koretz's Double Life," *Chicago Daily Tribune,* December 15, 1923.

150 Bayanoed "Koretz on Grill Here Today," *Chicago Daily Tribune,* December 1, 1924. The *Herald and Examiner* later tried to coin a term as well, dubbing Leo's victims "Bayanoes." See "Koretz Taken Ill in Prison," *Chicago Herald and Examiner,* January 6, 1925.

150 the most resourceful confidence man "Koretz Is Caught at Halifax Hotel," *New York Times,* November 24, 1924.

150 This is the greatest swindle "Was Preparing for Get-Away to South When Arrested," *Evening Mail,* November 25, 1924.

151 If I get any word "Mrs. Koretz Says She Never Can Forgive Husband," *Chicago Daily Tribune,* December 24, 1923.

151 We have pretty nearly run Ibid.

151 If—On New Year's The text of the card was quoted in various press reports, See, for instance, "Koretz Greeting Cards' Source Sought by U.S.," *Chicago Evening Post,* December 29, 1923.

151   Leo's last line   "Koretz Sends Yule Greetings to His Victims," *Chicago Daily Tribune,* December 29, 1923.

152   Joke or not   Ibid.

CHAPTER 19

153   hardly an equal for knowledge   Grant Richards, *Author Hunting, by an Old Literary Sportsman: Memories of Years Spent Mainly in Publishing, 1897–1925* (London: Hamish Hamilton, 1934), 74–77.

153   is one of the most potent   Temple Scott, ed., *The Friendship of Books* (New York: Macmillan, 1926), ix, xi–xii.

154   interested in opening a bookstore   Leo described his meeting with Scott in "Koretz Tells His Life Story," *Chicago Daily News,* December 2, 1924.

154   was one of the most interesting   "Koretz Posed as Man of Letters, Purchased New York Book Store," *Chicago Evening American,* November 26, 1924.

155   I suppose I took some chance   "Koretz Tells His Life Story," *Chicago Daily News,* December 2, 1924.

155   Leo checked the newspapers   Leo confirmed he followed newspaper coverage of his case in the transcript of evidence, pp. 21–22, In the Matter of the Estate of Leo Koretz in Bankruptcy, Nova Scotia Supreme Court (NSSC) (Halifax), Bankruptcy Court, RG 39 B, vol. 7, no. 72B, Nova Scotia Archives and Records Management (NSARM), Halifax, NS.

155   the metropolis of our planet   Ernest H. Gruening, "New York: 1. The City—Work of Man," in *These United States: Portraits of America from the 1920s,* ed. Daniel H. Borus (Ithaca, NY: Cornell University Press, 1992), 256–57, 265.

156   to make the height   Bryan B. Sterling and Frances N. Sterling, eds., *A Will Rogers Treasury: Reflections and Observations* (New York: Crown, 1982), 45.

156   In New York   Gruening, "New York," 265.

156   It just occurred to me   "'Guilty': To Be Koretz Plea," *Chicago Daily Tribune,* December 2, 1924.

156   often called him "kite"   Ibid.

156   Prefers jail, he says   From Pillar to Post, *Chicago Evening Post,* January 2, 1924.

156   Koretz was an insatiable reader   "Koretz Is Soviet Finance Minister, 'Hot Tip' to U.S.," *Chicago Evening American,* December 22, 1923.

157 I regarded him "Watson, Woman in Koretz Case, Found in India," *Chicago Daily Tribune*, January 31, 1924.

157 All the books he took "Koretz Posed as Man of Letters, Purchased New York Book Store," *Chicago Evening American*, November 26, 1924.

158 cozy rather than commercial "$49,000 Koretz Cash and Store Are Seized," *Chicago Daily News*, November 25, 1924.

158 It was a dud Ibid.

158 the city of the Good Time Ford Madox Ford, *New York Is Not America: Being a Mirror to the States* (New York: Albert and Charles Boni, 1927), 49.

158 city of booze and bankrolls Sterling and Sterling, eds., *A Will Rogers Treasury*, 45.

158 some place in the woods "Koretz Tells His Life Story," *Chicago Daily News*, December 2, 1924.

CHAPTER 20

160 citadel of The Leisure Class "The Theory of the A&F Class," *New York Times*, November 19, 1977.

160 an accomplished hunter Biographical information on Mitchell is drawn from his obituary, "L. D. Mitchell Dead; Noted Sportsman," *New York Times*, June 19, 1931.

161 veritable paradise Quoted in James Morrison and Lawrence Friend, *"We Have Held Our Own": The Western Interior of Nova Scotia, 1880–1940* (Ottawa: Parks Canada, 1981), 94. The photograph appears on p. 95.

161 Here is the new field Laurie D. Mitchell, "Where to Go for Atlantic Tuna," *Liverpool (NS) Advance*, April 22, 1914 (reprinted from *Rod and Gun*).

161 He was pleasant and agreeable "Women and $100 Tips Trapped Leo," *Chicago Herald and Examiner*, November 25, 1924.

162 If one has never been A. Byron McLeod, "Hunting in Nova Scotia," *National Sportsman*, n.d., p. 427. Undated copy of magazine article in manuscript file A97-58, Thomas Raddall Research Centre, Queens County Museum, Liverpool, NS.

162 fairy lakes Albert Bigelow Paine, *The Tent Dwellers* (Halifax: Nimbus, 1993), 33.

162 big game country Irvin S. Cobb, *Some United States: A Series of Stops in Various Parts of This Nation with One Excursion across the Line* (New York: George H. Doran, 1926), quoted in Mike Parker, *Where Moose and Trout Abound: A Sporting Journal* (Halifax: Nimbus, 1995), 31, 34.

162 John D. Rockefeller Jr James H. Morrison, "American Tourism in Nova Scotia, 1871–1940," *Nova Scotia Historical Review* 2, no. 2 (1982): 47.

163 commodious lodge Robert R. McLeod, *Pinehurst, or Glimpses of Nova Scotia Fairyland* (Boston: Bartlett, 1908), 11 (republished in the *Halifax Herald*, February 13, 1909).

163 Evening at Pinehurst William E. Marshall, *Brookfield and Other Verse* (Montreal: John Lovell and Son, 1919), 141. The poem was written in 1907.

164 a writer of reputation "Glancing over Nova Scotia—Liverpool," *Halifax Herald*, March 14, 1924.

164 L. Keyte, of New York "'Pinehurst Is Sold to New York Man," *Caledonia (NS) Gold Hunter and Farmers' Journal*, April 4, 1924.

165 nine miles out to sea Zane Grey, *Tales of Swordfish and Tuna* (New York: Harper and Brothers, 1927), 2, 13–14.

CHAPTER 21

166 He was an odd sight Raddall's recollections of Leo, unless otherwise noted, are drawn from his autobiography, *In My Time: A Memoir* (Toronto: McClelland and Stewart, 1976), 129–30; and "Pinehurst Lodge," in Thomas Head Raddall Fonds, MS-2-2002, series 14, research notes, box 31 file 1, 1–2, Dalhousie University Archives, Halifax, NS.

167 a printed menu card Raddall kept the signed card, which is included in the "Pinehurst Lodge" file in his papers. Raddall Fonds, series 14, box 31, file 1.

168 Money was nothing to him Quoted in Vernon L. Oickle, *Friends and Neighbours: A Collection of Stories from the Liverpool Advance* (Yarmouth, NS: Fundy Group, 1993), 135.

169 is now living at this beautiful "South Brookfield," *Caledonia (NS) Gold Hunter and Farmers' Journal*, May 16, 1924.

169 He spoke of the States Raddall, *In My Time*, 129.

170 to use later in his writings "'Why Don't the Women Leave Me to Myself?'—Koretz," *Chicago Daily Tribune*, November 28, 1924.

171 was known as one of the best "Swindler Led Merry Life of Country Squire," *Chicago Daily Tribune*, November 25, 1924. Descriptions of the renovated Pinehurst and its contents are drawn from reports and photographs published in Chicago newspapers and the Nova Scotia press, as well as "Pinehurst Lodge," Raddall Fonds, p. 2; and Robert Johnson, *Brookfield in the Wilderness: A History of North and South Brookfield, Queens County, Nova Scotia, Commemorating the 200th Anniversary of the Founding of Brookfield* (Caledonia: North Queens Heritage Society, 1999), 53.

172   He was a real fussy man   The Scott brothers' recollections, unless otherwise noted, are drawn from Oickle, *Friends and Neighbours,* 135. The author misspells Maurice Scott's name as Morris.

172   Getting me there   Interview with Maurice Scott, April 28, 1977, Kejimkujik Oral History Project. Recording in the possession of the Friends of Keji Cooperating Association, Hammonds Plains, NS. The author is grateful to the interviewer, Dr. James Morrison, for his assistance in tracking down this recording.

CHAPTER 22

174   prince of entertainers   "A Prince of Entertainers Was Millionaire Keytes," *Halifax Evening Mail,* November 24, 1924.

174   merry life   "Swindler Led Merry Life of Country Squire," *Chicago Daily Tribune,* November 25, 1924.

174   and seventeen were drunk   "Koretz Gives $200,000 to His Victims," *Chicago Daily Tribune,* November 28, 1924.

174   for fear he'd talk   Ibid.

174   Pinehurst became a northern version   See F. Scott Fitzgerald, *The Great Gatsby* (New York: Simon and Schuster, 1995), chapter 3. Fitzgerald wrote the novel in the summer and fall of 1924.

175   Everyone liked him   Oickle, *Friends and Neighbours,* 135 (see chap. 21 notes).

175   He was a rich bachelor   Interview with Maurice Scott, April 28, 1977, Kejimkujik Oral History Project (see chap. 21 notes).

176   a succession of dear friends   "Pinehurst Lodge," Raddall Fonds, p. 3 (see chap. 21 notes).

176   Keyte had a fickle   Ibid.

176   They send me urgent telegrams   "Koretz Hints Girl Loved and Betrayed Him," *Chicago Daily Tribune,* November 26, 1924.

176   a brilliant party   "Women and $100 Tips Trapped Leo," *Chicago Herald and Examiner,* November 25, 1924. Mitchell identified two of the prominent guests as George McClearn and J. J. Cameron. McClearn, a Liverpool hardware merchant just coming off a four-year term as the town's mayor, was Queens County's representative in the Nova Scotia Legislature. Cameron practiced law in Liverpool with W. L. Hall, the leader of one of the province's political parties; he would soon begin a thirty-year reign as the town's solicitor and magistrate.

177   Dancing . . . was the chief entertainment   "Glancing over Nova Scotia—Caledonia," *Halifax Herald,* September 2, 1924. The party was also noted in the Liverpool section of "Glancing over Nova Scotia" in the paper's August 30, 1924, edition and in "Nova Scotia Day by Day—Caledonia," *Halifax Morning Chronicle,* August 30, 1924.

177   Some people commandeered canoes   Thomas Raddall described the party and quoted Leo's comments about his past in "Pinehurst Lodge," Raddall Fonds, 2–3 (see chap. 21 notes).

CHAPTER 23

179   the most cruel, cowardly, dastardly   Baatz, *For the Thrill of It,* 3 (see chap. 8 notes).

180   love of thrills   Ibid., 91.

180   crime of the century   The case's claim to this overused title is discussed in Hal Higdon, *Leopold and Loeb: The Crime of the Century* (Urbana: University of Illinois Press, 1999), 7–8.

180   The Franks murder mystery   Ibid., 112.

181   a barbarous practice   Clarence Darrow, "The Futility of the Death Penalty," *Forum,* September 1928, reproduced in Wekesser, *The Death Penalty,* 48, 50 (see chap. 11 notes).

181   poor sons of millionaires   Quotations from Crowe's closing arguments are drawn from Sellers, *The Loeb-Leopold Case,* 234, 242–43, 247 (see chap. 2 notes). The reference to Koretz is on p. 293. In the 1956 novel *Compulsion,* a fictionalized account of the Leopold and Loeb case, a character modeled on Robert Crowe claims one of the thrill killers had aspired to become "a clever financial criminal, putting through gigantic stock swindles, like Koretz"—echoing Crowe's actual words from the 1924 trial. Meyer Levin, *Compulsion* (New York: Simon and Schuster, 1956), 465.

182   a crime of singular atrocity   Sellers, *The Loeb-Leopold Case,* 320–21 (see chap. 2 notes).

183   Arkansas land worth   Among the victims of the Arkansas scam was the widow of Leo's former law partner Daniel Belasco, the man who had introduced him to David Nieto in 1907. Belasco died in a car accident in 1915, and Leo, who administered the estate, convinced his wife to invest $31,000 in his Arkansas operations. Her investment was worthless. See "Find Koretz Trail in S. America, U.S. Hears," *Chicago Evening Post,* December 17, 1923; and "Koretz Fraud Grows by Millions," *Chicago Herald and Examiner,* December 18, 1923. Belasco's death was reported in "2 Killed, 8 Hurt in Auto Smashes; Lawyer a Victim," *Chicago Daily Tribune,* July 20, 1915.

183   mobbed the place all day   "Koretz Past Glories Sold for Creditors," *Chicago Daily Tribune*, April 30, 1924.

183   any other salesman   "Mrs. Koretz Earns Success," *Chicago Evening American*, November 25, 1924.

183   That woman is a brick   "Koretz' Wife Absolutely Penniless, Loyal Friends Assert," *Chicago Herald and Examiner*, November 26, 1924.

184   She has been remarkable   "Kin Hoped for Death, Not Cell, for Koretz," *Chicago Evening American*, November 26, 1924.

184   almost dispatched men to Paris   This was mentioned in several press accounts, including "Swindler Led Merry Life of Country Squire," *Chicago Daily Tribune*, November 25, 1924; and "Bank Clerk's Alert Eyes See Real Swindler under Beard," *Chicago Evening American*, November 25, 1924.

184   seen him in a hotel lobby   "Canada Moves to Give Koretz Back to U.S.," *Evanston News-Index*, November 24, 1924.

184   to a sanatorium in Montreal   While this was widely reported, the sanatorium was never identified and there is no evidence Leo traveled to any part of Canada besides Nova Scotia. See "Ask New Indictment Here as Captive Nears Break," *Chicago Evening American*, November 25, 1924; and "State and U.S. Claim Right to Punish Koretz," *Chicago Daily Tribune*, November 25, 1924.

184   a matter of conjecture   "$10,000 Reward Out for Koretz Capture in Million Swindle," *Chicago Daily Tribune*, September 12, 1924.

184   Klein provided a personal guarantee   Petition of Henry A. Klein, dated March 23, 1925, In the Matter of Leo Koretz, Bankrupt (Chicago) (see chap. 1 notes).

185   a poster announcing the new reward   The poster was reproduced in the *Halifax Evening Mail*, November 25, 1924. After Leo's arrest, Thomas Raddall clipped and kept a copy, now in the "Pinehurst Lodge" file in his papers. Raddall Fonds, series 14, box 31, file 1 (see chap. 21 notes).

185   an infernal place   Grey, *Tales of Swordfish and Tuna*, 12–13 (see chap. 20 notes).

185   with thrilling zest   Ibid., 13.

CHAPTER 24

186   just to make a splurge   "Women and $100 Tips Trapped Leo," *Chicago Herald and Examiner*, November 25, 1924; and " 'Why Don't the Women Leave Me to Myself?'—Koretz," *Chicago Daily Tribune*, November 28, 1924.

186   sending letters and expensive gifts   "Bare Secret Trips from Halifax for Huge Sums," *Chicago Evening American*, November 28, 1924. Elizabeth Mitchell was described as a student at Halifax's Convent of the Sacred Heart school in "Glancing over Nova Scotia—Liverpool," *Halifax Herald,* April 21, 1924. The *Chicago Daily Journal* went so far as to accuse Leo of "making love" to Mitchell's "young daughter;" see "Vote Indictment of Koretz," *Chicago Daily Journal,* November 28, 1924. Other press accounts alleged Leo was involved with an unnamed, underage girl who had been sent away to a convent, a possible reference to Mitchell's daughter.

187   I figured if this man   Abbott's recollections are found in Oickle, *Friends and Neighbours,* 137–38 (see chap. 21 notes).

187   too big-eyed   "No Signs of Treasure Hidden on the Koretz Estate at Pinehurst," *Halifax Morning Chronicle,* November 27, 1924.

188   practically made Zane Grey   "Biggest Confidence Man in U.S. Captured in Halifax," *Halifax Morning Chronicle,* November 24, 1924; "'Millionaire' Keytes Cuts Wide Swath in Province," *Halifax Morning Chronicle,* November 25, 1924.

188   I'll show you how   "Koretz' Arrest Halts $1,000,000 Scheme," *Chicago Daily News,* November 28, 1924.

188   I planned to make Zane Grey   "Bare Secret Trips from Halifax for Huge Sums," *Chicago Evening American,* November 28, 1924.

188   "ripped" into the author   "'Why Don't the Women Leave me to Myself?'—Koretz," *Chicago Daily Tribune,* November 28, 1924.

188   If it were possible   Grey, *Tales of Swordfish and Tuna,* 95 (see chap. 20 notes).

189   He didn't know a good book   "Didn't Know Good Books from Bale of Hay, Says Collector," *Chicago Evening American,* November 29, 1924. The *Evening American* reporter mistakenly identified him as F. J. Logan. John D. Logan's Acadia University connection is confirmed in William H. New, ed., *Encyclopedia of Literature in Canada* (Toronto: University of Toronto Press, 2002), 674.

189   cheap mystery and detective stories   "Koretz Canadian Home Looks Like a Furniture Showroom," *Chicago Herald and Examiner,* November 30, 1924.

190   have a tendency to demoralize   Quoted in Morrison and Friend, *"We Have Held Our Own,"* 94 (see chap. 20 notes).

190   the talk of the district   "Koretz Poses as Dramatic Critic and Fictionist," *Halifax Morning Chronicle,* November 25, 1924.

190   considering lodging a complaint   "How Leo Koretz Lived While a Fugitive," *Chicago Evening American,* November 25, 1924; and "Swindler Led Merry Life of Country Squire," *Chicago Daily Tribune,* November 25, 1924.

190   forbade their daughters   "Ask New Indictment Here as Captive Nears Break," *Chicago Evening American,* November 25, 1924.

190 soon had no use for him   "Women and $100 Tips Trapped Leo," *Chicago Herald and Examiner,* November 25, 1924.

CHAPTER 25

191 avid for a good time   "Pinehurst Lodge," Raddall Fonds, p. 3 (see chap. 21 notes). Raddall altered the name Mabelle Gene to Arabelle Lee in his account of Leo's time in Nova Scotia, but his description of her—and her relationship with Leo—confirms he was referring to Banks.

191 Stop knocking, you pessimists   Quoted in Morrison and Friend, *"We Have Held Our Own,"* 82–83 (see chap. 20 notes).

192 flattered with the notion   "Pinehurst Lodge," Raddall Fonds, p. 3 (see chap. 21 notes).

193 Visitors from England   Phyllis R. Blakeley, *Glimpses of Halifax, 1867–1900* (Halifax: Public Archives of Nova Scotia, 1949), 17.

193 Leo entertained as often   It was widely reported that Leo threw a party for American actress Edna Preston and her eighteen-member troupe when they performed in Halifax that summer. He hired cars to convey the players to the Waverley, a lakeside hotel north of the city, for dinner. A quart of champagne awaited each guest, and champagne "flowed in a golden stream" into the early hours of the morning. See "Chicago Hears Departure of Koretz May Be Delayed by Young Lady's Charges," *Halifax Morning Chronicle,* November 28, 1924.

193 foreign Johnny   "Delighted in Strolls with Waitresses, Domestics and the Girl He Called Topsy," *Chicago Evening American,* November 25, 1924.

194 Leo hobnobbed   Information about the club and its membership was found in the records of the Royal Nova Scotia Yacht Squadron, MG 20, vol. 3031, no. 7, NSARM. "Lon Keyte" is listed among ten new members elected at the April 28, 1924, meeting of the managing committee, and the misspelling persisted in references to Leo in other club records and publications. His membership was noted in "Koretz Remanded for 15 Days, Denies Guilt," *Chicago Daily News,* November 24, 1924, and other press reports.

194 No . . . you take one of mine   "Koretz Didn't Like W.M.P's Cigars," *Halifax Evening Mail,* November 24, 1924.

195 I noticed this very distinguished   "'Guilty': To Be Koretz Plea," *Chicago Daily Tribune,* December 2, 1924.

195 of all classes and standing   "Delighted in Strolls with Waitresses, Domestics and the Girl He Called Topsy," *Chicago Evening American,* November 25, 1924.

195 at a furious pace   "Pinehurst Lodge," Raddall Fonds, 3 (see chap. 21 notes).

195   as if the American Revolution   Charles Ritchie, *An Appetite for Life: The Education of a Young Diarist, 1924–1927* (Toronto: Macmillan, 1977), 33.

195   shut out of many Halifax clubs   "Zatzman No Ordinary Joe: Businessman Will Forever Be Linked with Dartmouth," *Halifax Daily News,* May 25, 2000. The exclusion of Jews in Nova Scotia is also documented in Sheva Medjuck, *Jews of Atlantic Canada* (St. John's, NL: Breakwater Books, 1986), 39–41. Population figures are drawn from Gerald Tulchinsky, *Canada's Jews: A People's Journey* (Toronto: University of Toronto Press, 2008), 199, 499; Medjuck, *Jews of Atlantic Canada,* 31; and Cutler, *The Jews of Chicago,* 285 (see chap. 4 notes).

196   as if he were going for a stroll   "Pinehurst Lodge," Raddall Fonds, 5 (see chap. 21 notes). Raddall mentioned his acquaintance with local hunters and guides in his memoir, *In My Time,* 124–25, 130 (see chap. 21 notes).

196   Jack Frost made his appearance   "Local and Other Items," *Caledonia (NS) Gold Hunter and Farmers' Journal,* November 21, 1924. The account that follows of events from November 21 to 23 is compiled from accounts in the Chicago and Halifax papers. George Banks's role as driver on the trip is recorded in Johnson, *Brookfield in the Wilderness,* 54 (see chap. 21 notes).

196   Weekend getaways to the city   Leo considered buying a new home closer to Halifax that fall and contacted at least one steamship line to inquire about voyages to the Caribbean or Central America. While journalists later speculated he had been planning another escape, Leo claimed he thought a southern vacation would "fit in with my character of a writer and one who was fond of wandering" and he had intended to return to Nova Scotia. See transcript of evidence, pp. 14, 20, In the Matter of the Estate of Leo Koretz in Bankruptcy (Halifax) (see chap. 19 notes).

197   His church-attendance record   "Halifax Men Figured," *Halifax Acadian Recorder,* November 25, 1924; and "Swindler Led Merry Life of Country Squire," Chicago Daily Tribune, November 25, 1924. Chapter 26

CHAPTER 26

201   repairing the lining   Details of how Leo was detected and even the names of those involved vary in the press reports, particularly in the rushed coverage immediately following his arrest. The description presented here is based on the best sources available—interviews with two of the key figures, Horace Flemming and William Davies. See "Ottawa Has Consented to the Extradition of Koretz," *Halifax Morning Chronicle,* November 26, 1924; "Fur-Trimmed Silk Pajamas for 'Lou Keytes,'" *Halifax Evening Mail,* November 25, 1924; "New Indictments for Koretz; He is Due Here Sunday," *Chicago Evening Post,* November 28, 1924; and "Koretz in Loeb Case Thought Banker," *Chicago Evening American,* November 28, 1924.

201 little coverage in the Halifax press The *Halifax Morning Chronicle* published two stories on the Bayano swindle. See "Oil Company a Huge Swindle, Chicago Hears," *Halifax Morning Chronicle*, December 14, 1923. Publication of a second article is referred to in "'Millionaire' Keytes Cuts Wide Swath in Province," *Halifax Morning Chronicle*, November 25, 1924.

203 What's wanted? Scriven described the arrest and what was said in two press interviews: "Was Preparing for Get-Away to South When Wrrested," *Halifax Evening Mail*, November 25, 1924; and "Koretz Wants to See Wife, but Won't Ask Her," *Chicago Herald and Examiner*, December 2, 1924. The account that follows also draws on other press reports.

203 For God's sake "Girl Affair Halts Koretz," *Chicago Daily Tribune*, November 27, 1924. Banks's release after questioning is also reported in "Koretz Tells Story; New Flight Blocked," *Chicago Evening American*, November 24, 1924.

203 He was very calm "Koretz Tells Story; New Flight Blocked," *Chicago Evening American*, November 24, 1924.

204 the greatest confidence man "Biggest Confidence Man in U.S. Captured in Halifax," *Halifax Morning Chronicle*, November 24, 1924.

205 ARREST KORETZ IN CANADA The *Chicago Herald and Examiner*'s first reports appeared the following day. See "Koretz Capture Nipped New Flight," November 25, 1924.

205 with a beautiful woman "Koretz Tells Story; New Flight Blocked," *Chicago Evening American*, November 24, 1924.

205 Leo was front-page news "Charged with Huge Swindle," *Wolfville (NS) Acadian*, December 4, 1924; and news item in the *Blairmore (AB) Enterprise*, December 11, 1924. See also "Arrest Chicago's Ponzi in a Hotel at Halifax," *Toronto Daily Star*, November 24, 1924.

205 Newspaper junkies in Paris "Dernière heure," *Le Petit Parisien*, December 6, 1924.

205 newest criminal sensation "Supreme Bluff: Chicago Duped by Story of Great Riches," *Straits Times* (Singapore), January 12, 1925.

205 reached readers in Brisbane "Men and Matters," *Worker* (Brisbane), December 11, 1924; "American Oil Fraud: Swindler on Its Simplicity," *Advocate* (Burnie), February 2, 1925.

205 far from destitute "Mrs. Koretz Owns Home," *Chicago Daily News*, November 25, 1924.

206 The children and I want only "Mrs. Koretz Earns Success," *Chicago Evening American*, November 25, 1924.

206   The family had hoped   "Kin Hoped for Death, Not Cell, for Koretz," *Chicago Evening American,* November 26, 1924.

206   I pray every night   "Koretz Arrest Kept from Mother, 80," *Chicago Evening American,* November 25, 1924.

206   It's been a pleasant day   "State and U.S. Claim Right to Punish Koretz," *Chicago Daily Tribune,* November 25, 1924.

207   a claim for $753,067   The tax claim and the receivers' objection were widely reported. See, for instance, "Koretz Remanded for 15 Days, Denies Guilt," *Chicago Daily News,* November 24, 1924.

207   to the *people from whom it was stolen*   Grace Katz to Harlan F. Stone, November 30, 1924. RG 60, Department of Justice records, Classified Subject Files, file 36-18-3 (Leo Koretz), box 9131, NARA, College Park, MD (emphasis in original).

207   May be the joke's on me   "Owns Bookstore in New York," *Halifax Morning Chronicle,* November 26, 1924; and "How Leo Koretz Bought a Bookshop," *Halifax Evening Mail,* November 26, 1924.

207   Mr. Grey . . . was very much perturbed   "Koretz Capture Nipped New Flight," *Chicago Herald and Examiner,* November 25, 1924.

208   as a respectable person   "Two of a Kind," *Halifax Morning Chronicle,* December 2, 1924.

208   who could have been knocked down   "News of Arrest Shocks People of Liverpool," *Halifax Morning Chronicle,* November 25, 1924.

208   flashed across the skyline   "Koretz Dies in Jail," *Liverpool (NS) Advance,* January 14, 1925.

208   The few Halifax people   "Ottawa Has Consented to the Extradition of Koretz," *Halifax Morning Chronicle,* November 26, 1924.

208   was never received with open arms   "Keyte Will Leave Friday," *Halifax Acadian Recorder,* November 26, 1924.

208   a bolt from the blue   "Mr. Keyte Arrested at Halifax," *Caledonia (NS) Gold Hunter and Farmers' Journal,* November 28, 1924. The seizure of Leo's car was reported in "Lawyer Asks Aid to Halt Delay Sought by Trust Firm," *Chicago Evening American,* November 26, 1924. The return of Banks and his daughter to Caledonia by train was noted in Johnson, *Brookfield in the Wilderness,* 54 (see chap. 21 notes).

208   Had Leo chosen to live   "Koretz Wasted Golden Opportunity to Escape Detection at Pinehurst," *Halifax Morning Chronicle,* December 1, 1924.

CHAPTER 27

209 Crowe's men "Arrest Koretz in Canada," *Chicago Daily Tribune,* November 24, 1924.

209 a notable achievement for law enforcement Ibid.

209 Crowe would not permit himself "Wedged Way into Elite Circles of Society," *Chicago Evening American,* November 24, 1924.

209 merely had to make the arrest "Koretz Remanded for 15 Days, Denies Guilt," *Chicago Daily News,* November 24, 1924.

210 Chicago's arch-criminal Asbury, *The Gangs of Chicago,* 341 (see chap. 2 notes). Details of Capone's Cicero takeover and the O'Banion and Tancl murders are drawn from Asbury, *The Gangs of Chicago,* 331–36, 342–51; and Curt Johnson and R. Craig Sautter, *The Wicked City: Chicago from Kenna to Capone* (New York: Da Capo, 1998), 161–72.

210 They tell me you are crooked Sandburg, "Chicago," in *Chicago Poems,* 1 (see chap. 2 notes).

210 Either the gunman Editorial page note, *Chicago Daily News,* November 28, 1924.

211 bribery was as much a fixture "Corruption Rife in State Courts, Olson Charges," *Chicago Daily Tribune,* January 10, 1925.

211 a system had been worked out Lewis and Smith, *Chicago,* 467–68 (see chap. 8 notes).

211 the gaudiest of all gangland's Asbury, *The Gangs of Chicago,* 351 (see chap. 2 notes).

211 Familiarity between judges and gangsters "Hits Judges Who Attend Crook Funerals," *Chicago Evening Post,* November 29, 1924.

211 We're going to have a Republican Johnson and Sautter, *The Wicked City,* 171.

211 a gangland favorite Ibid., 210. Sbarbaro's role in barring the press from the chapel was reported in "Chicago Gangsters Appear for Funeral," *New York Times,* October 16, 1926.

212 The gunmen merely take advantage "Bullets, Beer and the Law," *Chicago Daily News,* November 25, 1924.

212 teach the masters of crime "Who is Doing the Protecting?" *Chicago Evening Post,* November 19, 1924.

212   With the community aroused   "No Flowers for Crowe," *Chicago Herald and Examiner,* November 29, 1924.

212   the biggest smash   "Crowe Directs Police Raids in Big Chicago Cleanup," *Chicago Herald and Examiner,* November 26, 1924.

CHAPTER 28

213   Leo stood with his hands   Photographs of Leo in his beard appeared in the Chicago and Halifax newspapers. The description of his clothes and the reference to "last word in style" appeared in the caption of the photograph published under the headline FACE ON, in the *Halifax Evening Mail,* November 24, 1924. The change from brown suit to green is noted in "Koretz Admits His Guilt, Attorneys Declare," *Halifax Evening Mail,* November 24, 1924.

213   I want to go back   "Koretz Admits His Guilt, Attorneys Declare," *Halifax Evening Mail,* November 24, 1924.

214   Can I waive my right   Copy of Evidence, Judge Wallace's handwritten synopsis of the proceedings, in Department of Justice (Canada) Extradition Files, RG13-A5, vol. 2076, file 1914, Library and Archives Canada, Ottawa, ON.

215   a witty, big-hearted, flamboyant   Frank Manning Covert and Barry Cahill, *Fifty Years in the Practice of Law* (Montreal: McGill-Queen's University Press, 2005), 30–31.

215   something sinister   "Authorities Have Duty to People of Halifax and Nova Scotia in the Case of Leo Koretz," *Halifax Evening Mail,* November 25, 1924.

215   we are certain his record   The comment was widely reported. See, for instance, "Departure of Koretz is Held Up," *Halifax Evening Mail,* November 26, 1924.

215   spent money "like water"   "New Dupes of Swindler Sought in Nova Scotia," *Chicago Herald and Examiner,* November 26, 1924.

216   His dances, his dinners   "Koretz Remanded for 15 Days, Denies Guilt," *Chicago Daily News,* November 24, 1924.

216   a brave front   "Lawyer Asks Aid to Halt Delay Sought by Trust Firm," *Chicago Evening American,* November 26, 1924.

216   a secret plan   Ibid.

216   a modern version   "Koretz Start Home Set for To-morrow," *Chicago Daily News,* November 26, 1924.

216 **Koretz is not a gunman** "Was Preparing for Get-Away to South When Arrested," *Halifax Evening Mail,* November 25, 1924. Leo denied rumors he had buried money and employed bodyguards. Transcript, p. 15, In the Matter of the Estate of Leo Koretz in Bankruptcy (Halifax) (see chap. 19 notes). There were press reports, never confirmed, that he stole a revolver from a house detective at the St. Regis Hotel just before he disappeared in December 1923. See, for instance, "Koretz Fled with Million in Boat; Hunt Woman Accomplice," *Chicago Evening American,* December 14, 1923.

217 **Course I want to know him** "Koretz On Ship for Home," *Chicago Daily Tribune,* November 29, 1924.

217 **How is Mr. Koretz today?** "Koretz Puts to Sea and Thus Outwits Chicago Reporters," *Halifax Morning Chronicle,* December 1, 1924.

217 FUR-TRIMMED SILK PAJAMAS *Halifax Evening Mail,* November 25, 1924. The tailor's accounts, filed in a court action and published in several newspapers, reveal no such purchase between October 22, 1924, and Leo's arrest a month later. See "Keyte Will Leave Friday," *Halifax Acadian Recorder,* November 26, 1924; and the affidavit of Francis Hiltz, dated November 25, 1924, filed in Robert Stanford Limited v. Lou Keyte, NSSC (Halifax), RG 39 C no. 6383, NSARM.

The *Evening Mail*'s cartoonist, Donald McRitchie, later lamented the departure of the man who had thrust Nova Scotia into the spotlight—and pumped much-appreciated cash into the local economy. His cartoon on the front page of the paper's November 27 edition (reprinted in the *Chicago Daily Tribune* on December 4) depicted Leo in his beard and derby, strutting off to Chicago and leaving a trail of coins and banknotes in his wake. His body was a building labeled "'Lou Keytes' Inc.," and the caption read, "Nova Scotia Loses Another Industry." The arms and legs protruding from the building were clad, appropriately, in striped, fur-trimmed pajamas.

CHAPTER 29

218 **brilliant, literate, scholarly** Murray, *The Madhouse on Madison Street,* 237 (see chap. 14 notes).

218 **I had lost most** "First Interview with Leo Koretz," *Chicago Herald and Examiner,* November 28, 1924.

219 **There was no swindle** "Koretz Gives $200,000 to His Victims," *Chicago Daily Tribune,* November 28, 1924.

219 **The others can stand it** "Koretz' Arrest Halts $1,000,000 Scheme," *Chicago Daily News,* November 28, 1924.

219 **he never swindled any one** "Koretz Gives $200,000 to His Victims," *Chicago Daily Tribune,* November 28, 1924.

219   consummated a fraud   "State and U.S. Claim Right to Punish Koretz," *Chicago Daily Tribune,* November 25, 1924.

220   Koretz's victims   Editorial note, *Chicago Daily News,* November 29, 1924.

220   Tell a jury what I know   The comments of Kahnweiler, Weil, Decker, and Westerfeld were reported in "Will He Tell Jury of Koretz? He Will," *Chicago Evening American,* November 29, 1924.

221   may take that as a challenge   Hit or Miss, *Chicago Daily News,* November 29, 1924.

221   pull "innocent" verdicts   Hecht, *Gaily, Gaily,* 50, 52–53 (see chap. 10 notes).

221   It is to be hoped   Editorial note, *Chicago Daily News,* November 25, 1924.

221   slow, technical, antiquated procedure   Editorial, "An Example to State Courts," *Chicago Daily News,* December 1, 1924.

222   Leo Koretz is my prisoner   "'Hands Off,' Crowe Warns, 'Koretz is My Prisoner,'" *Chicago Evening American,* November 25, 1924.

222   If he were indicted   "State and U.S. Claim Right to Punish Koretz," *Chicago Daily Tribune,* November 25, 1924.

222   There really was nothing   "Koretz On Ship for Home," *Chicago Daily Tribune,* November 29, 1924.

222   daily press teem with inaccuracies   "Mr. Keyte Arrested at Halifax," *Caledonia (NS) Gold Hunter and Farmers' Journal,* November 28, 1924. Banks's editorial was republished under the headline "Says Reports Misleading" in the *Halifax Acadian Recorder,* December 1, 1924.

223   no grounds whatever   "Leo Koretz's Property in Nova Scotia is Valued at $100,000," *Halifax Morning Chronicle,* November 27, 1924. A rumor was widely reported, but never substantiated, that Leo had been involved with a teenage girl and that her parents had considered having him prosecuted for statutory rape.

223   Hail to the Cheat!   "Koretz's Homecoming," *Chicago Daily Tribune* cartoon republished in the *Halifax Evening Mail,* December 6, 1924.

224   a surprise in the morning   Descriptions of the jailhouse rendezvous and Connolly's conversation with the reporter appeared in "Koretz Party Evades Watchers; Go by Steamer," *Halifax Evening Mail,* November 29, 1924; and "Koretz Leaves by Caronia," *Halifax Acadian Recorder,* November 29, 1924.

224   I give you my solemn word   "Koretz Gives $100,000 to Avoid Reporters?" *Chicago Daily News,* November 29, 1924.

226 Every fugitive from justice "Sheriff Characterized as a Guardian Angel by Koretz, His Prisoner," *Halifax Evening Mail,* December 10, 1924.

226 ingratiating chap Murray, *The Madhouse on Madison Street,* 287 (see chap. 14 notes).

226 I knew you before "Koretz Tells How He Refused to Escape," *Chicago Evening American,* December 1, 1924.

CHAPTER 30

228 Say," asked the slim woman "Curious Crowds at Union Station to Get Peep at Leo Koretz," *Chicago Evening American,* December 1, 1924. The description of his arrival that follows is drawn from Chicago press reports.

228 the money magician "New Dupes of Swindler Sought in Nova Scotia," *Chicago Herald and Examiner,* November 26, 1924.

228 usually accorded a President "Koretz Grilled by Crowe," *Chicago Evening Post,* December 1, 1924.

229 Leo called the state's attorney Bob "Koretz Ready to Give Full Confession," *Chicago Daily News,* December 1, 1924.

229 Didn't buy any Bayano stock "Curious Crowds at Union Station to Get Peep at Leo Koretz," *Chicago Evening American,* December 1, 1924.

230 How did you keep The press briefings, photo session in Crowe's office, and details of Leo's confession that follow have been compiled from reports in the Chicago press. The confession does not appear to have survived—there is no copy in Leo's bankruptcy or criminal file—but his testimony before referee Harry Parkin the following day was described as "a virtual repetition" of what he told Crowe. The only difference was a "more explicit" description of financial matters in his testimony. See "'Guilty,' Is Koretz Plea," *Chicago Evening Post,* December 3, 1924.

231 Forget that I have ever lived Only one reporter claimed to have overheard what Leo discussed with his brothers. See "Mother of Koretz Is Stoical in Grief," *Chicago Evening American,* December 2, 1924.

231 I believe he is holding "Koretz on Stand Tells How He Worked Swindle," *Chicago Evening American,* December 2, 1924.

231 that people seemed to throw Ibid.

232 She is pathetically eager "Wife Anxious to See Koretz. He Wants to See Her. Both Wait," *Chicago Evening American,* December 2, 1924.

232 I've hurt her enough "Koretz Wants to See Wife, but Won't Ask Her," *Chicago Herald and Examiner,* December 2, 1924; and "'I Return Willingly, Short of Every Cent for Creditors,'" *Chicago Herald and Examiner,* December 2, 1924.

232 I don't think I've got "Koretz a Broken Man," *Chicago Daily News,* December 1, 1924.

232 Your father says "Koretz Wants to See Wife, but Won't Ask Her," *Chicago Herald and Examiner,* December 2, 1924.

233 probably constitutionally impossible Editorial page note, *Chicago Evening Post,* December 1, 1924.

233 one of the strangest bankruptcy "10 Year Prison Term Confronts Koretz," *Chicago Daily Tribune,* December 3, 1924.

237 I am indifferent "Koretz Pleads Guilty before Judge Hopkins," *Evanston News-Index,* December 3, 1924.

CHAPTER 31

238 Leo Koretz, in an indictment This account of the guilty plea and sentencing hearing, unless otherwise noted, is based on press reports and the official record of the hearing: Indictment No. 32273, The People of the State of Illinois v. Leo Koretz, docket 56, p. 499, criminal felony indexes, Archives of the Clerk of the Circuit Court of Cook County.

240 a veritable family farewell banquet "Koretz Gets 1 to 10 Years," *Chicago Evening American,* December 4, 1923.

240 transformed into a temporary White House "Coolidge Pays Tribute to Chicago and Pere Marquette in His First Speech Here," *Chicago Evening Post,* December 4, 1924.

241 That means death "Was Koretz Victim of Circumstances?" *Evanston News-Index,* January 9, 1925.

241 Koretz, who has never shown "Swindler, Broken in Health, Is Given Mercy," *Chicago Herald and Examiner,* December 5, 1924.

242 Steal two million dollars Letters from the People—Law, *Chicago Herald and Examiner,* December 10, 1924.

242 We frequently hear it said "Weakening Our Courts," *Chicago Daily Tribune,* December 18, 1924.

242 The criminal of today "This Too Is Vanity," *Wolfville (NS) Acadian,* December 11, 1924.

242 I have shown the defendant "No Parole in Less Than Six Years, Is Demand," *Chicago Herald and Examiner,* December 6, 1924.

243 All these investors "Judge Hopkins to Oppose Parole for Leo Koretz," *Chicago Evening Post,* December 5, 1924.

243 This seems to be my last Leo's statements during the drive to Joliet prison were widely reported in the Chicago papers.

CHAPTER 32

245 Bars, guards, sober faces "Prison Rigor Drives Mirth from Slayers," *Chicago Daily Tribune,* September 13, 1924.

245 The cells are small "Killers in 'Solitary' Cells," *Chicago Daily Tribune,* September 12, 1924. The cells are also described in S. W. Wetmore, *Behind the Bars at Joliet: A Peep at a Prison, Its History and Its Mysteries* (Joliet: J. O. Gorman, 1892), 20–22. Leo's first hours in prison were chronicled in the Chicago press.

246 He is very ill "Grooms Koretz to Be Waiter," *Chicago Daily Journal,* December 6, 1924. Details of Leo's medical condition were recorded in "Register of Prisoners, Joliet" (1923), inmate no. 9463, p. 98. RG 243.200, Illinois State Archives, Springfield.

246 Con men were among the lowest Nathan F. Leopold, *Life plus 99 Years* (Garden City, NY: Doubleday, 1958), 90.

247 no judge in Chicago Attorney General Harlan F. Stone authorized the dismissal of the charges on January 7, 1925. Edwin Olson to Harlan F. Stone, December 16, 1924; Assistant Attorney General William Donovan to Edwin Olson, January 7, 1925. RG 60, Department of Justice records, Classified Subject Files, file 36-18-3 (Leo Koretz), box 9131, NARA, College Park, MD.

247 Koretz's condition is serious His illness and treatments and Fletcher's comments were widely reported in the Chicago and Nova Scotia press and in the *New York Times.*

248 king of con men "'Guilty,' Is Koretz Plea," *Chicago Evening Post,* December 3, 1924.

248 the greatest swindler of all time "Koretz Capture Nipped New Flight," *Chicago Herald and Examiner,* November 25, 1924.

248 If I had only known "Return Body of Koretz to Chicago," *Evanston News-Index,* January 9, 1925.

248 No crowds "Simple Burial for Leo Koretz, Lavish Spender," *Chicago Daily Tribune,* January 10, 1925. Reports in other Chicago papers provided further details about the funeral.

251 REVEAL KORETZ KILLED SELF *Chicago Herald and Examiner,* January 11, 1925.

251 **extra servings of syrup** *"True:* Koretz, Leo," p. 22 (Swanberg Papers) (see chap. 7 notes).

251 **"uncommon" for diabetics** Michael Bliss, *The Discovery of Insulin* (Chicago: University of Chicago Press, 2007), 20, 38. Robert Allen Preston, a young Chicago university student and diabetic facing his own death sentence, felt he understood Leo's desperation. "God! the poor devil," Preston wrote in his diary when he heard the news of Leo's death. "He may have done wrong, but I pity him." Leo's diabetes was a "jail within a jail." "It is better he has gone. Maybe some day I, too, will journey to that happy land where there is no sorrow, pain, joy, or happiness." Preston soon made the journey—he committed suicide three months later. "Diary Reveals Plan of Youth to End His Life," *Chicago Daily Tribune,* April 13, 1925, quoted in Virginia A. McConnell, *Fatal Fortune: The Death of Chicago's Millionaire Orphan* (Westport, CT: Praeger, 2005), 61.

252 **I have heard** "Hear Koretz Lives; May Exhume Body," *New York Times,* March 7, 1925. The comments of Whitman and Fletcher that follow appeared in the Chicago press.

252 **This is certainly worth** Ibid.

EPILOGUE

255 **worthy of a brief news item** It was published in the *Chicago Daily Tribune,* April 10, 1927. Leo's headstone has been righted since the author's 2009 visit, exposing his name.

255 **greatest confidence man** "Leo Koretz Dies in Prison at Joliet," *Chicago Herald and Examiner,* January 9, 1925.

255 **Leo Koretz bears witness** "Imagination," *New York Times,* December 4, 1924. Republished in the *Halifax Morning Chronicle,* December 8, 1924.

256 **second Leo Koretz** "Rumor Gottlieb Fleeing toward South America," *Chicago Daily Tribune,* November 12, 1929.

256 **swindling brigade** George C. Atteberry, John L. Auble, and Elgin F. Hunt, *Introduction to Social Science: A Survey of Social Problems,* vol. 1 (New York: Macmillan, 1941), 291.

256 TOO MANY WOMEN! *Inside Detective,* October 1938.

256 **With oil he was master** Jack Wilder, "Artist of Flim-Flam," *Best Detective Cases* 1, no. 6 (1958): 10–12, 40–41. See also H. L. Spinner, "Guilt-Edge Genius," *Master Detective* 49, no. 5 (February 1955): 16–19, 59–63; and Sumner Plunkett, "The Phony Empire of Lover Boy Leo Koretz," *For Men Only* 5, no. 9 (September 1958): 26–29, 42–45, which was republished as "El Falso Imperio del Galan Leo Koretz," *Bohemia* 50, no. 35 (August 31, 1958): 32–34, 115–17.

256   **the swindler of the century**   Swanberg, "The Fabulous Boom of Bayano," 17, 28 (see chap. 1 notes). Swanberg toyed with the idea of turning the story into a book. When Sumner Plunkett borrowed his research notes in 1958 to write his article in *For Men Only,* Swanberg took pains to ensure they were returned. "I may want to do something with Koretz later on," he explained. "There's enough here for a book on the guy." Swanberg appears to have drafted an outline for a book—an undated, six-page typescript titled "Outline—LEO KORETZ" survives in his papers—but took the idea no further before his death in 1992. See *"True:* Koretz, Leo" file (Swanberg Papers) (see chap. 7 notes).

256   **prince of thieves**   Hecht, *A Child of the Century,* 154–55 (see chap. 15 notes). Hecht repeated Leo's story in 1958 when he hosted a short-lived television talk show in New York, only this time he claimed that Hearst himself and the top executives of the Marshall Field department stores and the Yellow Cab Company were among Bayano's investors. The editor who prepared transcripts of the shows for publication described the story as "an amalgam of memory and imagination" in which Hecht "embellishes, judiciously." See Ben Hecht and Bret Primack, *The Ben Hecht Show: Impolitic Observations from the Freest Thinker of 1950s Television* (Jefferson, NC: McFarland, 1993), 65–66. The show aired on November 3, 1958. Hecht also mentioned "Leo Koretz, who peddled millions of dollars of stock in the Bayano oil fields, that didn't exist," in his 1963 memoir, *Gaily, Gaily,* 186 (see chap. 10 notes).

Some of Hecht's embellishments appear in Jay Robert Nash, *Hustlers and Con Men: An Anecdotal History of the Confidence Man and His Games* (New York: M. Evans, 1976), 212–13 (expanded and republished on the Internet as "Leo Koretz: Colossal Swindler of Tycoons," available at www.annalsofcrime.com); Carl Sifakis, *The Encyclopedia of American Crime* (New York: Facts on File, 1982), 403–4; George C. Kohn, *Dictionary of Culprits and Criminals,* 2nd ed. (Lanham, MD: Scarecrow, 1995), 170; and Carl Sifakis, *Frauds, Deceptions and Swindles* (New York: Checkmark Books, 2001), 107–8.

For an example of the influence of the pulp-magazine stories, see Nat Howard, "Panama Hat Trick: A Con Man Who Swindled Even His Mother," *D & B Reports* 42, no. 6 (Nov/Dec 1993): 62. Another writer erroneously subjected Leo to a thirty-day trial and had him arrested not in Halifax but a continent away, in the Pacific coast port of Vancouver, British Columbia. See Carlson Wade, *Great Hoaxes and Famous Impostors* (Middle Village, NY: Jonathan David, 1976), 28, 35–36, 44.

257   **recognized the term** *Ponzi scheme*   Zuckoff, *Ponzi's Scheme,* 314 (see chap. 10 notes).

258   **The average person thinks**   Quoted in Diana Henriques, "The Lasting Shadow of Bernie Madoff," *New York Times,* December 10, 2011.

258   **expected his lucky clients**   Diana Henriques, *The Wizard of Lies: Bernie Madoff and the Death of Trust* (New York: St. Martin's Griffin, 2012), 59, 214.

258   a time of madness   Galbraith, *The Great Crash 1929,* xxiv, 9 (see chap. 1 notes).

259   a safari into Panama's   "Safari into Panama's Untamed Green Hell," *Chicago Tribune,* February 23, 1975.

259   a perfect gateway   Don Winner, "Patrolling the Bayano River Basin for Drug Traffickers," article posted August 5, 2010, and available online at www.panama -guide.com.

260   ties between politicians and organized crime   To the authors of the *Illinois Crime Survey,* an investigation into the tainted justice system of 1920s Chicago, McSwiggin's death exposed the "unholy alliance . . . between criminal gangs and the political machine" at the heart of Chicago's epidemic of crime. *The Illinois Crime Survey* (Chicago: Illinois Association for Criminal Justice, 1929), 841.

260   Not only had Capone ordered   Crowe's allegation, published in the *Chicago Daily Tribune* on May 5, 1926, is reproduced in John Kobler, *Capone: The Life and World of Al Capone* (New York: G.P. Putnam and Sons, 1971), 177.

260   I didn't kill him   *The Illinois Crime Survey,* 829.

260   Crowe was accused of protecting   Wooddy, *The Chicago Primary of 1926,* 136–37, 140 (see chap. 8 notes). Crowe's failure to secure convictions in gangland killings is noted in Bukowski, *Big Bill Thompson,* 203–4 (see chap. 8 notes).

261   no one ever by proof   "City Bar Board Opposes Crowe for Bench Post," *Chicago Daily Tribune,* October 1, 1942.

261   a smashing blow   "Robert Crowe Services Set for Tomorrow," *Chicago Daily Tribune,* January 20, 1958.

263   jolly millionaire   Raddall, *In My Time,* 130 (see chap. 21 notes).

263   It was quite a big blow up   Interview with Maurice Scott, April 28, 1977, Kejimkujik Oral History Project (see chap. 21 notes). The description of Leo's time in Nova Scotia appeared in Morrison and Friend, *"We Have Held Our Own,"* 81–82 (see chap. 20 notes). Years after Leo's arrest, members of the Caledonia Women's Institute organized a lecture that recalled the "spectacular social activities" at Pinehurst. See "Pinehurst—A Beauty Spot. Remember 'KORETZ'?" undated newspaper clipping, file 76 (Pinehurst), North Queens Heritage House Museum, Caledonia, NS.

263   The claims of 147 creditors   Details of the settlement of Leo's estate are drawn from documents filed in In the Matter of Leo Koretz, Bankrupt (Chicago) (see chap. 1 notes). The losses of individual investors have been calculated using figures recorded in this file.

264   Lewy Brothers fought the case   In re Koretz (Lewy Bros. Co. v. Chicago Title & Trust Co.), 6 F. (2d) 225 (7th Cir. 1925). Lewy Brothers' victory was short lived: the jeweler was struggling to stay afloat and, in a final irony, was petitioned into bankruptcy within months of the ruling, leaving creditors to swallow losses of $750,000. See "Lewy Bros., Jewelers, Fail," *New York Times,* November 24, 1925.

264 What a devastating thing Author's interview with Andrew Goodman, August 16, 2012.

265 had this look on his face Author's interview with Bill Goodman, August 30, 2012.

265 It was a terrible thing Author's interview with Jane Siegel, September 12, 2012.

265 left a modest estate Transcript of testimony of Mari (Koretz) Green in Probate Court of Cook County, December 4, 1941, p. 2; Inventory, dated February 6, 1942; and petition of executor Milton R. Simon, dated June 16, 1942. Probate File 8637 (Mae Koretz), YR41P, p. 324, docket 408, Archives of the Clerk of the Circuit Court of Cook County.

265 He was a personality Andrew Goodman interview.

265 Red Kearns and His Rinky Tink Piano See advertisements in the *Wisconsin State Journal,* June 15, 1966, and the *Montreal Gazette,* July 25, 1969.

266 I discovered the whole story Carol Stelzer, e-mail communication with the author, August 29, 2012.

266 I'm not ashamed Bill Goodman interview.

266 a great story to tell Andrew Goodman interview.

INDEX

Page numbers in italics refer to photos.

Abagnale, Frank, 78
Abbott, Richard, 187
Agatstein, Louis, 101
Allard, Leola, 232
Allen, Frederick Lewis, 74, 77
Arkansas rice farms
    bogus mortgages, 34–36
    investor earnings, 48, 59, 183
    Koretz's sales position and land hold-
        ings, 33–34
    land boom, 33–34
arrest. *See* manhunt and capture
Asbury, Herbert, 19
Auerbach, Anna
    affair with Koretz, 92, 129–30, *131*
    disappearance and warrant for arrest,
        133–34
    on Koretz's charm, 6
    on Koretz's popularity with women,
        57–58, 128
    losses, 263–64
Auerbach, Salo, 128, 130
Austrian, Alfred, 28
automobiles, 74–76

bankruptcy proceedings. *See also* crimi-
    nal proceedings
    creditors' petition, 138
    estimate of losses and claims, 143–45,
        183, 233
    federal income tax claim, 207, 263
    final distribution of cash and assets,
        263–64
    jeweler's claim, 264
    Koretz's testimony, 233–37
    Mae Koretz's testimony, *136,*
        137–38
    newspaper accounts, 141, 142–43
    recovery of assets, 141–43, 157, 183,
        207
    referee and receiver, 138
    return of cash by Koretz family, 114,
        122–23, 142, 263
Banks, George, 191–92, 196, 208, 222,
    262
Banks, Mabelle Gene "Topsy," 191–92,
    197, 203, 222, 262
Barrett, Charles, 64, 66, *85,* 87
Barrett, George, 64, 66

Bayano River region, Panama
exports, 38, 102
oil exploration, 101–2
Panama Canal project, 37, 38, 43
photograph of, *40*
remoteness and harsh conditions,
37–38, 39–41, 109, 259
timberland, 43, 107
Bayano River Syndicate. *See also*
bankruptcy proceedings; criminal
proceedings; investors
account of oil discovery, 12
Big Five investors, 48–49, 89
Chicago offices, 11, 56, 70–71, 90,
115, 131
destruction of evidence, 104
dividends, 5, 52, 59–60, 72, 93, 233
executive team, 96, 100–101
expansion of timber scam, 60–61,
71–74, 96
impending collapse, 82, 97–98, 112
inspiration for, 38–42, 43–44, 46
investors' inspection trip and discovery of swindle, 96, *100,* 100–101,
107–9, 139–40
Koretz's confession, 230–31
Koretz's denial of wrongdoing,
218–19
Koretz's pledge to make restitution,
243
Koretz's self-deception, 96–97,
235–36
limitation of shares sold, 11, 50–51,
73
longevity of swindle, 60, 81–82
mention of Standard Oil, 4, 12,
72–73, 76, 89, 94
New York office, 91, 105
prospectus for investors, 44–46
refunds to Koretz family and friends,
103, 104, 106, 142–43
secrecy, 11, 48–49, 58

select group of investors, 51–52, 53,
70–71, 82
state's attorney's cognizance of, 114–15
stock certificates, 12, *50*
suspicions concerning, 58–59
as template for subsequent swindles,
81, 257–59
true-crime and detective magazine
features about, *254,* 256
trust and loyalty of investors, 13,
52–53, 59–60
Belasco, Daniel, 31, 38, 43
Bergman, Eda, 92–93
Berkson, Maurice, 31, 58, 138, 143,
233, 236
Blakeley, Phyllis, 193
Boysen, Harry, 101, 107, 109
Brisbane, Arthur, 145
Bronson, Al (Koretz alias), 13, 48–49,
127–28

Canada. *See* Nova Scotia hideaway
Capone, Al, 9, 75, 88, 209, 211, 260,
263
capture. *See* manhunt and capture
Caverly, John, 181–82
Chicago
crime and corruption, 8–9, 19, 66,
69, 86–87, 210–12
Bobby Franks murder, 179–82
gang violence, 87–88, 209–10
immigrants, 20
Irish domination of local politics, 24,
66
Jewish community, 20, 32
newspapers and newsmen, 120–22
vice and depravity, 9, 19, 67
wealth and booming economy, 8,
9–10, 21, 258
Janet Wilkinson murder, 62–64
Eugene Williams murder and riots,
68–69

Chicago Daily Journal, 119, 120, 121–22, 131

Chicago Daily News
among Chicago's six newspapers, 120–21
on corruption, 212
on gangland violence, 210
on Koretz's ability to sway jury, 221
on Koretz's health, 247
on Koretz's womanizing, 130, 131–32, 216
on Mae Koretz's financial status, 205–6
on mail-fraud indictment, 149
on manhunt for Koretz, 151
party credited for Koretz's capture, 209
on reluctance of Bayano victims to testify, 220
ridicule of Bayano investors, *117,* 140, 141

Chicago Daily Tribune
on auction of Koretz's belongings, 183
on automobile deaths in Chicago, 74
on Bayano bankruptcy proceedings, 233–34, 236
on Bayano swindle and victims, 119, *120,* 133, 143, 150, 151, 206–7
among Chicago's six newspapers, 120
on Crowe's death, 261
exposure of city hall corruption, 86
on Koretz's capture and extradition, 205, 209, 223
on Koretz's denial of wrongdoing, 219
on Koretz's funeral and burial, 248, *250,* 250–51
on Koretz's health, 247
on Koretz's popularity, 6
on Koretz's prison life, 245
on Koretz's sentence, 242

on Koretz's womanizing, 130, 133, 157
on manhunt for Koretz, 184
on missing child and sentence for murderer, 62, 63, 64
outlook on new century, 23
on train wreck, 110–11

Chicago Evening American
on Bayano swindle and victims, 52, 119, 124, 125, 139–40, 141, 142, 144, 145
among Chicago's six newspapers, 120, 121
on Koretz's capture, 205, 209
on Koretz's womanizing, 6, 128, 133, 134
on Mae Koretz, 125
on Mentor Koretz, 139
praise of Crowe, 68
on return of cash by Koretz family, 123

Chicago Evening Post
on Bayano victims' petition for Koretz's pardon, 242–43
among Chicago's six newspapers, 120, 121
on corruption, 66, 148, 212
on Koretz's extradition to Chicago, 228
on Koretz's lying, 233
on Koretz's womanizing, 126, 134
on manhunt for Koretz, 157
prediction of Koretz's surrender, 156
ridicule of Bayano investors, 141

Chicago Herald and Examiner
on Bayano swindle and victims, 112, 140, 255
among Chicago's six newspapers, 120
on corruption, 212
on Zane Grey at revelation of Koretz's deception, 207
on Koretz's capture, 216
on Koretz's death, 251, 252

Chicago Herald and Examiner (continued)
on Koretz's denial of wrongdoing, 218–19
on Koretz's sentence, 241–42
on Koretz's womanizing, 133, 150
on Mae Koretz, 125
Mentor Koretz on mother's wishes, 232
praise of Crowe, 67
Chicago Title and Trust Company. *See* bankruptcy proceedings
Church, Harvey, 84–85
Cockran, Bourke, 27
Cohen, Samuel, 7, 13, 110, 143
Cohn, Charles
banquet in honor of Koretz, 4, 124
Bayano investment and losses, 4, 7, 104, 124, 263
trust in Koretz, 13, 52
Cohn, Milton, 112
Collins, Morgan, 148
con men
affinity fraud, 258
as American cultural heroes, 79
Bayano template for, 81, 257–58
characteristics, 78–79
first use of term, *confidence man,* 79
greed of victims, 258–59
Koretz's skills, 6, 22, 34, 52, 78–79, 81–82
notorious swindlers, 10–11, 79–82, 221, 257–58
Connolly, Joseph
acquaintance of Koretz, 194–95
as defense counsel, 215, 230, 235, 240–41
Koretz's departure from Nova Scotia, 223–24
in later years, 262
Cook County state's attorney. *See* Crowe, Robert
Corbin, Arthur, 27

criminal proceedings. *See also* bankruptcy proceedings
federal mail-fraud charges, 148–49, 220–21, 247
guilty plea, 231, 238, *239,* 240
imprisonment, 243–48
indictments, 116, 148–49, 220–22, 240, 243, 247
Koretz with prosecution team, *227*
petition for pardon, 242–43
questioning by state's attorney, 229–30
sentence, 241–42
testimony by investors and doctors, 240–41
Crowe, Frank, 64
Crowe, Patrick, 23–24
Crowe, Robert
background, personality, and style, 14–15, 23–25, 64–65, 85
crackdown on crime and corruption, 86–88, 212
death, 261
election as state's attorney, 83, *85,* 87, 209
judgeship, 68–69, 261
Koretz's confession to, 230–32
law studies and early legal experience, 14, 27–29, 64–67
manhunt and credit for capture of Koretz, 133–35, 147–49, 209
at news of Bayano scam, 114–16
political ambition, 15, 64, *65,* 65–67, 86–87, 148, 260–61
power as state's attorney, 66
proceedings against Koretz, 219–22, *227,* 229–30, 238, *239,* 242–43
tough-on-crime reputation, 9, 63–64, 84, 148, 179–82
underworld connections, 9, 19, 211–12, 260–61
Curran, Basil, 6, 90–91

Daily Journal (Chicago), 119, 120, 121–22, 133
Daily News. See Chicago Daily News
Daily Tribune. See Chicago Daily Tribune
Darrow, Clarence, 87, 181–82
Davidson, Charles, 127–28, 129
Davies, William H., 202, 262
Davis, Abel, 202
death and burial, 248–53, *250*
Decker, Alfred, 220
Delehanty, Joseph, 242
Dever, William, 87
disappearance. *See* manhunt and capture
Doherty, Jim, 259–60
Drake Hotel
   banquet in honor of Koretz, 3, 6–8, 10, 12–13
   Bayano offices, 11, 70–71, 104, 115
   female visitors to Koretz's suite, 99, 129–30
Duffy, Sherman, 139–40
Duffy, Tom, 259–60

economic prosperity, 8, 74–77
Eisenstaedt, Milton, 60
Evening American. See Chicago Evening American
Evening Post. See Chicago Evening Post
Ewing, Donald, 219
extradition. *See* manhunt and capture

Field, Marshall, 10
Fischel, Isaac, 73
Fisher, Harry, 94–95, 96, 125
Fitzgerald, F. Scott, 8, 174–75
Fitzgerald, Thomas, 62–64
Fitzhugh, Alex, 90
Fitzmorris, Charles, 86
Fleming, Joseph, 233, 234–35
Flemming, Horace, 201–2, 262
Fletcher, W. R., 246, 247, 251–52, 253
Foreman, Oscar G., 145

Fox, Anna, 51
Franks, Bobby, 179–82
Fraser, Millie, 131–32
Fuller, Henry Blake, 8
Fuller, William, 33

Galbraith, John Kenneth, 8, 258
Goodman, Andrew, 264, 265, 266
Goodman, Bill, 265, 266
Gorman, George, 88, 240–41
Great Gatsby, The, 174–75, 256
Grey, Zane, 164–65, 185–86, 188–89, 207, 216, 262
Gruening, Ernest, 155–56
Gumbiner, Stella, 220, 238–39, 270, 243

Halifax Evening Mail, 215, 217
Halifax Herald, 164, 169, 177
Halifax Morning Chronicle, 199, 204–5, 208
Hamlin, Harry F., 149, 156
Harding, Warren, 77, 83
Hargrave, George, 99, 129
Hearst, William Randolph, 121
Hecht, Ben, 80, 121–22, 125–26, 221, 256
Henriques, Diana, 258
Heppner, Henry and Company, 56, 201, 263
Herald and Examiner. See Chicago Herald and Examiner
Herrick, Genevieve Forbes, 233–34, 236, 248, 250–51
Hiltz, Francis, 201, 217, 262
Hopkins, Jacob, 241, 242
Hoyne, Maclay, 67

imprisonment
   declining health and death in, 246, 247–48
   living conditions, 245–46
   sentence, 241–42

Insull, Samuel, 9–10
investors. *See also* bankruptcy proceedings; Bayano River Syndicate
  banquet in honor of Koretz, 3, 6–8, 10, 12–13
  on capture of Koretz, 124–25, 206
  eagerness to testify against Koretz, 220
  formal complaint against Koretz, 114–15
  Koretz's contempt and lack of remorse for, 219, 236, 258
  public ridicule of, *117,* 140–41, 143–44
  search for Koretz, 184–85
  small investors, 92–93, 219, 263
  unidentified investors, 144–45, 183
Irrmann, John, 52, 124

Kahnweiler, Leo, 102
Kahnweiler, Sidney, 124, 151–52, 220
Katz, Grace, 207
Kaufman, Herbert, 140–41, 148
Kennedy, Charles, 172, 173
Keyte, Lou (Koretz alias), 13, 153–56, 157–59. *See also* Nova Scotia hideaway
Kindleberger, Charles, 82
Kipling, Rudyard, 19
Kitzinger, Emil, 100, 140
Klarkowski, Stanley, 115, 129, 131–33, 151, 156
Klein, Henry
  Bayano investment, 7, 101, 109, 140, 141, 264
  financial help for Mae Koretz, 184
  inspection trip to Panama and discovery of swindle, *100,* 101, 109, 139–40
  liquor business, 7, 47
  partnership with Koretz, 47
  purchase and sale of Pinehurst Lodge, 261

reward for capture of Koretz, 184–85
  trust in Koretz, 47–49
Klein, Leon, 57, 137, 142
Klein, Maude, 53, 103
Koretz, Adolph, 7–8, 16, 123, 231, 239, 248, 264
Koretz, Blanche, 123, 184
Koretz, Emil
  Bayano investment and losses, 8, 52–53, 264
  loyalty to and affection for Koretz, 123, 148, 231, 248
  return of investment to, 103, 114, 122–23, 142
  search for Koretz, 112
Koretz, Ferdinand, 7, 16, 103, 114, 122, 264
Koretz, Heinrich (later Henry), 16, 20, 32, 249
Koretz, Julius
  Bayano investment and losses, 7–8, 52, 264–65
  as boy in Bohemia, *17*
  death, 266
  return of investment to, 103, 106, 114
  search for Koretz, 113
Koretz, Leo. *See also* Bayano River Syndicate
  arrest (*see* manhunt and capture)
  bases of operations, *35*
  Bronson alias, 13, 48–49, 127–28
  con man's skills, 6, 22, 34, 52, 78–79, 81–82
  death and burial, 248–53, *250,* 255
  diabetes, 97, 170, 184, 240–41, 246, 247, 251
  disappearance (*see* manhunt and capture; New York hideaway; Nova Scotia hideaway)
  education, 22–23, 26–27
  family background, 15–18, 20–21

farm mortgage scam (*see* Arkansas rice farms)

first scam, 31–32

headaches, 33, 185, 187

imprisonment (*see* prison)

jewelry acquisitions, 57, 102–3, 113, 115, 236, 264

Keyte alias and persona, 13, 153–56, 157–59

law career, 26–27, 29–31, 55–56

marriage and children, 32–33, 42, 54

notoriety and magazine features about, *254*, 256–57

passion for detective stories, 5, 14, 55, 156, 189

physical appearance, 5, 14–15, *17, 146,* 185

trial (*see* criminal proceedings)

as victim of scam, 38–42, 43–44

wealth and opulent lifestyle, 5–6, *7,* 53–57

women (*see* women and womanizing)

Koretz, Ludwig, 7–8, 103, 124, 264

Koretz, Mae

  at bankruptcy hearing, *136,* 137–38

  Bayano investment, 53

  community service, 57

  death and estate, 265

  devastation and disgrace, 125, 183–84, 205–6, 232, 265

  at Koretz's death, 248, 249

  marriage, 32–33

  receipt and return of assets, 113, 115, 138, 143, 236

  search for Koretz, 112–13

Koretz, Mari Bertha, 125, 265

Koretz, Marie, 53, 114, 123, 255, 264

Koretz, Max, 16, 19, 249, 255

Koretz, Mentor Henry, 42, 139, 232, 248, 249, 265–66

Kraus, Adolph, 26, 28

Kroch, Adolph, 53

Le Bosky, Leo, 122

Lee, Robert Morton, 111

Leonard, Michael, 248

Leopold, Nathan, 180–82, 257

Levy, Felix, 52, 249–50

Lewy Brothers Jewelers, 57, 102–3, 113, 264

Light, Leland, 240–41

Lindberg, Gary, 79

Liverpool Advance, 208

Loeb, Richard, 180–82, 257

Logan, John D., 189

Loomis, Francis, 93

Lundborg, Alfred, 92–93, 263

Lundin, Fred, 68, 83, 86, 87

MacArthur, Charlie, 122

Madoff, Bernie, 81, 257–58

Majestic Building, 90, 104, 115, 131

Mandel, Milton, 57, 90, 97, 206, 241

Mandel, Sarah, 90, 104

manhunt and capture

  arrest and extradition, *199,* 203–5, *204,* 213–17, *214,* 223–25

  confession, 230–31

  credit for capture, 209, 212

  disappearance, 105–7, 111–14

  identification of Koretz, 201–2

  return to Chicago, 223–26, 228–29

  reward, *146,* 149–50, 184–85, 262

  tips and leads, 147–48, 149–51, 184, 185

Marshall, Thomas, 223, 230

Matthews, Francis

  as Bayano investor, 7, 49, 72, 89, 240

  discovery of swindle, 109, 114

  formal complaint against Koretz, 114

  in indictment against Koretz, 220, 239

  on Koretz as victim of scam, 42

  on Koretz's planning of swindle, 44

  losses, 116, 140

Matthews, Francis *(continued)*
  public ridicule of, 140–41
  trustee position with Bayano, 96
  trust in Koretz, 93–94, 124, 140–41
Maurer, David, 78–79
Mayer, Arthur, 51, 206
Mayer, Bertha, 32, 53, 103, 142
Mayer, Edwin, 100, 101–3, 108, 139
Mayer, Henry, 32, 53
Mayer, Levy, 28–29
Mayer, Oscar, 21
Mayer, Pearl, 53, 105
McCullough, David, 37
McKay, W. B., 169–70 186
McLeod, Byron, 162
McPhaul, John, 121, 129
McSwiggin, William, 203–4, 211, 224, 227, 259–61
Mell, Clayton, 107
Mencken, H. L., 121
Miller, Donald, 18
Miller, William Franklin, 80, 81–82
Mitchell, Elizabeth, 172, 186–87
Mitchell, Laurie
  death, 262
  on Koretz's womanizing, 190, 216
  on lavish entertaining at Pinehurst, 176, 216
  management of Pinehurst Lodge, 164, 172, 186–87
  relationship with Zane Grey, 165, 185, 186, 188–89, 216, 262
  as sportsman and promoter of tourism, 160–65
Mitchell, Malcolm, 203, 204, 213, 262
Moran, Thomas, 26

Newman, Jacob, 202
New York hideaway
  Abercrombie and Fitch, 159–60
  alias and persona, 153–56
  Bayano branch office, 91, 105

friends and diversions, 91–92, 158
Neighborhood Book Shop, 154, 157–58, 207
St. Regis Hotel, 90–91
New York Times
  on Abercrombie and Fitch, 160
  on Bayano victims, 144
  on Koretz as con artist, 150, 255–56
  on manhunt and capture of Koretz, 155, 205
  on Janet Wilkinson murder, 63
Nieto, David, 36, 38–39, 41, 42, 43–44
Nova Scotia hideaway
  alias and persona, 164, 165, 169–70, 188, 189, 196
  capture and extradition, 199, 203–5, 204, 213–17, 214, 223–25
  community reactions to deception, 208
  community wariness and disapproval, 189–90, 195
  discrimination against Jews, 195–96
  extravagant lifestyle and lavish entertaining, 166–69, 172–77, 175, 193–94, 215–17, 226
  at Halifax Hotel, 192, 193, 197
  identification of Koretz, 201–2
  moose-hunting expedition, 196
  Pinehurst Lodge and estate, 162–64, 169, 170, 171–72, 207, 261
  revelation of source of fortune, 178
  suspicious behavior and disputes, 186–87
  women, 175, 175–76, 195, 197, 222, 231

O'Banion, Dion, 210, 211
O'Brien, James "Ropes," 63, 84
O'Hearn, Walter, 215, 223
oil scam. *See* Bayano River Syndicate
oil-stock mania, 75–77

Olson, Edwin, 210–11, 221, 247
O'Malley, Austin, 218, 223

Paine, Albert Bigelow, 162
Panama. *See* Bayano River region,
    Panama
Panama Canal, 24, 37, 38, 39, 43,
    45–46, 101, 108, 189
Parkin, Harry. *See* bankruptcy proceedings
Patterson, Charles, 111
Peck, C. L., 108
Pegler, Arthur, 121
Pegler, Westbrook, 8
Philipsborn, Clara, 58, 124
Pinehurst Lodge and estate, 162–64,
    169, *170,* 171–72, 207, 261
Platt, Henry, 141
Polachek, Victor, 112, 145
Ponzi, Charles, 10–11, 80–82, 221,
    257
prison
    declining health and death in, 246,
        247–48
    living conditions, 245–46
    sentence, 241–42
Prohibition, 9, 71, 86, 158, 164
Pullman, George Mortimer, 9

Raddall, Thomas
    career as author, 262–63
    as friend and confidant of Koretz,
        166–67, 169, 177–78, 208
    on Koretz's fondness for women,
        176, 191–92, 195
    on Koretz's moose-hunting expedi-
        tion, 196
    at Pinehurst housewarming bash,
        177–78
    at revelation of Koretz's deception,
        208
Republic of Panama. *See* Bayano River
    region, Panama

Reutlinger, Harry, 226
rice farms. *See* Arkansas rice farms
Richman, Samuel
    Bayano investment, 51, 52, 72, 240
    in indictment against Koretz, 203,
        222, 238, 240
    rental of office space from Koretz, 56
    trust in Koretz, 53, 141
Ritchie, Charles, 195
Rockefeller, John D., 3, 12, 76,
        100–101, 138
Rockefeller, John D., Jr., 162
Roosevelt, Theodore, 23, 28, 38, 160
Rosenhaupt, Harry, 124–25
Rosenthal, Bessie, 60
Rosenwald, Julius, 95, 145

Sandburg, Carl, 19, 210
Sante, Luc, 79
Sbarbaro, John
    arrest and extradition of Koretz,
        203–4, 215, 216, 224
    Leopold and Loeb case, 180, 184
    on magnitude of Bayano swindle,
        144, 150
    manhunt for Koretz, 133–34, 149,
        151, 156, 184
    prosecution of Koretz, *227,* 230
    underworld connections, 211
Schaeffer, Mrs. Alwin, 30
Schoener, Marcy, 51, 91–92, 105, 144
Schoener, Mary, 91, 105, 132, 155
Scholl, William, 21
Schon, Harriet, 197
Schroeder, Josephine, 49, 92–93
Schwartz, Sylvia, 129, 132, 133,
        134–35
Scott, Maurice, 172, 175, 263
Scott, Temple (Isaac Henry Solomon
        Isaacs), 153–54, 157–58, 163,
        193, 207
Scott, Walter, 168, 172, 175

Scriven, Rainard, 203, 223–24, 225–26, 261–62
search for Koretz. *See* manhunt and capture
Sheboygan Press-Telegram, 242
Shirley Apartments, 127–28, 129–30
Siegel, Jane, 265
Simon, Aimee, 53, 103, 113, 115
Simon, Milton, 53, 103, 113
Simon, Percy, 220, 239
Small, Lennington, 86
Smith, Henry K., 34
Smith, Milton, 100, 108
Speyer, Etta, 42, *50,* 142
St. Regis Hotel, 90–91
Standard Oil, 3, 4, 72–73, 74, 76, 89, 93, 101, 115, 138, 162
Stanford, Allen, 257
state's attorney. *See* Crowe, Robert
Stelzer, Carol, 266
Stern, Daniel, 93
Sting, The (movie), 78–79, 80
stock mania, 75–77, 258
Straits Times (Singapore), 205
Sutherland, Edwin, 78, 79, 82
Swanberg, W. A., 6, 221, 256
swindlers. *See* con men

Taggart, Jessie, 157
This Side of Paradise (Fitzgerald), 6
Thompson, William Hale "Big Bill," 67–69, 79, 83, *85,* 86–87, 95, 260
timber scam, Koretz's. *See* Bayano River Syndicate
timber scam, Nieto's, 38–42, 43–44
Torrio, Johnny, 88
trial. *See* criminal proceedings
Twain, Mark, 19–20, 70, 162

United Fruit Company, 38

victims. *See* investors

Wallace, William B., 214–15
Wanderer, Carl, 84
Wayman, John, 66–67
Weil, Joseph "Yellow Kid," 79–80, 97, 119
Weil, Leon, 220
Weisberg, Samuel, 124
Westerfeld, Simon, 220
White, Frances, 176, 177
Whitman, John, 253
Wilbraham, Isaac J., 92, 263
Wilkinson, Janet, 62–64
women and womanizing
    callers at Halifax County Jail, 217
    community disapproval of Koretz's behavior, 190, 195
    detective surveillance of hotel, 99, 129
    "find the woman" strategy in manhunt, 129–34, 157
    in Halifax, 191–92, 195, 197, 203, 222, 262
    Mae Koretz's awareness of, 58, 137
    Koretz's lies about, 231
    letters to Koretz, 131–32, 157
    love nests, 127–30, *131,* 133
    true-crime magazine stories about, *254,* 256
    visitors to Pinehurst Lodge, 176, 190, 216
    weekend getaways from Chicago, 92, 132
    women's attraction to Koretz, 6, 57, 175, *175*
Woolf, Elias B., 104, 106

Zinner, Shandor, 101, 109, 140